GRACE
THE GIFT OF THE HOLY SPIRIT

DAVID COFFEY

GRACE
THE GIFT OF THE HOLY SPIRIT

MARQUETTE
UNIVERSITY
PRESS

MARQUETTE STUDIES IN THEOLOGY
NO. 73
ANDREW TALLON, SERIES EDITOR

LIBRARY OF CONGRESS CATALOGING-IN-PUBLICATION DATA

Coffey, David (David Michael)
  Grace : the gift of the Holy Spirit / by David Coffey.
    p. cm. — (Marquette studies in theology ; no. 73)
  New, revised, and updated version of the edition originally published in
1979 by the Catholic Institute of Sydney, Australia.
  Includes bibliographical references and index.
  ISBN-13: 978-0-87462-787-9 (pbk. : alk. paper)
  ISBN-10: 0-87462-787-7 (pbk. : alk. paper)
  1. Holy Spirit. I. Title.
  BT121.3.C643 2011
  231'.3—dc22

                                                    2011009386

⊗The paper used in this publication meets the minimum requirements of the
American National Standard for Information Sciences—
Permanence of Paper for Printed Library Materials, ANSI Z39.48-1992.

MARQUETTE UNIVERSITY PRESS
MILWAUKEE

The Association of Jesuit University Presses

TO THE MEMORY OF MY FATHER AND MOTHER

TABLE OF CONTENTS

"The true aim of our Christian life is to acquire the Holy Spirit of God."
St. Seraphim of Sarov, Conversation with Nicholas Motovilov

ABBREVIATIONS

ASS   *Acta Sanctae Sedis* (Rome, 1865 ff.)

AAS   *Acta Apostolicae Sedis* (Rome, 1909 ff.)

CCSL   *Corpus Christianorum, Series Latina* (Tournai, 1954 ff.)

DS   *Enchiridion Symbolorum Definitionum et Declarationum de Rebus Fidei et Morum* (ed. H. Denzinger and A. Schönmetzer)(34th ed., Barcelona, etc., 1967)

DTC   *Dictionnaire de Théologie Catholique* (Paris, 1903 ff.)

HTG   *Handbuch theologischer Grundbegriffe* (Munich, 1962 f.)

LTK   *Lexikon fur Theologie und Kirche* (2nd ed., Freiburg im Br., 1957 ff.)

PG   *Patrologia Graeca* (ed. J. Migne) (Paris, 1857 ff.)

PL   *Patrologia Latina* (ed. J. Migne) (Paris, 1844 ff.)

RGG   *Die Religion in Geschichte und Gegenwart* (3rd ed., Tübingen, 1956 ff.)

SM   *Sacramentum Mundi* (London, 1968 ff.)

INTRODUCTION

When first invited by Marquette University Press to pre-pare a new edition of this, my first book, I was immediately confronted with the difficulty of the decision that lay before me. On the one hand it would give me an opportunity to correct mistakes and to drop material that I no longer agreed with or considered appropriate. And more importantly, it would give those interested in the theological "system" that I had developed over a life-time—almost without intending it—an opportunity to examine its foundations laid down here for the first time. The first edition, from 1979, was no longer in print. In any case, being of necessity published in Australia, having had a limited print run, and not having been prop-erly distributed overseas, the book had never been readily available, and, apart from those university libraries that stocked it, had in the intervening years become well-nigh inaccessible. True, a reprint was undertaken in 1988, but this did little to alleviate the situation. It too was small, it was still not distributed abroad, and very few people knew of its existence.

On the other hand the problems associated with a second edition were formidable. It would have been relatively easy to authorize an-other reprint, but the original was couched in a non-inclusive language that could no longer be reproduced. Even just recasting the text in inclusive language presented thorny problems at times. How was I to maintain a reasonable standard of expression without undergoing some loss of meaning? On this I could only do my best, and doubt-less, what I have produced will not please everyone. The question of updating the theology presented the biggest challenge of all. I did not want to write a new book on grace, nor was that my brief. It was to be a second edition of my first book. I took this to mean that it was to remain a book of 1979 and not become a compendium of my life's work, as was, for example, Rahner's *Foundations of Christian Faith*. At the same time certain developments in my thinking over the years could not be ignored. Here I settled for a compromise, and decided to incorporate the more important advances made, like the Lonerganian methodology for distinguishing the biblical, immanent and economic understandings of the Trinity, and the theandric nature of Christ, to name just two. Where such updating has taken place, I have taken care, in the text or the notes, to draw attention to it explicitly. The bibliography reflects the same compromise: I have updated it only to include this kind of material.

The perceptive reader will notice that my book begins and ends with references to Karl Barth's well-known attack on the Catholic doctrine of grace for its lack of unity. When I first read this critique, I had felt forced to admit the truth of its main point, though I remained as convinced as ever of the truth of the Catholic doctrine and as impressed as ever with its logic and beauty. But, it was true, it was so fragmented into divisions and sub-divisions as to appear incapable of genuine synthesis. A Catholic, when asked the simple question, what is grace? would be hard put to it to give a straightforward answer. The motive of the book, therefore, was to find a way of synthesizing the Catholic theology of grace, which in the first place meant discovering the appropriate principle of synthesis. The principle which I have elaborated I offer tentatively as my contribution to this theology. The following paragraph is devoted exclusively to a brief summary of it.

The paradigm of all grace is Jesus Christ. In him took place the Incarnation of the divine Son, Second Person of the Blessed Trinity. The union of divinity and humanity in him must be understood as the elevation of the sacred humanity to divine Sonship, so that it is precisely in his humanity that Jesus is the Son of God. This elevation was brought about through the bestowal, by the Father, of the Holy Spirit as Spirit of Sonship, on Jesus, in the act which at the same time created his humanity, sanctified it and united it in person with the pre-existent divine Son. This was a theme known in part already to the Eastern Fathers: for them it was the anointing of Jesus, by the Father, with the ointment of the Holy Spirit, an anointing that was identical with the Incarnation. The divine Sonship forged in his humanity is no threat to his eternal Sonship, to which it stands in the relationship of first effect and last disposition. This more exact understanding of the relationship was achieved not in the first edition of the book, but only subsequently. Symbolic of the Incarnation itself, it stands as the prime example of the updating referred to above.

Christian theology has long known that the grace of ordinary people is a participation in the Holy Spirit, Spirit of filiation, whereby they become "sons—and daughters—in the Son", even if it is only recently that this truth has again come into its due prominence. But now we no longer need see this grace as lacking direct relationship to the Incarnation. With the help of our principle of synthesization we can see that the grace that Jesus possessed in all fullness as his proper grace, the grace of the Incarnation, is the same grace as that in which other people share in their own way. Grace, all grace, is the Gift of the Holy Spirit or its created effect.

It is very much my hope that, whatever its shortcomings, my book will be judged ultimately in the light of its success or failure in relation to the achievement of its main aim. Is my principle true in itself? If it is, it must surely mean something for Christology, even apart from other considerations. But have I adequately established it from the sources? Is it capable of synthesizing the Catholic doctrine of grace, and have I in fact satisfactorily synthesized it? The whole plan of the book is explained in terms of this principle. And involving, as it necessarily does, Christology and the Trinity as well as grace, the book ranges in some way over the whole field of theology, which it also attempts to present as a synthesis—and hence as a "system" of some kind.

To carry out my project I found it necessary to take Scholastic theology as the point of departure and even to complete certain arguments begun within Scholasticism. This may not please those who like to think that the ghost of Scholasticism has finally been laid. However, to those who understand the progress of theology in terms of organic growth rather than abrupt revolution, my procedure, far from requiring justification, will appear obvious and necessary. Even if the Scholastic revival is now over, and theology is finding new methods by which to continue its task, the theologian cannot overlook the fact that the Catholic doctrine of grace largely took shape within a Scholastic framework. Hence any attempt to synthesize this doctrine, even in terms of some other theology, must take respectful account of the Scholastic achievement.

It will be clear from the book itself that the two theologians, both Catholics, to whom, after St. Thomas, I owe the most, are Karl Rahner, whom I had the privilege of hearing during my student days in Munich, and Heribert Mühlen. As each of them has come in for some criticism in the course of the book, I want to make it clear at the outset that I am most conscious of my debt to them and grateful for the illumination they have provided me. It was they, Rahner with his transcendental theology and his key concept of the self-communication of

God, and Mühlen with his research into the patristic theology of the anointing of Jesus with the Holy Spirit, who set my feet on the path which led to the theology propounded in this book.

For the preparation of the second edition I have really only two people to thank, for, apart from them, the onus rested squarely on myself. They are Maura Hearden and Andrew Tallon, both of Marquette University. Maura Hearden, graduate student and my assistant at Marquette at the beginning of the work—and now an assistant professor at DeSales University—undertook the laborious task of transferring the printed text, the only form in which the original survived, to CD-ROM, in order to simplify the work of editing for me. To her I obviously owe a debt of thanks. And to Andrew Tallon, philosophy professor and Director of Marquette University Press, I also express heartfelt thanks for his inspiration, encouragement, technical advice and endless patience in bearing with the many interruptions that punctuated the project, which was carried out in the first years of my retirement.

David Coffey
Sydney, NSW, Australia
January 1st, 2010

PART I

THEOLOGY OF THE TRINITY

THE PROCESSION MODEL AND THE RETURN MODEL

I SOME TRINITARIAN PRINCIPLES

A glance at the table of contents of this book will reveal that what purports to be a book about grace is in fact as much a book about Christ. No apology, however, is needed for this, as the union between the man Jesus and God must be what Christians are basically talking about when they speak of grace. If ordinary human beings are to experience the grace of God, it can only be by participation in Christ, the supreme and unique recipient of grace. Too often theology has tried to understand grace apart from the mystery of the Incarnation. Small wonder, then, that it has experienced such difficulty when it comes to examine the relationship which Scripture affirms to exist between other humans and Christ, and has had to have recourse to extrinsic (albeit biblical) categories such as "Savior" or "Redeemer" to grasp this relationship.

Many will be aware of Karl Barth's searing critique of Catholic theology of grace.[1] However intemperate and in some ways unfair this may be, it must be admitted that it is basically justified, since even the best Catholic theology has not succeeded in overcoming the dichotomy between ordinary humans and Christ which there remains affirmed. The most that this theology can do is to say that the principal grace of Christ, the "grace of union," is the divine Son, while the principal grace of other humans is the Holy Spirit. This distinction at the heart of Catholic theology of grace is the real reason, uncomprehended by Barth, for the fragmentation which he there discerns. The present book, an effort of specifically Catholic theology, hopes to overcome this dichotomy and to unify the various elements of the theology of grace in a genuine synthesis.

An adjustment at the centre of theology might be assumed to have its repercussions at the periphery. Here, therefore, we shall be at pains to show that the hard-won positions of the Scholastic theology of grace are not only not contradicted but capable of assimilation into the broader synthesis. At the same time we shall show that whatever we have to say about the Incarnation and grace reflects the inner, i.e., trinitarian, being of God, which stands revealed in his gracious action

---

1 Cf. K. Barth, *Church Dogmatics* 4/1 (Edinburgh, 1956) 84-88.

among human beings. First we offer some observations on the method we shall use in the execution of our task.

Commenting in the course of his own work on Christology on that of P. Schoonenberg, W. Kasper approves the theological method enunciated by Schoonenberg: "Our whole thinking moves from the world to God, and can never move in the opposite direction ... We never conclude from the Trinity to Christ and his Spirit given to us, but always the other way round."[2] This position is undoubtedly correct. It will determine the method used in this book, and most obviously in Parts Three and Four, which are devoted to ascending Christology and its corresponding theology of grace. Kasper goes on to observe that also the principle of the consistency of God has to be upheld: "The theologian, however, has to proceed not from a 'critique of pure reason' but from the New Testament witness, according to which God has revealed his innermost being and mystery to us in Jesus Christ in an eschatological and definitive manner ... If, therefore, God reveals himself in Jesus Christ eschatologically and definitively as self-communicating love, then the self-communication of God between the Father and the Son is the eternal essence of God itself."[3] The same is affirmed by K. Rahner when he speaks of the "axiomatic unity of the 'economic' and 'immanent' Trinity."[4] While the traditional Catholic theology of Christ and of grace has in some measure proceeded from the Godhead to Christ (and hence has been a descending Christology) and to grace, i.e., it understands the Incarnation and grace as respective prolongations into the world of the trinitarian processions of the Son and the Holy Spirit, it does not, however, necessarily stand condemned by the methodological principle just enunciated. Provided that this theology does not make the blunder of moving from God to the world in so far as the discovery of new material is concerned, legitimate and useful purposes remain for a trinitarian model whose correctness is independently certain, e.g., to impart form to material which otherwise would remain unordered, and thence to provide illustration of the necessary consistency of God in his inner being and his saving intervention in the world. Thus, while we know from revelation that the Incarnation is the union of the divine Son with the humanity of Christ, and that grace is in the first instance the union of the Holy Spirit with human

---

2   W. Kasper, *Jesus the Christ* (London, 1976) 180.

3   Ibid. 181.

4   K. Rahner, *The Trinity* (London, 1970) 21-24.

persons, our knowledge receives new order and intelligibility from the fact that we can invoke the principle of the consistency of God and hence see the Incarnation as precisely the prolongation into the world of the procession of the Son in the Trinity, and grace as the prolongation of the procession of the Holy Spirit. The model of the Trinity used here may be called the "procession" model because it grasps the Trinity in terms of two ordered processions, viz., that of the Son from the Father and that of the Holy Spirit from the Father and (or through) the Son. Obviously, it lends itself to application only to descending Christology and its implied theology of grace, which is the familiar Scholastic theology. Much, however, is to be learned in both Christology and the theology of grace by use of the complementary method of ascending Christology, and it would be advantageous to be able to order this knowledge also by showing that it too corresponds formally to the inner being of God. This, however, could only be done with the aid of a different trinitarian model.

The first part of this book, therefore, will be an inquiry in the field of trinitarian theology, specifically a search for a trinitarian model which will complement the procession model, and which will be able to order the yield of ascending Christology and its attendant theology of grace and at the same time show that it too reflects the inner being of God. If we can show that the two trinitarian models are compatible and complementary, and that every part of our work in the fields of descending and ascending Christology and their corresponding theologies of grace harmonizes with one or the other of them, we can be assured both that we have covered the field of the theology of grace systematically and comprehensively and that we have provided adequate checks on the correctness of the new theological material that we bring to light.

The second part is devoted to carrying through, for completeness' sake, the project of applying the traditional trinitarian model to the theology of Christ and of grace, and we shall take pains to ensure that the methodological principle enunciated above is not violated there, where it might be considered most at risk.

These particular observations on method do not apply directly to the fifth and last part, for it is concerned simply with treating the various matters normally considered in a theology of grace (and until then not treated in this book) and showing how they are integrated into the synthesis without loss or diminution.

We begin, then, with the Trinity, and for the remainder of this chapter will be satisfied with enunciating some basic principles of trinitarian theology which we will be applying in the next chapter, where we elaborate our new trinitarian model. The first of these is the "homoousion," the identity of each of the divine persons with the one divine substance.

A great danger in the trinitarian theology of the East during the patristic age was the tendency to subordinate the Son and the Holy Spirit to the Father.[5] This tendency was inevitable, for the theology flowed immediately from the New Testament, in which the starting point was the manifest humanness of Jesus, of whom, certainly, a oneness of some kind with the transcendent God was confessed, but as a baffling mystery of faith. The distinction of persons was the given; their unity was a problem for faith and theology. Moreover, while the distinctness of the personality of the Holy Spirit was not very clear, it *was* clear that his sanctifying work among human beings depended on the events that climaxed Jesus' earthly life and on the latter's action in sending him on his mission. And to the later writers of the New Testament God the Father appeared as the fount of all being, including that of the Son and the Holy Spirit. The earlier Eastern Fathers, therefore, can scarcely be blamed for a certain tendency to subordinationism, evident even in so sophisticated a thinker as Origen. This tendency attained its extreme and heretical formulation in Arianism, in which the strict divinity of the Son was denied.

The corrective for this tendency was supplied by the anti-Arian Council of Nicaea in its teaching of the homoousion, the assertion that the Son was "of the same substance," or "stuff," as the Father (DS 125). It is probably true that for the majority of the participants at the Council this meant no more than that the Son was strictly divine, like the Father. However it was soon realized by St. Athanasius and his followers (and by the time of the First Council of Constantinople it was recognized as orthodoxy) that the word implied that the Son was *identical* in substance with the Father. From this it was only a short step for Athanasius to maintain that the Holy Spirit was of the same substance as the Father and the Son. The homoousion, therefore, came to designate the realization that the Father, the Son and the Holy Spirit were "the same," not just in the sense in which three

---

5   J.N.D. Kelly, *Early Christian Doctrines*, 5th edn. (London, 1977) 252-279; G.L. Prestige, *God in Patristic Thought* (London, 1936) 197-300.

human beings might be said to be the same, but in the sense that each was identical with the one divine substance.

Logically connected with the full understanding of the homoousion are the three following doctrines. The first is that the unity of the triune God is to be seen not as rooted in the Father as the principle of the other two divine persons, as in the earlier thinking, but as founded in the unity of the divine substance. The second is that the will and energy, or principle of operation, in the Godhead is located primarily in the divine substance, not in the persons as such, so that there is only one operation in the triune God. And the third is the conclusion drawn by the eighth-century writer known as Pseudo-Cyril, of the co-inherence or inter-penetration of the three divine persons, which he called the "perichoresis." These important doctrines will be invoked from time to time in the course of this book.

Our second trinitarian principle is the "per filium," i.e., the fact that it is through the Son that the Holy Spirit proceeds from the Father.

The Cappadocian Fathers, St. Basil, St. Gregory of Nazianzus and St. Gregory of Nyssa came out of the so-called semi-Arian tradition, the starting-point of which was the distinction of the divine persons, but in the development of their theology they came to embrace the homoousion in the Athanasian sense. In their intellectual journey they achieved a trinitarian doctrine of remarkable comprehensiveness and balance. They taught the traditional doctrine of the generation of the Son by the Father, and did not hesitate to say that the Father was the "cause" of the Son, as of the Holy Spirit. The term that they used for the origination of the Holy Spirit was "procession." Though confident of the doctrine that the Holy Spirit proceeds from the Father, they were unable to describe the manner of his procession beyond saying that it was not by generation. Basil thought that the Holy Spirit came from the Father "as the breath of his mouth," but said that the manner of the procession was "ineffable."[6]

The question that had to be answered was, how is the procession of the Holy Spirit from the Father differentiated from that of the Son? One suggestion was that the Son played some part in the origination of the Holy Spirit. This was rejected by the "creed of Theodore" and by Theodoret, both representative of the school of Antioch. Like the Son, they said, the Holy Spirit proceeds immediately from the Father, but they were quick to say that this did not make another Son of the

---

6   *Liber de spiritu sancto* 18, 46 (PG 32, 152; *Sources chrétiennes* 17, 195).

Holy Spirit. But it may well be asked, how not? Origen, of the school of Alexandria, on the other hand, in a manifestation of the subordinationist thought spoken of above, held that the Son does play a part in the origination of the Holy Spirit. The Cappadocians followed Origen in attributing such a function to the Son, but did not follow him in his subordinationism. Gregory of Nyssa was finally able to describe the Holy Spirit as "proceeding from the Father, receiving from the Son."[7] Thereafter in Cyril and other writers the formula "out of the Father through the Son" became the regular way of expressing the procession of the Holy Spirit.

In this book we shall have reason to make frequent reference to the manner of the procession of the Holy Spirit as understood in the East, and to compare it with the Western conception, that the Holy Spirit proceeds from the Father *and* the Son. For these purposes it will be convenient to use the Latin expressions, per filium: *through* the Son, and filioque: (from the Father) *and* the Son.

It is clear from their treatment that the Cappadocians were able to speak of the Father as "cause" and of the other divine persons as "caused" without the overtones of subordination of the caused to the cause that would inevitably accompany our use of this terminology. We shall therefore follow the Latin preference for saying "principle" (*principium*) rather than "cause," and by analogy with the latter term we shall also adopt certain derivatives, such as "principial," "principiality," etc.

This brings us to the other way of conceiving the procession of the Holy Spirit, viz., that he proceeds from the Father *and* the Son as from one principle.

It can be argued that the great Father of the West, St. Augustine of Hippo, took as the starting point of his trinitarian thought the unity of the divine "essence" (a term that he preferred to "substance"). As we have pointed out, this approach is soundly scriptural, though less obviously so than that of the Eastern tradition. By starting in this way Augustine was able to avoid the danger of subordinationism that had threatened Eastern writers.

One of Augustine's greatest contributions was his recognition of the existence of analogy in respect of spiritual operation between the human being, a creature, and God the triune creator. Distinguishing in humans the two spiritual operations of knowledge and love, and

---

7   *Adversus Macedonios* 10 (PG 45, 1513).

applying them analogously to the Trinity, he was able to describe the two processions, the generation of the Son as being according to knowledge and the procession of the Holy Spirit as being according to love. This is not to say that the Trinity of God can be proved from reason: it simply means that once revealed it can be elaborated by the use of analogy.

The other main contribution of Augustine was his realization that the Holy Spirit proceeds from the Father and the Son acting as one. Given Augustine's starting point, it was a logical development. For him it was demanded by the unity of the divine operation. It had been adumbrated in Western thought before him, but he was the first to grasp it thus and to express it clearly.

It is important to note that Augustine held as a corollary of the doctrine of Scripture that the Holy Spirit is the mutual love of the Father and the Son: "According to the holy scriptures this Holy Spirit is not of the Father alone, nor of the Son alone, but of both, and therefore he conveys to us the common love by which the Father and the Son love each other."[8] As such he is the "bond" that unites them. From this mutual love must be distinguished the "common" love of the Father and the Son, by which the two together love some object, be it a divine person or persons or the divine essence. It is unfortunate that in this context Augustine uses the word "common" in the sense in which we have just defined "mutual" precisely in order to distinguish it from the proper sense of "common." That Augustine held the Holy Spirit to be in fact the mutual, rather than the common, love of the Father and the Son is remarkable, for his starting point of the unity of the divine essence and of the divine operation might have been expected to lead him to the other conclusion. Later we shall be concerned with the question whether and in what way love may be said to be "bestowed" within the Trinity. The answer from Augustine is that in the Trinity love is bestowed by the Father and the Son on each other, this mutual love being the Holy Spirit. The apparent paradox of Augustine's position is that when he considers the *fact* of the procession of the Holy Spirit, he says that the Holy Spirit proceeds from the Father and the

---

8   *De trinitate* XV, 17, 27 (PL 42, 1080; CCSL 50A, 501). Cf. *ibid.* V, 11, 12 (PL 42, 919; CCSL 50, 219); ibid. XV, 19, 37 (PL 42, 1086; CCSL 50A, 513). Cf. B. de Margerie, "La doctrine de saint Augustin sur l'Ésprit-Saint comme communion et source de communion," *Augustinianum* 12 (1972) 111-113.

Son acting together; but when he considers the *manner* of this procession, he says that the Holy Spirit proceeds as the love of the Father and the Son acting now not in unison but distinctly, even, in a sense, in opposition to each other, i.e., in loving each other. Whether this is really paradoxical will emerge later in our study.

At this point a comparison may be made of the per filium and the filioque. It is sometimes said that the difference between East and West on this matter is purely terminological. This, however, is not fully true. Reflection on the per filium on its own, that is, without consideration of other factors, leads to a sense of the filioque that is only part of what is meant by this term in the West. The Western position, on the other hand, begins with an understanding of the filioque that is simply unacceptable in the East. The Western position, being more comprehensive, includes the per filium logically, though, given that sufficient distinction between the Father and the Son is made already when it is said that the Son proceeds from the Father alone while the Holy Spirit proceeds from the Father and the Son, it is questionable whether the full Western position on the filioque would have had the impetus to develop had not the per filium been established independently.

The two positions are now presented in their logically developed forms, first the Eastern, then the Western.

As has been seen, the standard formula of the developed thought of the East was "out of the Father through the Son." When the per filium here is awarded its full value, it is realized that the Holy Spirit comes from the Son as well as from the Father. In this sense the filioque is admitted. But this is not to concede that the dignity of principle or co-principle accrues to the Son. "Principle" means "ultimate origin", and as the Son himself is principled, it is argued that the term must be reserved to the Father alone. For the same reason the idea of the Son as a co-principle is also rejected. Therefore the filioque is not admitted in the sense that the Father and the Son are recognized as constituting a single principle in relation to the Holy Spirit. The protagonist of the West would say at this point that the Western sense of the filioque is required by the unity of the divine operation, but the East would reply that this unity is assured already by the fact that the operation originates from the Father and is only mediated by the Son.

The Western position is given here in roughly the terms in which it was enunciated by the Council of Florence (cf. DS 1301). The Son pertains to the principle of the Holy Spirit. (This is not to deny that the Son himself is principled, or to assert that the distinction of persons in the Father and the Son is abolished.) Now everything that the Son has he has from the Father. Therefore that he pertains to the principle of the Holy Spirit is something that the Son has from the Father. It is in this sense, therefore, that the Father may be said to principle the Holy Spirit through the Son.

It will be appreciated that the Eastern position overlaps the Western without simply coinciding with it. It is futile to hope that the Eastern position is capable of further linear development so that it will eventually coincide with the Western. Each position has a legitimate, though radically different, starting point: in the West the unity of the divine essence, in the East the distinction of the divine persons. As the homoousion in the Athanasian sense coincides materially in designation with the unity of the divine essence, it is evident that the homoousion would have been a more productive basis for continued trinitarian thought than was the actual Eastern starting-point of the distinction of persons; but in the East in the question of the procession of the Holy Spirit the distinction of persons remained the regulative concept despite the development of the homoousion.

As representing unity and distinction in God respectively, both the filioque and the per filium are to be upheld. Each will play an important part in the theology of grace presented in this book.

We now embark on a brief reflection on two trinitarian axioms which were known basically to the Fathers and which have important application to this book.

The first, for which there is no standard formulation, states that the works of God in the world are done by all three divine persons. The second is commonly cited in Latin in roughly the form in which it was expressed by the Council of Florence: *In Deo omnia sunt unum ubi non obviat relationis oppositio*, which may be translated as: In the Godhead all things are one except where the opposition of relationship rules this out (DS 1330).

The first axiom sounds Augustinian, and indeed it is to be found in that Father's works. Because of the unity of the divine operation the triune God acts as one principle in relation to the world.[9] The axiom

---

9   *De trinitate* V, 14, 15 (PL 42, 921: CCSL 50, 223); cf. *Enchiridion ad Laurentium* 12, 38 (PL 40, 251; CCSL 46, 71); *Contra sermonem Arianorum* 3, 4 (PL 42, 685); *De trinitate* I, 4, 7 (PL 42, 824; CCSL 50, 35-36).

is basically concerned with creation. As the work of the Godhead in the world, it is done by all three divine persons. If it is linked with one of them, as it sometimes is with the Father, this is by "appropriation." This means that because of what is proper to him, viz., that he is the principle of the other two persons, it is fitting that of the three he alone be named as the source of all created being, the creator, though in fact the others create no less than he, and indeed with him constitute the single creator.

While the axiom applies without difficulty to creation, its application to the Incarnation and to grace creates a problem; for, to take up the first example only, the Incarnation is to be confessed by faith as that of the Son alone, but at the same time has to be recognized to be a work of the Godhead in the world, and so in some sense to be done by all three divine persons. The problem, in relation both to the Incarnation as proper to the Son and to grace as proper to the Holy Spirit, will be taken up when we turn to the question of the categories in which the divine action on the world is most appropriately conceived.

The second axiom also has an Augustinian ring. It reflects that Father's concern for the unity of the divine essence and also his conviction that distinction in the Godhead is explained by the opposition of relationships. Thus the Father and the Son are distinct in that their relationship maintains between them an opposition that prevents them from merging as long as the one remains the Father who begets the Son and the other remains this Son who is begotten of the Father. It should be noted, however, that the substance of the axiom was held also in the East, and is there traced back to Gregory of Nazianzus.[10]

While it expresses a profound truth, the axiom could convey by its wording the impression that the unity of the Godhead is the prime consideration and the distinction of persons secondary. It has been pointed out that the axiom was formulated in the Decree for the Jacobites of the Council of Florence for the purpose of condemning tritheism. It would be unwarranted to generalize from this by saying that in all circumstances this emphasis has to be maintained.[11] In fact

---

10   Cf. M. Schmaus, *Katholische Dogmatik* 1/1, 4th edn. (Munich, 1948) 433.

11   Cf. H. Mühlen, "Person und Appropriation. Zum Verständnis des Axioms: In Deo omnia sunt unum, ubi non obviat relationis opposition," *Münchener Theologische Zeitschrift* 16 (1965) 43-44.

in the East the emphasis has always been on the distinction of the persons rather than their unity. While the Athanasian development of the homoousion was a great advance, it by no means negatived the previous emphasis on the distinct persons. The homoousion was the achievement of unity from the standpoint of diversity, and not just an assertion of unity. As has been observed, despite the homoousion the distinction of persons remained the regulative concept in the East.

The theology of grace offered in this book has its roots in the Eastern tradition. This can be seen in the emphasis placed on the distinction of the divine persons. As has been said, this is a more obvious and direct way of taking up the statements of the New Testament than that of the West. While the unity of the Godhead is to be kept before our eyes, it should be remembered that it is in what might be called the "natural" activity of the Godhead, the creation of the world, that this unity is most evident. But grace pertains to the "supernatural" activity of the Godhead. If this is to be safeguarded, it must be linked with how the Godhead exists in itself, i.e., as Father, Son and Holy Spirit, three distinct persons in the one divine essence. Only thus is a reduced "monotheistic" theology of grace avoided, a theology that would remain such despite nominal linking with one of the divine persons, as would happen, for example, if grace were said to be the grace of Christ simply because he was linked with it by an extrinsic bond such as, for example, merit.[12] In addition to the Eastern patrimony, however, the insights of Augustine, "doctor of grace," are incorporated into our theology where applicable and will be seen to play an important part in it.

---

12   Cf. K. Rahner, "Some Implications of the Scholastic Concept of Uncreated Grace," *Theological Investigations* 1 (London, 1961) 346.

2 THE PROCESSION MODEL AND THE RETURN MODEL

This chapter is devoted to an exercise in traditional trinitarian theology, the conclusion to which will be that in addition to the usual "out-going" way, or model, of conceiving the Trinity, i.e., that the Son proceeds from the Father, and the Holy Spirit proceeds from the Father and (or through) the Son, there is another legitimate model, a "circular" one, viz., that the Father bestows his love on the Son generated by him, and the Son in return bestows his love on the Father, this mutual love being the Holy Spirit. The former model we call the "procession model," and the latter the "return model," because it is concerned with the return of the Son and Holy Spirit to the Father.[1] Our point of departure is the trinitarian theology of St. Thomas Aquinas. In the context of a critique of his thought, we will have the opportunity of extrapolating the new model. The purpose of the exercise is that, in accomplishing it, we will be in the position to apply the procession model, in Part Two, to descending Christology and its implied theology of grace, and the return model, in Parts Three and Four, to ascending Christology and its theology of grace, respectively. Thus we will be able to organize our knowledge of the economy of salvation and to show that it reflects the inner being of God.

Because of its relation to the question of the procession of the Holy Spirit, the nature of love is the first matter to consider in the thought of Aquinas; and because of the intrinsic dependence of love on knowledge, the exercise begins with a consideration of his position on the nature of knowledge.

---

1   In the first edition I called this model the "bestowal" model because in it the Father and the Son bestow the Holy Spirit on each other. Later I came to see that while this is a fitting name, it does not bring out the model's contrast with the procession model. For while in the procession model the Son and the Holy Spirit come out from the Father, in this one they return to him, or better, the Son, having come out from the Father, returns to him in the power of the Holy Spirit. Hence I renamed it "the return model." See Introduction.

In the Thomistic philosophy knowledge is a perfection of the knowing subject. In the knower there takes place the operation of knowing, by which indeed the external world becomes known, but which terminates in knowledge as an enrichment of self that is identified as the concept or the word. Further, it is in the acquisition of knowledge of the world that the knower becomes known to self. Ultimately, knowledge is self-knowledge, although acquired in knowledge of the world.[2]

In Scholastic philosophy such an operation is called a *processio operati*, literally a "procession of the thing operated," to be distinguished from a *processio operationis*, a "procession of the operation." The former is an operation that terminates in a "thing operated," an immanent term, i.e., an end-point that is contained within the operation, but as a static point is distinct from it. Also, though it is a perfection of the principle, the term is distinct from the principle of the operation as accident from substance. In the case of knowledge the principle is the knower, the operation the act of knowing, and the immanent term the concept or word. Knowledge, therefore, is clearly a *processio operati*. In a *processio operationis*, on the other hand, there is no immanent term, but simply the operation, directed to an object in the world.

In his early work Aquinas espoused the view that knowledge is a *processio operati* and love a *processio operationis*. Thus: "This is the difference between the intellect and the will, that the operation of the will terminates at things, in which are good and evil, whereas the operation of the intellect terminates in the mind, in which are truth and falsehood, as is said in the Metaphysics 6, 8. Therefore the will does not have proceeding from it anything which is in it after the manner of an operation, but the intellect does have in itself something proceeding from it, not only after the manner of an operation, but also after the manner of a thing operated. Therefore the word is signified as a thing proceeding, but love is signified as an operation proceeding."[3] Knowledge, therefore, may be characterized as centripetal, and love as centrifugal. As is clear from the quotation, Aquinas derived this view from Aristotle. Love is an operation emanating from the lover as principle and terminating not in an immanent term but in the person or object loved, resulting in an adaptation of the lover to the loved and thus in a certain union between them. Knowledge and love are

---

2   Cf. Rahner, "Some Implications of the Scholastic Concept of Uncreated Grace," *Theological Investigations* 1 (1961) 327-28.

3   *De veritate* 4, 2 ad 7.

contrasted, and the contrast is expressed succinctly by Aquinas in the statement that truth, the object of knowledge, is in the mind, while good, the object of love, is in things.

While Aquinas continued to maintain his doctrine of the nature of knowledge, in his later work he changed his position on the nature of love, and began to regard it also as a *processio operati*, with an immanent term. On this view knowledge and love are no longer to be fundamentally contrasted, but are to be compared as fundamentally parallel. Each is centripetal. The following is a well-known example from the *Summa theologiae* that reflects the change in his thought: "As when someone knows something there proceeds in the knower a certain intellectual conception of the thing known, which is called the word, so when someone loves something there proceeds in the affection of the lover what might be called an impression of the thing loved, according to which the thing loved is said to be in the lover, just as the thing known is in the knower."[4]

Since in the Trinity the Son proceeds by knowledge and the Holy Spirit by love, this change had far-reaching effects on Aquinas's trinitarian theology. Consistently with his philosophical position, he never changed his view on the Son as the immanent term of the first procession. The personhood (for Aquinas distinctness, subsistence) of the Son is understood from the analogy of human knowledge, by exploiting the distinction of the concept or word from both the knower and the act of knowing. Likewise consistently with the change in his philosophical position, Aquinas changed his view on the Holy Spirit. In the early works the Holy Spirit is not the term of the operation of love, but the operation itself: "He (the Holy Spirit) proceeds as a subsistent operation."[5] In the later works the Holy Spirit is the immanent term of the operation of love in the Trinity: "In God there are two processions, viz., the procession of the word and another one. To see this, one has only to consider that in God procession is given only according to an action which does not tend toward something outside him but remains in the agent himself. In an intellectual nature this kind of action is that of the intellect and that of the will. The procession of the word takes place according to the action of knowing. According to the operation of the will, however, there is found in us another procession, viz., of love, according to which the thing loved is in the lover, just as

---

4   *Summa theologiae* I, 37, 1.
5   "Ipse procedit ut operatio subsistens." In *I Sententiarum* 32, 1, 2 ad 4.

through the conception of the word something said or known is in the knower. Therefore in God in addition to the procession of the word [that of the Son], there is another procession [that of the Holy Spirit], viz., of love."[6]

Thus we are brought to ask two questions: 1) why did Aquinas change his mind on this subject? and 2) what is the truth of the matter?

It is difficult to answer the first of these questions. However, the last-given quotation provides some justification for suggesting that Aquinas reasoned in the following way. The Holy Spirit is immanent to the Trinity. Also, as he is a person (subsistent), he is the term of an operation in God. Therefore he is the immanent term of a divine operation. But the Holy Spirit proceeds according to love. Therefore the operation of which he is the immanent term is that of love. Since in God love has an immanent term, and since there exists analogy between human beings and God, in human beings also there is an immanent term in the operation of love. Even if this is not in fact the thought of Aquinas, the argument itself merits our attention.

In the first place, since this argument proceeds from God to the world, it stands condemned by the methodological principal enunciated in the preceding chapter. Moreover, it is not legitimate to deduce from the fact that he is a person that the Holy Spirit is the term of a divine operation. A principled being can be conceived either in relation to that from which it proceeds or in relation to the operation by which it proceeds. While it is true that there is no real distinction of being and operation in God, nevertheless their distinction must be maintained in language if confusion and error are to be avoided. In the Trinity, therefore, the Son can be conceived as the person whose principle is the Father. Here the Father and the Son are conceived in terms of subsistent relational being, the one as principle, the other as principled. Alternatively, the Son can be conceived in relation to the operation of knowing by which he proceeds. In the late thought of Aquinas, as will soon be seen in greater detail, God knowing himself is seen as the formal reason (*ratio formalis*) of the procession of the Son, and the Son is seen as the divine Word, immanent term of this operation. Now it is not permissible to conclude from being to operation. It is therefore not legitimate to deduce from the fact that the Son is a divine person that he is the immanent term of a divine operation. The converse procedure, however, is legitimate: one may

---

6   *Summa theologiae* I, 27, 3.

conclude from operation to being. Given, therefore, that the Son is the immanent term of a divine operation, it may be concluded, on the ground that there can be no accidents in God, that he is a person (subsistent). Hence, when one comes to speak of the Holy Spirit, one may not argue from the fact that he is a divine person to his being the immanent term of a divine operation. The question as to whether he is a term remains open, even when it is accepted that he is a person, whose principle is the Father and the Son.

Further, the fact that he is immanent to the Trinity does not require the Holy Spirit to be an immanent *term*, but is adequately explained on other grounds, by a factor unique to the Trinity, viz., the homoousion, that each of the three divine persons is identical with the one divine substance. Given the homoousion, each person has to be immanent to the Trinity. The question as to whether the Holy Spirit is the immanent term of the operation of love in God is therefore not settled by the two facts that he is immanent to the Trinity and that he proceeds by love.

The second question, as to the truth of the matter in itself, may now be dealt with. Here we concentrate on the primary analogue, the operation of the human spirit. We accept that knowledge is centripetal. It can be argued that it is a simple datum of experience that love is centrifugal, that it has no term within itself, but that its term is the loved one. This is not to deny the "two faces" [7] of love, i.e., that love implies a spontaneous inclination toward the loved one and the affective "impression" of the loved one in the lover. But it is to deny that this impression is an immanent term distinct from the act of love itself, as is the word in relation to knowledge. As, however, this appeal to experience does not pass unchallenged, it needs to be supported by argument; and this is at hand in the failure of language to provide a word for this alleged immanent term. Although the following text of Aquinas is primarily concerned with the lack of a word to denote the relation of this term to its principle, it also recognizes that there is no accepted word for the term itself. "On the part of the intellect words have been found to signify the relation of the knower to the thing known, as is clear from the fact that I say 'to know'; and also other words have been found to signify the process of intellectual conception, viz., 'to say' and 'word' . . . But on the part of the will, besides 'to love' (*diligere* and

---

7   H.-F. Dondaine, *La Trinité* (Saint Thomas D'Aquin, *Somme Théologique*)
     2 (Tournai, 1962) 406.

amare) there are no words to convey the relation to its principle or vice versa of this impression or affection of the thing loved, which proceeds in the lover from the fact that he loves."[8] This admission is very damaging to Aquinas's case. When one considers that the discussion is about two such fundamental and universal human activities as knowing and loving; that popular speech and philosophy have experienced no difficulty in assigning apt words to the term of knowing, viz., , "concept" and "word;" but that in the long history of the human race neither has been able to produce any suggestion for the alleged immanent term of love: it may be safely concluded that this term is no more than an assertion, for whose real existence convincing evidence is lacking.

On the nature of love, therefore, the position of the younger Aquinas is preferable to that of the older. Knowledge is a *processio operati*, love a *processio operationis*. Applying this to the Trinity, again the younger Aquinas is to be preferred. The conclusion is that the Son is understood as a distinct person in that he is the immanent term of the operation of knowing within the Trinity, but the Holy Spirit is understood as a distinct person in a different way, as the subsistent operation of love in the Godhead. We understand him as distinct from his principle, the Father and the Son, by exploiting the analogy of the distinction of an operation from its source. This conclusion will suffice for the present, though it is realized that it does not fully explain the distinction of the Son and the Holy Spirit from each other, as knowledge and love are not simply distinct in God. The distinction will be argued fully later in this chapter.

As a corollary, attention should now be given to an expression based remotely on Augustine[9] and used by Aquinas to describe the way in which a person or thing may be present to spiritual being: "as the known is in the knower and the loved is in the lover."[10] This expression, which is important for the understanding of the manner of the presence of God to humans in grace, is explained differently by Aquinas according to his changing theory of the nature of love. If knowledge and love are to be contrasted, the loved is not present to the lover in the same way as is the known to the knower. The known is present to

---

8 *Summa theologiae* I, 37, 1.

9 Cf. *De trinitate* IV, 20, 28-29 (PL 42, 907-908).

10 "...secundum quod cognitum est in cognoscente, et desideratum in desiderante." *Summa theologiae* I, 8, 3. "...sicut cognitum in cognoscente et amatum in amante." Ibid. I, 43, 3.

the knower in the concept, but the loved is present to the lover only as an "impression" that is not distinct from the act of loving. It could perhaps be more justly said that the converse of the second half of the expression is true, that the lover is in the loved, in that the centrifugal movement of love tends to adapt the lover to the loved. When, however, the two movements are seen as parallel, the manner of presence of the loved to the lover is seen as the same as that of the known to the knower. The latter psychology is exemplified in the *Summa theologiae* 1, 37, 1, and the former in the *Compendium theologiae* 46.

Granted that the Holy Spirit is the subsistent operation of love in the Godhead, it may now be asked whether this statement can be given more precision, so that a deeper appreciation of the procession of the Holy Spirit may be gained. In order to answer this question it will be necessary first to look more closely at the divine operation and then to explore the limits of the Augustinian psychological analogy.

In the divine operation Aquinas made a distinction of essential and notional acts. By an essential act he meant an act performed by the Godhead as such. This is the same as an act done by all three divine persons, although in an essential act one thinks of the divine agent in his unity of essence rather than in his Trinity of persons. In the following quotation the knowing and loving referred to are essential acts: "From what has been said it is clear that the Son proceeds from the Father after the manner of the knowledge by which God knows himself, and the Holy Spirit proceeds from the Father and the Son after the manner of the love by which God loves himself."[11]

In order to understand what Aquinas meant by "notional acts," it is necessary first to explain why he used the word "notion." "A notion," he said, "is the proper idea by which we know a divine person."[12] There are five notions: ingenerateness, fatherhood, sonship, common spiration (breathing-forth) and procession. By the first and the second the Father is known, by the third the Son, by the fourth the Father and the Son are known, and by the fifth the Holy Spirit is known. From this it can be seen what Aquinas meant by "notional acts:" "The distinction of the divine persons is had according to their origin. But origin can be fittingly designated only by certain acts. Therefore to designate origin in the divine persons it has been necessary to attribute notional

---

11   *Summa contra Gentiles* 4, 23.
12   *Summa theologiae* I, 32, 3.

acts to the persons;"[13] and "Every origin is designated by some act. Now a twofold order of origin can be attributed to God. The first is had according as creatures proceed from him, and this is common to the three persons. Therefore the actions that are attributed to God to designate the origin of creatures from him pertain to his essence. But the other order of origin in the Godhead is had according to the procession of person from person. Whence the acts designating this order or origin are called notional, for the notions of the persons are the relations that they bear to one another."[14] For Aquinas, therefore, notional acts are those that designate the origin of divine persons by procession of person from person or persons. They are the acts performed in the Godhead that are not common to the three divine persons, concretely the act of the Father by which he generates the Son, and the act of the Father and the Son by which as one principle they breathe forth the Holy Spirit. We may leave aside the other two "acts" traditionally added to these, to be generated and to be breathed forth, since they are merely the passives of the two already mentioned, and as such, strictly speaking, should not be termed acts.

We now make a further distinction in the divine acts, viz., of constitutive and concomitant acts. This distinction is based on a statement of Aquinas that when something is said to happen by the will this can denote either that the action of the will accompanies the event or that it is its principle. The human examples that he gives are: "I am a human being by my will," where the action of the will only concurs in the given state of being a human, and therefore is merely concomitant to the action that constitutes this state; and "The workman works by his will," where the action of the will is the principle of the work, and therefore constitutive of it.[15] On this basis we may define a constitutive act in the Godhead as an act that constitutes a divine person, and a concomitant act as an act that is not constitutive but that accompanies a constitutive act. Concretely, constitutive acts coincide with notional acts, and concomitant acts with essential acts, but in each instance the basis of comparison is different.

While the statement of a concomitant act may be true and meaningful, e.g., that the Holy Spirit loves the Father, it should be remembered that in a sense that must still be affirmed there is in the Godhead only

13   Ibid. I, 41, 1.
14   Ibid. I, 41, 1 ad 1.
15   Ibid. I, 41, 2.

one subject, one psychological centre, with which each person (object) is identical. Therefore the act by which the Holy Spirit loves the Father is concretely the single act of love by which God loves himself.

This leads us to ask whether there is any distinction in reality in regard to all these divine acts, or whether the distinctions that we have made are merely in thought and language. The only real distinction in the Godhead is that of the three persons, distinguished from each other by relationships of opposition: "In the Godhead all things are one except where the opposition of relationship rules this out." The distinction of persons, however, is established only through the two processions, by which the Son and the Holy Spirit are constituted as distinct not only from the Father but from each other. Therefore the two processions must also be really distinct from each other. This is not to posit in the Godhead real distinction in addition to that which exists among the persons. It is simply to state the distinction of the persons in another way. As the two processions are respectively identical with the two constitutive acts, it is further concluded that the constitutive or notional acts are really distinct from each other. Having said this, however, for reasons of method we leave the notional acts aside for the present, and revert to the question of the distinction of the two processions. How, we ask, can this distinction be upheld without sacrificing the unity of the divine operation?

Aquinas answered this question by making within the one divine operation a distinction of order, where the order is according to origin, and not essence or time.[16] His principle is that "nothing can be loved by the will unless it is conceived in the intellect." Thus in the procession of knowledge and the procession of love there is an order, in which everything pertaining to the former, therefore both principle and term, the Father and the Son, is presupposed for the latter. This is the adequate explanation of the distinction of the Holy Spirit from the Son. It is not sufficient to say that the procession of the Son is by knowledge and the procession of the Holy Spirit by love, but it must be added that the Son proceeds from the Father alone whereas the Holy Spirit proceeds from the Father and the Son. This order of the two processions allows a real distinction between them without destroying the unity of the divine operation. In God, then, there is a single operation identical with his essence, given, however, in the two "modalities" of knowledge and love, between which there is a real distinction. One

---

16   Cf. ibid. I, 27, 3 ad 3.

speaks loosely of the two operations in the Godhead when it would be more correct to speak of the two modalities of the one divine operation. However, as this expression is somewhat cumbersome, it will not be rigorously adhered to here.

Aquinas's principle, invoked above, that "nothing can be loved by the will unless it is conceived in the intellect," coupled with the fact of the unity of the spiritual operation, shows that the order of intellect and will implies in the spiritual operation a dynamism inherent in its first phase which impels it forward until the second is accomplished, and an impossibility of accomplishing the second unless the first is already given. This is why Aquinas is able to say that "every agent, whatever it be, accomplishes every action out of love of some kind."[17] Applying this to the Trinity, we see that the order of the two processions is more than just a fact. Rather, the generation of the Son is the necessary first phase of the breathing-forth of the Holy Spirit. It is not an action that comes to rest once it is accomplished, but it is carried forward irresistibly by its inner dynamism until it comes to rest in the breathing-forth of the Holy Spirit. Then, as Aquinas says, "the circle is closed."[18] Thus it may be said that not only the Holy Spirit, but also the Son, proceeds by love, and this without prejudice to the fact that formally he proceeds by knowledge. As H. Mühlen writes, "One is entitled to say that the Father produces the Son *ex aliquo amore*, i.e., out of the love with which he wills that the Son together with him produce the Holy Spirit."[19]

At this point a more detailed consideration of the psychological analogy of the Trinity is called for. In this analogy, as we have said, the primary analogue is the human spirit in its operations, and the secondary analogue is God as infinite spirit in his Trinity of persons. Because the human spirit has two operations, knowing and loving, it is inferred that this is the case also with God. Given, therefore, from revelation that there are two originated persons in the Godhead and also certain basic information about them, it is reasoned that the one, the Son, proceeds by knowledge, and the other, the Holy Spirit, by love. If the analogy is to be developed in a purely linear way, without introducing any extraneous factor, it is concluded that the knowledge by which the Son proceeds is that by which God knows himself, and

---

17   Ibid. I-II, 28, 6.

18   Cf. *De potentia* 9, 9.

19   H. Mühlen, Der Heilige Geist als Person (Münster, 1966) 124.

the love by which the Holy Spirit proceeds is that by which God loves himself. In technical terms, therefore, the formal reasons of the processions are the essential divine acts.

Having used the expression "formal reason" now more than once, we should reflect on its meaning and on its applicability to the two processions. The formal reason of a thing is its exact, precise and immediate explanation. Properly speaking, therefore, it indicates not the thing itself, but what is immediately prior to it, not in time but in logical sequence. In that the Son is the immanent term of the divine self-knowledge and not the act of knowing itself, the divine self-knowledge is clearly the formal reason of the procession of the Son. The expression, therefore, is applied properly to the first procession. But in the case of the second procession the Holy Spirit is not the term of the divine love but the act of love itself. This raises the question as to whether the divine self-love can be said to be the formal reason of the second procession in any proper sense. However, because there is no action prior to the divine self-love that could be invoked as the formal reason of the procession of the Holy Spirit as distinct from that of the Son, and because tautology is avoided in that in explanation of his personhood the Holy Spirit is advanced not as person (being) but as operation (the act of love), which in this instance (subsistent operation) is logically prior to being, the divine self-love can, after all, be said to be the formal reason of the second procession, but not in precisely the same sense as that in which the expression is used in relation to the first procession. The expression "formal reason" is applied properly but *analogously* to the second procession, and this is the case ultimately because of the fundamental contrast that exists between knowledge and love.

Augustine, from whom the psychological analogy comes, did not apply it rigorously, as for him, as has been seen, the Holy Spirit proceeded as the mutual love of the Father and the Son. It was St. Anselm who carried the analogy through to its logical conclusion, which makes the essential acts of knowledge and love the formal reasons of the processions.[20] This position does not dispute the fact that the Father alone generates the Son, or that the Father and the Son alone breathe forth the Holy Spirit; but when the matter is stated thus the analogy of the human spirit is set aside, and the actions are called generating and breathing-forth, not knowing and loving. It is argued that if one wishes to use the analogy, in which the operations are those of a single

---

20   Cf. *De divinitatis essentia monologium* 49-51 (PL 158, 200-201).

intellectual subject; if, therefore, one wishes to speak of the Son as proceeding by knowledge and the Holy Spirit by love: one must remain within the limits of the analogy and respect the fact that there is only one subject of action, not several; and therefore one must conclude that the formal reasons of the processions are the essential operations of knowledge and love. This is clearly how Aquinas was thinking in the following passage: "That something proceed, remaining within its principle, is found only in the operation of the intellect and will, as is clear from what has been said. Therefore the divine persons cannot be multiplied except according to what is demanded by the procession of intellect and will in God. But it is not possible that there be in God any more than one procession according to intellect, because his understanding is one and simple and perfect, for knowing himself, he knows all other things; and thus there cannot be in God more than one procession of word. But likewise it is also necessary that there be only one procession of love, because also the divine will is one only and simple, for loving himself, he loves all other things. Therefore it is not possible that there be in God other than two persons proceeding, one by the manner of knowledge, as word, viz., the Son, and the other by the manner of love, viz., the Holy Spirit."[21] In this passage the emphasis on the distinct persons, which is characteristic of the early work, is replaced by emphasis on the unity of the divine essence. This is the approach also of the *Summa theologiae*, with the apparent exception of I, 37, 1 ad 3, to which we will return.

It is maintained that it is not legitimate to extend this argument by introducing the factor that the originated persons proceed from respectively different persons, from the Father alone in the case of the Son, and from the Father and the Son in the case of the Holy Spirit, to draw the conclusion that the Son proceeds according to *the Father's* knowledge, and the Holy Spirit according to the love of *the Father and the Son*.[22] The objection to this is that the extension depends on the introduction of a factor that is foreign to, and incompatible with, the analogy: unity of subject is surrendered in favor of multiplicity. When this is done, the guarantee of a valid theological method is lost, so that the results of such argumentation are, at best, dubious. It is permissible to say that the Holy Spirit is the mutual love of the Father and the Son on the ground that this has become part of the fund of theological

---

21   *Summa contra Gentiles* 4, 26.
22   Cf. Dondaine 393-401.

tradition, and indeed, as we will see, Aquinas continued to hold it even in his late works; but he relegated statements of this order to a plane that was clearly secondary to that to which belonged statements deduced strictly from the analogy. For this reason it is maintained that the formal reasons of the processions are not the notional acts but the essential ones. This conclusion is sometimes invoked as the explanation of the fact that the Father and the Son constitute a single principle of the Holy Spirit even though they are two distinct persons, for the essential act of love is declared to remain one and the same in the two persons who breathe forth the Holy Spirit.[23]

The thinking of the older Aquinas is well exemplified in the passage referred to above, *Summa theologiae* I, 37, 1 ad 3. The question is whether "love" is the proper name of the Holy Spirit. The objection runs as follows: "Love is the bond of lovers, for according to Denis it is 'a certain unitive force' (*De Div. Nom.* 4). But a bond is an intermediary between the things that it joins together, not something proceeding from them. Therefore, since the Holy Spirit proceeds from the Father and the Son, as has been shown, it seems that he is not the love or the bond of the Father and the Son." To this Aquinas replies: "The Holy Spirit is said to be the bond of the Father and the Son in so far as he is love. For since with a single love the Father loves himself and the Son, and the Son loves himself and the Father, in the Holy Spirit as love there is brought about a relationship of the Father to the Son and of the Son to the Father. But from the fact that the Father and the Son love each other mutually, it is demanded that their mutual love, which is the Holy Spirit, proceed from them both. Therefore according to origin the Holy Spirit is not an intermediary, but the third person in the Trinity. But according to the aforesaid relationship he is the intermediary bond of the two, proceeding from them both."

In this passage we see not an exception to Aquinas's late thought but an ingenious harmonization of the old Augustinian view that the Holy Spirit is the mutual love of the Father and the Son with the Anselmian view that the formal reason of the procession of the Holy Spirit is the essential act of love, which by this time Aquinas has made his own. His thinking in this answer becomes clearer when it is sorted out on to two planes, the essential and the notional, with the latter subordinated to the former. Uppermost in his mind is the consideration that the formal reason of the second procession is the essential

---

23   Cf. P. Parente, *De Deo Uno et Trino* (Rome, 1949) 273-74.

act of love. He then sets about integrating notionalist thinking into this essentialist framework. The Father and the Son love each other with a single love, not with two acts emanating from each of them, for their love is the essential act of love, which is one. As the divine love, this act can be identified as the Holy Spirit. Aquinas does not use the analogy to deduce that the Holy Spirit proceeds from the Father and the Son, or that he proceeds as their mutual love. For Aquinas he proceeds as the essential love of the Godhead. Rather he argues conversely, that the fact that the Holy Spirit is the mutual love of the Father and the Son shows that he proceeds from them both. That the Holy Spirit proceeds as the essential divine love is a statement on the essential plane, and is primary in Aquinas's thought; that he proceeds from the Father and the Son is implied by the fact that he is their mutual love, and is a statement on the notional plane, and is secondary in his thought, not at odds with the former statement, but reconciled with it. The thought of Aquinas here is perfectly consistent with his late thought as expressed elsewhere. It can be summed up thus: the Holy Spirit is the mutual love of the Father and the Son, but he *proceeds* as the divine self-love.

Certain aspects of Aquinas' teaching on the two processions underwent change, his thought moving from the notional to the essential plane. Thus in the early works he held that the formal reason of the second procession was the notional love, and concretely, the mutual love of the Father and the Son. This is the position in the Commentary on the Sentences. In the *De potentia* the change is evidently taking place, and by the *Contra Gentiles* he has settled firmly into the other view, that the formal reason is the essential love. This can be accounted for at least partly as a movement away from the influence of the twelfth century Parisian theologian, Richard of St. Victor, in the direction of Augustine, and beyond him to Anselm. It has been observed how in the writings of Aquinas Richard is progressively demoted, from the body of the article to the *Contra*, and finally to the objections, while at the same time and in inverse proportion Augustine is promoted.[24] It is true that the influence of Richard was not entirely wholesome, as his trinitarian thought was marred by a certain rationalism and anthropomorphism. Aquinas never succumbed to the rationalism of Richard, but in his early period he does appear to have been misled to some

---

24   Cf. M.T.-L. Penido, "Gloses sur la Procession d'Amour dans la Trinité", *Ephemerides Theologicae Lovanienses* 14 (1937) 51.

extent by his anthropomorphism, particularly in the matter of the relative value of the love of friendship and self-love in the Godhead. Richard's strong point, however, was that he transmitted the spirit of the Eastern Fathers, being more interested in the divine persons than in the divine essence; and while Aquinas was under his influence his theology too breathed the Eastern spirit, which was largely lost as he fell more under the sway of Augustine. It must also be said that Aquinas always accepted the Augustinian psychological analogy, which Richard did not, holding that the Son and the Holy Spirit both proceeded by love. Perhaps the gradual appreciation of the implications of the analogy played a part in separating Aquinas from Richard. However, it seems that in rejecting the weak points of Richard's theology, Aquinas was unable to retain his strong points, with the result that his theology suffered some diminution.

We now set out to criticize the position of the late Aquinas. The conclusion of this will be that the notional acts of knowing and loving, and not the essential ones, are the true formal reasons of the two processions. Our special interest is the procession of the Holy Spirit.

For the sake of clarity we recognize at the outset that objection can be made against the terminology of notional acts of knowing and loving. Generating and breathing-forth are the only true notional acts, in as much as only the Father can be said to generate, and in so doing constitutes the Son, and only the Father and the Son can be said to breathe forth, and in so doing constitute the Holy Spirit. It is not possible to make these claims for knowing and loving, as each divine person may be said to know and to love both himself and each of the other two. Strictly speaking, then, there are no notional acts of knowing and loving. In what follows, however, we will attempt to show that two acts of knowing and loving respectively, when specified precisely in regard to subject and object, are constitutive acts, and thus is supplied the ground on which they can also be called notional. We are constrained to accept and use this terminology, first because "notional" is the accepted contrary of "essential," and secondly because the only serious alternative, "personal," is no less objectionable, since the breathing-forth of the Holy Spirit is clearly not a personal act, performed as it is by two persons acting as a single principle. The word that corresponds precisely to what we mean, "constitutive," cannot be used, as it is the contrary of "concomitant," not "essential." Despite the defects of the terminology, however, no risk of confusion or error is incurred when in what follows we speak of certain divine acts of knowing and loving as "notional" or as belonging to the "notional plane," etc., for what is then meant by the word "notional" is clearly enough defined: it denotes the inner-trinitarian activity, expressed in whatever appropriate terminology, that is not common to the three divine persons and that is constitutive of a divine person.

First, we criticize the position that the psychological analogy requires the formal reasons of the processions to be the essential acts. The reason advanced for this is that the analogy calls for unity of subject. This unity we recognize to be required. But we maintain that it is not sacrificed when one begins to speak of the several divine persons. Admittedly it would be sacrificed if we were speaking of anything but the Godhead, but there is present in the Godhead a unique factor that guarantees that this unity is not sacrificed, viz., the homoousion, with its logical corollary of the unity of the divine operation. It is not an error of *method*, therefore, to pass from saying that the formal reason of the first procession is the divine self-knowledge to saying that it is precisely God the Father's self-knowledge, though the correctness of the *content* of this statement remains to be established. Similarly, it is not an error of method to pass from saying that the formal reason of the second procession is the divine self-love to saying that it is precisely the mutual love of the Father and the Son, though that too remains to be established in content. For, as Aquinas said, it is with a single love that the Father loves the Son and the Son loves the Father. These "two" loves are in fact one and indivisible, not because they simply coincide with the essential love, for the love of the Father and Son, which, as we will show, is constitutive of the Holy Spirit and therefore excludes him as agent, is not simply coincident with the essential love, which includes him as agent; they are one because in the Trinity there are not three psychological subjects, three centers of consciousness from which numerically different acts of knowledge and love flow, but only one subject, one center of consciousness, one act of love, which can be conceived as performed now simply by God (or the three persons), now by the Father alone, now by the Son alone, now by the Father and the Son alone, etc. With the psychological analogy left thus intact, the way remains open for showing that, precisely and only as performed by the Father and the Son in relation to each other, the single act of divine love is constitutive of the Holy Spirit.

Since in the unique case of the Godhead unity of subject is not sacrificed when the psychological analogy is extended from the essential to the notional plane, there is left no methodological objection against so extending it. Indeed, if this may be done, it must be done, as it allows the possibility of determining more precisely the formal reasons of the processions.

This procedure is supported by an examination of the two terms that are universally accepted as notional, viz., generation and breathing-forth. These terms developed in Eastern theology, and served as the preparation for the achievement of the psychological analogy in the West. It is therefore hardly surprising that there exists a close correspondence, commented on by Aquinas himself,[25] between generation and knowledge on the one hand, and breathing-forth and love on the other. Of itself this suggests that knowledge and love also have a place on the notional plane.

We are not suggesting that Aquinas was simply incorrect in proposing the essential acts as the formal reasons of the processions. It remains true that the Son proceeds according to the divine self-knowledge and the Holy Spirit according to the divine self-love; but while these statements are true, they lack a precision that they are capable of having; and as a formal reason has to be as precise a formulation as possible, they do not merit to be accepted as the formal reasons of the processions. Because it is justified to extend the psychological analogy from the essential to the notional plane, the latter stands as the determination or specification of the former. Notionalist statements, therefore, do not simply eliminate or invalidate essentialist ones, but rather make an advance on them. In relation to the processions, therefore, it is preferable to speak on the notional plane; and in determining their formal reasons it is necessary to do so.

The difference between the position of Aquinas and that which we are taking here is that for reasons that we have noted he judged the essential plane to be primary and the notional plane to be secondary, whereas in the argument that we present the notional plane is primary and the essential plane secondary. Logically, each position assigns the formal reasons of the processions to the plane that it considers primary.

As we have seen, Aquinas himself recognized that when speaking of the origin of divine persons it is necessary to speak in terms of notional

---

25   Cf. *Summa theologiae* I, 27, 2, in corp., and 4, in corp. and ad 3.

acts. This is an admitted principle. He did not follow it in relation to the divine knowing and loving, because he did not regard these acts as notional. Having shown that certain acts of knowing and loving in the Godhead can in fact be notional, it now remains for us to specify precisely which acts are to be so designated. Because the Father alone is the principle of the Son, the knowing according to which the Son is generated must be the Father's act of knowing; and because the Father and the Son are the principle of the Holy Spirit, the love according to which the Holy Spirit is breathed forth must be the act of loving of the Father and the Son. These two statements determine the subjects of the notional acts of knowing and loving, but leave their objects undetermined. In order to specify these notional acts precisely, we need to know their objects as well as their subjects. It is this task to which we now turn. There is, however, a preliminary statement that needs to be made. This is that it is an error of method to confuse essentialist with notionalist language. When making statements about the Godhead it is necessary to realize which plane, the essential or the notional, the language used belongs to, and to avoid mixing the two sets of terms. In this connection we repeat that in trinitarian discourse it is imperative to observe the distinctions dictated by the laws of thought, even when corresponding distinctions are lacking in reality. The absence of real distinction in God save for the three persons may not be used as an excuse for confusing, and therefore applying indiscriminately, concepts that are logically distinct, for only the observance of these distinctions provides the guarantee of correct method necessary to ensure the correctness of the results achieved.

Hence, to take up again and dispose of a point raised earlier, it is not legitimate to advance the essential act of love as the reason for the fact that the Father and the Son together constitute a single principle with respect to the Holy Spirit even though remaining two distinct persons. For to say that the essential act is the same in the two persons who breathe him forth is to confuse the essential and the notional planes. An essential act is one that is performed by the Godhead as such. When one speaks of an act as performed by the Father and the Son alone one can no longer be speaking of an essential act. The true reason for the fact that the Father and the Son constitute a single principle with respect to the Holy Spirit is that "in the Godhead all things are one except where the opposition of relationship rules this out." Now in relation to the Holy Spirit the Father and the Son are not opposed; they are opposed only in relation to each other. Thus it is that they constitute a single principle in relation to the Holy Spirit. Hence that the Father and the Son constitute a single principle of the Holy Spirit does not require the formal reason of the second procession to be the essential act of love. The true formal reason of this procession is the notional act of love, performed by the Father and the Son alone.

We now take up the question as to the object of the Father's knowledge that is constitutive of the Son. It cannot be the divine essence, for to say that would be to introduce essentialist language into a notionalist proposition. Neither can it be the Son or the Holy Spirit, for to introduce into the answer of the question as to what constitutes a particular divine person that same person or one who actually proceeds from him would be to beg the question. By a process of elimination, therefore, we come to the only possibility left, the Father himself. That is to say, the act constitutive of the Son is the Father's act of knowing himself. This, however, can also be shown positively, for, as has been said, in the Thomistic epistemology knowledge is ultimately self-knowledge. The primal object of the Father's knowledge is himself. The Father knows himself, and this knowledge is the divine Word, his Son, in whom he knows himself. In a passage in the *Summa theologiae* Aquinas speaks on the notional plane about the formal reason of the first procession: "The Father, knowing himself and the Son and the Holy Spirit and all other things that are contained in his knowledge, conceives the Word."[26] This statement, surprising for the late Aquinas, is unquestionably true, but it is lacking in precision so far as the formal reason of the first procession is concerned. For in as much as the Father is the principle of all other things, knowledge of himself is knowledge of the Son, the Holy Spirit and all created things, and hence it is superfluous to mention them. It is more precise simply to say that knowing himself, the Father conceives the Word.

We come now to the question of the object of the love of the Father and the Son that is constitutive of the Holy Spirit. In his early works, where Aquinas accepted the notional act of love as the formal reason of the second procession, this object was the Son and the Father respectively. That is to say, the formal reason of this procession was the

---

26   Ibid. I, 34, 1ad 3.

mutual love of the Father and the Son.[27] This is the position for which we now argue. By the same kind of reasoning as we used above in relation to the first procession, we rule out the divine essence and the Holy Spirit as the object of the notional love. We are left with the alternatives of the love with which the Father and the Son love themselves, and the love with which they love each other, their mutual love. The former is ruled out as not unitive; the latter is accepted as unitive. The dogmatic principle that guides us here is the filioque. The Father and the Son are one principle of the Holy Spirit. Therefore the Father and the Son must be one in being, and this is guaranteed by the homoousion. But if they are to be truly one principle, they must also be one in the act of love by which they breathe forth the Holy Spirit. The act of love that unites them is their mutual love. Therefore the formal reason of the procession of the Holy Spirit is the mutual love of the Father and the Son.

There is a danger of conceiving the mutual love of the Father and the Son as a meeting of two distinct acts, the love of the Father for the Son and the love of the Son for the Father. It is therefore apposite to cite again the observation of Aquinas that "with a single love the Father loves himself and the Son, and the Son loves himself and the Father." We are speaking of the one and indivisible act of divine love, and saying that it is constitutive of the Holy Spirit in so far as it is performed by the Father and the Son in relation to each other.

Hence, while we stress the unity of the act of the mutual love of the Father and the Son, we must not allow its unity to threaten in our minds the genuineness of its mutuality. Although it is true to say, as Aquinas does, that the Father loves the Son with the Holy Spirit, it is also true that by this statement alone the formal reason of the constitution of the Holy Spirit is not yet given. It is imperative that he be recognized to be not just the love of the Father for the Son, or of the Son for the Father, but their mutual love.

If with the one indivisible act the Father loves the Son and the Son loves the Father, there must exist between the two phases of this act an order, depending on a priority not in time or in essence but in the origin of persons as elaborated in Aquinas's psychological argument

---

27   For Aquinas on the essential mutuality (*amicitia*) of supernatural love see A. Stévaux, "La doctrine de la charité dans les Commentaires des Sentences de Saint Albert, de Saint Bonaventure et da Saint Thomas", *Ephemerides Theologicae Lovanienses* 24 (1948) 85-87.

based on the principle "nothing can be loved by the will unless it is conceived in the intellect," translated to the notional plane. We make this translation now, in order both to use it in relation to the present question, and to return to it for another purpose later. Thus the Father is the absolute beginning, and the Son proceeds from him as the immanent term of his self-knowledge. Thus constituted, the Son is the object of the Father's love. Loved by the Father, the Son loves him in return. The Holy Spirit proceeds as the mutual love of the Father and the Son. Our immediate conclusion is that in the single act of the mutual love of the Father and the Son there are two "moments" (to borrow a Rahnerian term), which are given in the following order: the Father's love of the Son, and the Son's love of the Father.

Because of this order, the Son's love of the Father is to be conceived as an answering love, requiring the Father's love for him as its condition of possibility. In one sense the Son's love of the Father is determinative, in that it is the ultimate moment required to complete the constitution of the Holy Spirit; but in another sense the Father's love of the Son is determinative, in that it is the basic or primordial instance of love, in the light of which all love within the Godhead and therefore also in the world is comprehended. *Therefore the most basic, even if not the most adequate, statement that can be made about the Holy Spirit is that he is the love with which the Father loves the Son.* These observations will be seen to be important when we come to invoke them in the theology of grace.

The real distinction of order that was discerned between the two processions when considered as modalities of the divine spiritual operation on the essential plane is reinforced when they are considered on the notional plane. In the first place all that was said of them on the essential plane continues to stand. Then on the notional plane the further distinction can be made that the first procession is from the Father alone whereas the second is from the Father and the Son. But also the fact of the order and the order itself of the two processions as elaborated in Aquinas' psychological argument on the essential plane is confirmed when this argument is translated to the notional plane as we have done two paragraphs above.

We have seen that there are two acts within the Trinity that may be designated as constitutive, viz., the Father's self-knowledge, which is constitutive of the Son, and the mutual love of the Father and the Son, which is constitutive of the Holy Spirit. It should be noted, however, that these two acts are not constitutive in exactly the same way. The former is constitutive in that it is productive of the Son, in as much as he is the immanent term of the Father's self-knowledge. The latter has no immanent term, and therefore cannot be said to be productive. The Holy Spirit is the mutual love of the Father and the Son. Therefore this act is constitutive in the sense of *merely* constitutive (i.e., not productive). We have by now seen several instances of how words applied in one sense to the first procession may be applied only in an analogous sense to the second. This should cause no surprise. It underscores the difference between the two processions, which are too lightly compared as parallel. Given that any difference exists within the regulative homoousion, it is precisely difference and not repetitive sameness that we should expect to find in the most basic and primordial data of the Godhead.

We now reproduce a text of the young Aquinas taken from his commentary on the first book of the Sentences of Peter Lombard, firstly because it witnesses to his early view that the formal reason of the procession of the Holy Spirit is the mutual love of the Father and the Son, and secondly because in distinguishing between the procession and the *manner* of the procession of the Holy Spirit it will assume considerable importance for the theology of grace. "In the procession of the Holy Spirit there are two things to be considered, viz., the procession itself and the manner of the procession. And because the Holy Spirit proceeds as something distinct and self-existent, he does not have it from the procession as such that he is from the Father to the Son or vice versa, but he has it that he is subsistent in himself. But if the manner of the procession is considered, i.e., that he proceeds as love (as we said in the preceding article in reply to the second objection), since according to the nature of the intellectual process the loved one is that in which love is terminated, and the lover that from which love goes forth: since the Father loves the Son, the Holy Spirit can be said to be the love of the Father for the Son; and since the Son loves the Father, the Holy Spirit can be said to be the love of the Son for the Father."[28]

In this text, though the emphasis on the distinct persons shows the influence of Richard, it is Augustine's distinction of the procession and the manner of the procession of the Holy Spirit that is taken up and developed. What the Holy Spirit owes to the procession is his personhood, his subsistence. As this concerns the Father and the Son only

---

28　*In I Sententiarum* 10, 1, 2.

in as much as they constitute the single principle of this subsistence, it has nothing to do with the reciprocal relationship between them. But if the manner of the procession is considered, it must be said that the Holy Spirit proceeds as love, and indeed as the mutual love of the Father and the Son. Here the relationship between the Father and the Son is of vital importance.

We come now to the distinction that is important for the theology of grace. This is the distinction between the procession and the bestowal of the Holy Spirit in the Trinity. The bestowal corresponds to the manner of the procession in Aquinas's distinction. The Holy Spirit *proceeds* from the Father through the Son, from the Father and the Son; he *is bestowed* as love, by the Father on the Son, and by the Son on the Father. As the procession occurs only in its concrete mode, the order of encounter or what we might call the epistemological order, is first the bestowal, then the procession; the logical order, however, is the inverse, first the procession, then its mode, bestowal, of love.

The basic position for which we have opted above, that the Holy Spirit proceeds as the mutual love of the Father and the Son is not novel or eccentric. It was the position of the young Aquinas, and, as we hope to have shown, was abandoned by him for reasons which, though understandable, were ultimately inadequate. It was also the position of others, Augustine, Bonaventure and John of St. Thomas, to name a few.[29] Though it must stand on its intrinsic merits, it is at least worth noting that it is a position which has received support in the history of theology. We hope to have shown that it does not necessarily involve the anthropomorphism with which it has been, and still is, associated in the minds of some.

Thus we have two ways, or models, of conceiving the Trinity: the procession model, in which the Son proceeds from the Father, and the Holy Spirit proceeds from the Father and (or through) the Son; and what I now call the return model, in which the Father bestows his love on the Son generated by him, and the Son in reply bestows his love on the Father, this mutual love being the Holy Spirit.

The validity of the procession model needs no defense: it has been, as we have shown, the standard way of conceiving the Trinity since patristic times. What we have done in this chapter has been to propose another model, which, however, is not meant in any way to stand as a challenge to the procession model. The two models, as we will

---

29   Cf. Penido 48-68.

show, have different uses, and neither should ever come into conflict with the other. Difficulty will occur, as we will show, only when one is made to do the work of the other, concretely when the procession model is wrongly used instead of the return model. We believe that by the preceding argumentation we have justified the acceptance of the return model. Its complementarity to the procession model is shown from the fact that whereas the latter corresponds to the *fact* of the procession of the Holy Spirit, the former corresponds to the *manner* of this procession.

We conclude by pointing to one advantage that the return model has over the procession model, and to do this we reduce each to a diagram, the latter to a linear diagram (and this whether the per filium or the filioque is invoked), and the former to a circular diagram (remembering that Aquinas said that with the procession of the Holy Spirit "the circle is closed").

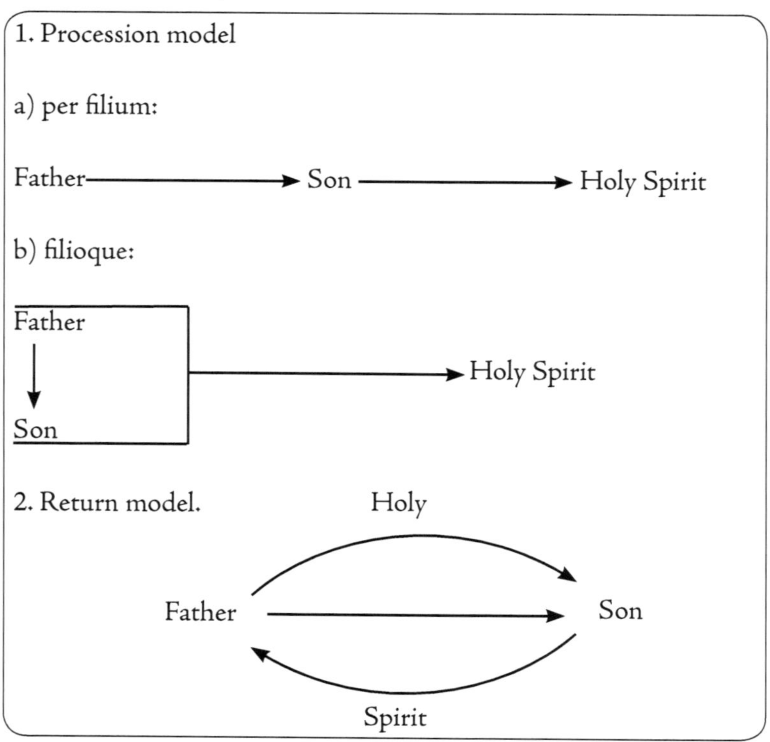

The procession model has the disadvantage of neither stating nor implying the purpose of the breathing-forth of the Holy Spirit, and so inevitably conveys the impression that he is breathed forth purposelessly into the void. The solution lies in turning to the return model. There it is readily seen that the Trinity is self-enclosed and self-sufficient, and that the breathing-forth of the Holy Spirit has a purpose in the Trinity, for he is breathed forth as the mutual love of the Father and the Son. The process is seen to terminate at the Father (in receiving the bestowal of the Son's love), from whom it began (in generating the Son).

3 ASSESSMENT OF THE TRINITARIAN THEOLOGY OF MÜHLEN AND RAHNER

In this chapter we present a critique of the attempts of two recent theologians, H. Mühlen and K. Rahner, to grasp the mystery of the Trinity in terms other than those of the Augustinian psychological analogy. Though neither denies the validity of this model, each sees his own theology as improving on it significantly. We acquiesce in this judgment more wholeheartedly in the case of Rahner than in that of Mühlen. We present the latter's thought on this question because it corresponds to a widely felt desire to conceive the Trinity in a more personal way than hitherto; and we present Rahner's thought because his key-concept of the self-communication of God is carried over by him most fruitfully into the field of the theology of the economy of salvation, i.e., to the Incarnation and grace, resulting in a highly admirable theological synthesis. We begin with Mühlen.

In his book *Der Heilige Geist als Person* Heribert Mühlen presents for the understanding of the Trinity the analogy of personal relations that he draws from the philological research of von Humboldt and from the theology of von Hildebrand and Malmberg, with due recognition of the contributions of Ebner and Buber.[1] In this analogy the Father is the "I",[2] and the Son the "Thou."[3] The Father is the I-relation[4] and the Son the Thou-relation.[5] The question is: How is the Holy Spirit properly characterized within this scheme? From the fact that the Holy Spirit proceeds from the Father and the Son as from a single principle, Mühlen concludes that the "I" that is the Father and the "Thou" that is the Son combine to become the "We" that is the principle of the Holy Spirit.[6] As in the psychological analogy the Holy Spirit proceeds as the subsistent operation of the Father and the Son,

---

1   H. Mühlen, *Der Heilige Geist als Person* (Münster, 1966) 44-82, 100-69.

2   Ibid. 126-31.

3   Ibid. 131-36.

4   Ibid. 129.

5   Ibid. 133.

6   Ibid. 142.

in the terms of the new analogy he is "the subsistent We-act between Father and Son," the "We-act in person."[7] He is "the 'We' in person," the "We-relation,"[8] "one person in two persons."[9]

This analogy has the advantage of enabling the relations of the persons to be expressed in a truly personal way. Thus the Father-Son relation is an I-Thou relation, the Son-Father a Thou-Thou relation,[10] the single relation of the Father and the Son to the Holy Spirit a We-Thou relation,[11] and that of the Holy Spirit to the Father and the Son an I-You (plural) relation.[12] The naming of the relation of the Father and the Son to the Holy Spirit and vice versa is something new in trinitarian theology. Augustine and Aquinas had confessed themselves unable to assign any name to this relation.[13]

In the psychological analogy the relation of the Father and the Son to the Holy Spirit and vice versa remains not only unnamed in fact but unnameable in principle. This is because a relation normally presupposes two fixed beings between which the relation can exist. This is exemplified in the first procession, with the Father and the Son and their relations of fatherhood and sonship. But in the second procession there is only one fixed being, viz., the Father and the Son as the single principle of the Holy Spirit, while the other being, the Holy Spirit, in as much as he is an operation, is not fixed. Of course the Holy Spirit is fixed in that he is subsistent, but his subsistence does not pertain to his property, all three persons being subsistent. Now the trinitarian relations can be expressed only in terms of the properties of the persons. Because the Holy Spirit is subsistent there does exist a relation between his principle and himself and vice versa, but because he is not by his property a fixed being, within the limits of the psychological analogy it is not possible to express this relation. To state the same thing in different words, in the psychological analogy the relation of the Father to the Son and vice versa can be expressed, because the first procession is a *processio operati*, i.e., with an immanent term;

---

7   Respectively, "der subsistierende Wir-Akt zwischen Vater und Sohn", "Wir-Akt in Person." Ibid. 157.

8   "Das Wir in Person." Ibid. 157.

9   "Eine Person in Zwei Personen." Ibid. 164.

10   Ibid. 135.

11   Ibid. 155.

12   Ibid. 158.

13   Cf. ibid. 4.

but the relation of the Father and the Son to the Holy Spirit and vice versa cannot be expressed, because the second procession is a *processio operationis*, i.e., with no immanent term.

Mühlen does not claim to have said the last word on the new analogy, or suggest that as a key to the Trinity it is sufficient in itself. It has received an enthusiastic reception in some quarters, and indeed it does have some good points. On the other hand, however, objections can be sustained against it in regard both to the particular way in which Mühlen has developed it and to its aptness in itself.

The analogy may be described as the assignation of pronouns to, or the "pronominalization" of, the three persons, so that they may be thus distinguished from each other and their relations precisely expressed. Since the Father is the absolute beginning within the Trinity, he is aptly pronominalized as I. As the first of the two persons who proceed from him, the Son is suitably pronominalized as the Thou who stands over against him. As the Father and the Son are a single principle of the Holy Spirit without thereby sacrificing their personhood, it is fitting that they be pronominalized as We. Invoking now the trinitarian theology of subsistent relations, we may call the Father the I-relation, and the Son the Thou-relation. In maintaining that the Holy Spirit is the subsistent We-act in the Godhead and the We-act in person, Mühlen complements the analogy of personal relations from the psychological analogy, and indeed in the form adopted by the younger Aquinas and without discussion as to whether the early or the late form is the correct one. We let this latter point pass, however, as Mühlen's choice coincides with our own conclusion reached in the preceding chapter; and we raise no objection to the combining of the two analogies, as there is no incompatibility between them.

However, we query the correctness of calling the Holy Spirit the We in person, as though he were the hypostatized We of the Father and the Son. The We is the principle from which the Holy Spirit proceeds. Therefore, far from being the We, he stands in a relation of opposition to it. Neither may he be characterized as the We-relation. As subsistent relations the Father and the Son can be characterized as the I-relation and the Thou-relation, because I-Thou expresses the relation between them. In order to express the Holy Spirit as a relation in this scheme it would be necessary to express accurately the single relation between the Father and the Son on the one hand and the Holy Spirit on the other. For the Father and the Son We is certainly appropriate, but it is far from easy to find a suitable pronoun for the Holy Spirit. Mühlen rightly excludes He and It as removing the Holy Spirit from the inner-trinitarian life and making him an external object of dialogue.[14] But in settling for Thou, Mühlen has assigned him the same pronoun as he did the Son. In principle this may not be done. The analogy will be useful only if worked out consistently. If the Father is I and the Son Thou, some other pronoun must be found for the Holy Spirit if he is to be distinguished from them within the framework of the analogy. If he is Thou he is not distinguished from the Son. It may be responded that the Thou of the Holy Spirit does not coincide with the Thou of the Son, as the Son has ceased to be Thou in being included in the We, but against this it must be pointed out that the We is precisely I and Thou. In the end it has to be conceded that there is no suitable pronoun for the Holy Spirit. This means that the analogy of personal relations is only of limited use in understanding the Holy Spirit within the Trinity, and then only in conjunction with the psychological analogy.

Furthermore, within this scheme a personal relation can only be expressed as between an I or a We on the one hand and a Thou or a You (plural) on the other. Under this limitation the only relation that can be named within the scheme is the I-Thou relation of the Father and the Son. The Thou-Thou relation which Mühlen claims is that of the Son to the Father has to be rejected as meaningless and impossible, while the We-Thou and the I-You relations which he claims are those of the Father and the Son to the Holy Spirit and vice versa have to be rejected because each duplicates Thou and the second has the Holy Spirit taking over I from the Father. Hence, far from improving on the psychological analogy so far as the naming of the relations is concerned, the analogy of personal relations is actually less successful than it, and, like it, is incapable of naming the relation of the Father and the Son to the Holy Spirit and vice versa.

These observations, it is realized, apply in the field of what we may call "proper" pronominalization, i.e., the assignation of distinctive pronouns to the three persons so that they may be distinguished and their relations expressed. This procedure belongs with constitutive and notional acts to the level of what we may call primary trinitarian data. Another possibility, of course, is "common" pronominalization, whereby each person is made an I over against the Thou or the You

14   Cf. ibid. 158.

of the other or the others, and each pair is made a We over against the Thou of the other. This is a legitimate procedure, but it belongs with concomitant and essential acts to the level of secondary trinitarian data, where no contribution can be made to the real questions of trinitarian theology, which stand at primary level. The great disadvantage of the analogy of personal relations is that at the primary level of proper pronominalization the exercise cannot be carried through to a point where any significant contribution can be made to trinitarian questions.

We now wish to examine critically Mühlen's understanding of the Holy Spirit as the We-act of the Father and the Son. While there is no difficulty in accepting the concept itself, the way in which Mühlen explains it is open to criticism. He understands the We-act as a common, as distinct from a mutual, act.[15] The Father and the Son stand, as it were, side by side, performing the act together. They are not mutually the object of each other's act. In fact, as we have shown in the case of notional love (We love each other), the We-act does not have to be a common act. Indeed insoluble problems occur if, like Mühlen, one insists that it does. The question is immediately raised, who or what is the object of this act? Mühlen himself rules out the example of two people making a request of a third, as in regard to the Trinity this involves a begging of the question, since the matter under investigation is the formal reason of the procession of the third person, the Holy Spirit.[16] He then gives another example, which he considers free of this objection: the love of a father and a mother directed to their child.[17] Apparently he does not realize that this example is open to the same criticism as the other. The love of the father and the mother is directed to the child only when the latter already exists. As the act constitutive of the child, their love cannot be directed to the child, indeed it is a mutual love, directed to each other. It is most important that this point be taken, for when it comes to the theology of grace, it must be understood that basically and primarily the love of God is not directed beyond the Trinity, or, seeing that it is the Holy Spirit, even beyond the Father and the Son. The Trinity is sufficient to itself. Human beings and the world are created not out of some need felt by God, but out of his freedom. If the love of God is directed beyond the Trinity to

15   Cf. ibid. 142-154.

16   Ibid. 76.

17   Ibid.

humans, this is only that they be drawn into the trinitarian life, to be identified in some way with the Son, and thus made the object of the Father's inner-trinitarian love.

If we take the acceptable results of the new analogy and combine them with the appropriate elements of the psychological analogy, a procedure that is methodologically unimpeachable, we can express the two constitutive acts thus:

1. I (the Father) know myself in Thee (the Son);

2. We (the Father and the Son) love each other (this love being the Holy Spirit).

This appears to be the principal contribution of Mühlen's analogy of personal relations. While it is not without merit, its value is considerably less than is claimed by its author.

We now take up Karl Rahner's concept of "the self-communication of God" (*die Selbstmitteilung Gottes*). Rahner uses this expression mainly in relation to the two supernatural activities of God in the world, the Incarnation and grace/beatific vision.[18] However he also points out that the self-communication of God to the world presupposes and continues the primordial self-communication of God that takes place within the Trinity. It is precisely because the self-communication of God is given in the Trinity that it can be, and is, given in the world.[19]

"To communicate" means "to give to another as partaker; to impart, confer, transmit."[20] The communicating person gives to the recipient something of himself, which is received in the same condition as that in which it was bestowed, i.e., without diminishment. Rahner gives a helpful illustration of communication when he compares the reception of a human word by a human being to its reception by an animal.[21] The former case is an example of communication, because the human being receives the human word *as* a human word; the latter case is not a proper example of communication, or is communication only in a "deficient mode,"[22] because the animal receives the word only in the reduced form of an animal signal.

---

18   Cf. "Selbtmitteilung Gottes," LTK 9, 627; "Revelation. II. God's Self-Communication," SM 5, 353 b-355 b.

19   Cf. Rahner, *The Trinity* 99-103.

20   *The Shorter Oxford English Dictionary* (London, 1970).

21   Rahner 89.

22   "Selbstmitteilung Gottes", LTK 9, 627.

As it takes place in the world, communication may be described, admittedly inadequately but nevertheless correctly, as an exercise of formal causality, in that the imparted reality is received as a form, i.e., not reduced in the process of bestowal and reception.[23] Where, however, the reality is reduced by the recipient to its own level of being, as happens in the example above of the human word received by an animal, or in the case of a painting, which receives and reflects the personality of the painter not in itself but only in the arrangement of pigments, the causality is efficient, a deficient mode of formal causality.

From what we have said it is clear that communication denotes assimilation. The communicating person gives something of self to the recipient, which means that instead of merely casting out in a centrifugal action some pale reflection of self, they draw the recipient in a centripetal motion into the ambit of their own being, so that the recipient begins to share in that being. However if the recipient has their being in the world, there will have to be a centrifugal action, as they have to be reached somehow. Before electricity can be communicated from one object to another a physical link has to be established between them. The human word will be received by a human person also as an animal signal but not only so. Efficient causality provides the basis and condition of possibility of formal causality. Hence in communication in the world centrifugal action and efficient causality are given, but only that the recipient be engaged, so that in a simultaneous centripetal action and by the higher formal causality, which, however, includes the efficient causality within itself, he or she may be assimilated to the communicator.

Communication is a useful concept for helping us understand the two supernatural activities of God in relation to humans. In the Incarnation divinity is communicated to the humanity of Jesus, so that the result is the hypostatic union; and in grace divinity is communicated to humans, so that they become united to God as he is in himself, though not in a hypostatic union. We shall say more of this later, when we shall be at pains to show why each of these communications is a communication of both the Son and the Holy Spirit. For the present we shall be satisfied with observing that in each of these instances formal causality may be invoked, in that God is communicated to a created reality, the sacred humanity in the first instance and believers

---

23   Cf. D. Coffey, "The Gift of the Holy Spirit", *Irish Theological Quarterly* 38 (1971) 202-23.

in the second, and efficient causality is included in it, as is evident from the fact that in each instance there is a "new creation," the sacred humanity itself in the first and "created grace" in the second.

The observations made so far enable us to dispose of the problem raised by the first of the two theological axioms of which we spoke earlier: the works of God in the world are done by all three divine persons. There is a sense in which the Incarnation and grace must be acknowledged as works of God in the world, i.e., to the extent that they are done by efficient causality. In this respect they must be said to be done by all three persons. This means that the creation of the sacred humanity and what we call created grace are the work of the three persons. But as we have intimated above, this is only part of the truth about the Incarnation and grace, even in the categories of infra-personal Aristotelian philosophy. They may also be explained as instances of formal causality, of the self-communication of God, and precisely as the latter, are not works of God in the world, but the assimilation of created realities to the inner life of God. In this respect, therefore, the axiom does not apply to them, and there is no problem in principle in seeing the Incarnation and grace, as what we know them by faith to be, communications of the Son and the Holy Spirit to the sacred humanity and to ordinary humans (though in respectively different ways).

Hitherto we have spoken of communication. We must now justify Rahner's term, "self-communication." Is not the "self" redundant in that every communication is necessarily a self-communication? This is true, but only in the sense that in the secular usage it can never be more than part of the self that is communicated, e.g., a thought; whereas, though God can also communicate his thoughts if he so desires, he can also communicate himself, i.e., in the totality of his divinity, and this even outside the Trinity. The use of the word "self" expresses the difference that exists between the limit of divine communication and that of human communication.

Self-communication is likewise a useful concept for helping us understand the two modalities of the divine operation within the Trinity that give rise to the Son and the Holy Spirit. It is clear that within the Trinity the self-communication of God is identical with the divine operation. It is also clear that here there is no question of causality of any kind. Instead there is pure principiality. It is only when the two modalities of the self-communication of God are projected beyond the Trinity into the sphere of the non-divine that principiality extends to include formal causality. Hence within the Trinity there is no centrifugal and centripetal motion but only pure immanence. This explains why the personhood of the Son and of the Holy Spirit is constituted by, and does not logically precede, the self-communication. In the self-communication of God each receives himself.

The first modality in which the self-communication of God in the Trinity is given is that by which the Father constitutes the Son. The Father communicates himself to the Son, and the Son receives himself from the Father. This, then, is a self-communication of the Father, in which the word "self" stands for the Father. It may also be said that the Father communicates the divine essence to the Son, and the Son receives this essence from the Father. Both the Father and the Son are identical with this essence, but this does not make them identical with each other, for they are relationally opposed as communicator and recipient respectively. Indeed the Father is pure communicator or bestower, *principium sine principio*, the unprincipled principle. This explains why, even though the Father communicates himself to the Son, the Son does not receive the Father. As pure communicator the Father cannot be received. Hence it follows that it is not simply a fact but in principle impossible that the Father be received in the world, i.e., in a hypostatic union. He must always remain the invisible God of Scripture and tradition.[24]

The Son is both recipient and communicator, *principium principiatum*, the principled principle. As communicator he becomes one with the Father, and the single principle of the Holy Spirit. This is not to say that the personhood of the Son is surrendered, for as recipient to communicator he remains opposed to, and therefore distinct from, the Father. It is only as co-principle of the Holy Spirit that he makes one with the Father. The Father and the Son communicate themselves, or alternatively the divine essence, to the Holy Spirit, and the Holy Spirit receives himself, or alternatively the divine essence, from the Father and the Son. The same kind of remark applies to the second modality of the self-communication of God as to the first, and readers are left to make such adjustments for themselves. We make the observation, however, that the Holy Spirit is pure recipient, *principiatus*, the principled one, and thus the circle of the Trinity is closed. Applying the principle of the necessary consistency of God, we note that in his role

---

24   Cf. Jn 1:18; Rom 1:20; Col 1:15; 1 Tim 1:17; 6:16; Heb 11:27; Origen, *Contra Celsum* 7, 43 (PG 11, 1484).

of pure communicator the Father sends the Son into the world, and in his role of communicator the Son sends the Holy Spirit, but as pure recipient the Holy Spirit can only be sent, he cannot send himself or either of the other persons. This is important for the theology of grace.

In speaking of the self-communication of God to the Holy Spirit we have so far considered only the filioque, the Father and the Son as a single principle. We must now take the other aspect, the per filium, into account. The statement that the Father and the Son communicate themselves to the Holy Spirit can without prejudice to the singularity of principle be reduced to two statements, the Father communicates himself to the Holy Spirit, and the Son communicates himself to the Holy Spirit. Thus already it may be said that the Father communicates himself to the Son, and the Father communicates himself to the Holy Spirit, which means that both modalities of the self-communication of God in the Trinity are self-communications of the Father. Admittedly this leaves the self-communication of the Son out of account. However, if the Father communicates himself to the Son, and the Son communicates himself to the Holy Spirit, it is clear that the self-communication of the Son *can* be taken into account and seen as the *means* by which the Father communicates himself to the Holy Spirit. The Father, then, communicates himself both immediately and mediately to the Holy Spirit.[25] Hence, without prejudice to the fact that the Father and the Son together communicate themselves to the Holy Spirit, we may draw the conclusion that both modalities of the self-communication of God in the Trinity are ultimately self-communications of God the Father, or, more precisely, that in the Trinity there is only one self-communication of God, which is the self-communication of the Father, given, however, in two modalities.

In thus assessing the trinitarian theologies of Mühlen and Rahner, we have seen to what extent Mühlen's analogy of personal relations is valid and able to be retained in support of the positions reached in the preceding chapter, and we have embraced Rahner's theology of the self-communication of God as helpful in understanding the processions of the Son and the Holy Spirit in the Trinity and their respective prolongations into the world as Incarnation and grace. In the next part of the book we subject this idea to close scrutiny in order to be able to understand better the theology of the divine economy, particularly that of grace, and to see it as the revelation of the inner being of God.

---

25   Cf. *Summa theologiae* I, 36, 3 ad 1.

The Christology will be of the descending kind, the theology of grace will correspond to it, and the relevant model of the Trinity will be the procession model.

PART II

THEOLOGY OF THE INCARNATION AND GRACE IN THE LIGHT OF THE PROCESSION MODEL

4 ASSESSMENT OF SCHOLASTICISM AND PERSONALISM

We have now reached the point where we may begin our inquiry into the revelation and the operation of the Trinity in the world and among human beings. In this part we restrict our conception of the Trinity to what we know from the procession model, and in the next two parts we will explore the same subject from the standpoint of the return model. In this first chapter, which is introductory to all three parts, we examine the categories, philosophical and biblical, in which we may speak of the action of God in the world, culminating in the Incarnation (the revelation of the Trinity) and grace (the operation of the Trinity).

Until recently Catholic theology in the West has been satisfied to conceive this action of God in simply physical categories, viz., in the terms of infra-personal Aristotelian philosophy. For instance, Scholasticism regarded sanctifying grace as an accident, i.e., something which has its being in another, as distinct from a substance, which has being in itself; and it went on from there to categorize it as a quality, a habit, indeed an entitative habit. There is now a reaction against this approach at least partly because of its inadequacy to express the reality of grace as presented in Scripture, i.e., as something highly personal, viz., the favor and merciful love of God. In this connection the attempt of Mühlen to personalize the essentially infra-personal category of efficient causality and so arrive at the new category of "personal causality" must be said to be a failure.[1] Mühlen describes personal causality as "the *species infima* of the *genus* of *causa efficiens*,"[2] the lowest species of the genus of efficient cause. The concept of efficient cause itself is apersonal, i.e., it prescinds from whether the cause is personal or infra-personal. (More precisely, it applies directly to the infra-personal agent, and only by transference to the personal agent.) When a person exerts a purely mechanical influence on infra-personal being, it is impossible to tell from the effect alone whether the cause is personal

---

1   Cf. Mühlen, *Der Heilige Geist als Person* 274-80.

2   Ibid. 279.

or not. Sometimes, however, the effect clearly bespeaks a personal cause, e.g., a work of art. In this latter case it may well be admissible to speak of the causality as personal and as a species of efficient causality. However, the important factor is not so much the personhood of the cause, which here is taken for granted, as the non-personhood of the being on which the influence is exerted. When we have personal being as the recipient of the influence, unless we are speaking of the act of creation, the concept of purely efficient causality is no longer applicable. A person has something caused in them, or is caused to do something, only if their personhood is overlooked or abused and they are treated as infra-personal being. When a person is persuaded to do or to allow something, so that the consequence flows, at least in part, from their own free decision, it is no longer appropriate to speak simply in terms of efficient causality. Admittedly, some theologians of the Scholastic tradition have made use of the category of "moral causality" to cover just this situation, but in fact this expression is a contradiction in terms. If this is so of moral causality, it is likewise so of Mühlen's personal causality. We have to accept the fact that if we speak of grace in terms of efficient causality, we thereby reduce a personal reality to an infra-personal level, at least on the side of the recipient.

To some extent the same must be said of Rahner's concept of divine formal causality ("quasi"-formal causality, as he called it[3]) as a way of grasping the action of God in the Incarnation and grace, for here too an infra-personal concept from Aristotelian philosophy is put to work in the service of theology. However, formal causality is less open to objection than efficient causality, since it is the highest kind of causality, the one most akin to personal action and interaction, and in the appropriate (i.e., personal) circumstances can be expounded in terms of personal communication. It is therefore a bridge-concept, with links to both Aristotelianism and Personalism. In theology it leads to the key concept of the self-communication of God, and provides a way of understanding the spiritual union of God and humans, and hence is suited to be a model for their union in both the Incarnation and grace. In the latter field, e.g., it enables us to give some account of what is meant by the expression "receiving the Holy Spirit."

The use of the concept of formal causality in regard to the Incarnation and grace is connected with the transcendental method as

---

3   Rahner, "Some Implications of the Scholastic Concept of Uncreated Grace," *Theological Investigations* 1, 330.

developed by Rahner.[4] In his approach the human being is no longer simply an objective observer of the physical universe (who from that point has to be related somehow to God), but the primordial subject, transcendentally oriented to God in a relationship which is realized through the self-communication of God in grace. The concept of formal causality serves as an aid, albeit a limited one, for explaining how this takes place. It would be wrong to conclude from this that Scholasticism was simply in error in characterizing created habitual grace as an accident, as though that by which a human being is perfected precisely as human could never be so characterized.[5] A fact too easily forgotten is that in Scholasticism the word "accident" has two meanings: one metaphysical, where it is opposed to "substance," the other logical, where it is opposed to "essence." When created grace is said to be an accident, the term is intended only in the former sense; and all that it affirms in reality is that a human being in union with God by grace retains their distinct human personhood, so that in grace there is a union of persons, viz., the human and God (the Holy Spirit), not, as in the Incarnation, a union of person (the human and the divine natures in the single person of the Son). Even though the terminology of substance and accident sounds inappropriate to ears attuned to personal categories, the truth thus asserted is fundamental, and should never be lost to sight. The objection mentioned above, viz., that that by which a human being is perfected as human cannot be termed an accident, understands "accident" in the logical sense, but it is a caricature of Scholasticism to maintain that it used the word in this sense when speaking of grace.

These brief remarks will, it is hoped, suffice to show that there is a great need for a theology of grace which is as systematic as the efforts of Scholasticism but which surpasses them by presenting grace in genuinely personal terms. Scholarly works of biblical theology of grace, though indispensable, are no substitute for this. They constitute only the first and preparatory stage of a comprehensive theology of grace, which must interpret the biblical truth in the light of contemporary culture, particularly philosophical culture.

---

4   For an account of this by Rahner, see "Transcendental Theology," SM 6, 287a-289b. Cf. also O. Muck, *The Transcendental Method* (New York, 1968).

5   For example, F. Malmberg, *Über den Gottmenschen* (Freiburg im Br., 1960) 84-85.

Having seen something of the importance of personal categories for the conceptualization of grace, we now look at the limitations inherent in these categories where they remain unintegrated into an adequate philosophy. At the outset, however, we ought to remind ourselves of the change that has taken place in the concept of person itself from ancient to modern thought. The classical definition of person, which arose in specifically Christian thought, is that of Boethius from the sixth century: *rationalis naturae individua substantia*, the individual substance (supposit) of a rational nature. Evident here is the emphasis placed by the ancient world on the subsistence and incommunicability of the person, with its consequence that the spirituality of the person, while remaining essential, took second place. The modern concept contains roughly the same elements, but the emphasis is inverted, so that the spirituality, freedom and relatedness of the person come to the fore. The assumption that the modern meaning of "person" holds also for the ancient world results in confusion and at times also in doctrinal error, e.g., when made in regard to the trinitarian dogma of three persons in one God it issues in tritheism.

For Aquinas, who inherited the thought of Boethius, the problem of person was to understand its capacity to be a universal, seeing that it signified a thing precisely in its particularity. He put the question, what is the quality of that thing which certain things have in common which enables each of them to be called person?[6] This thing in common, or "community," he says, cannot be something real, as otherwise there would be only one person in God, whereas in fact there are three. Nor is it a "community of intention," to which belong genus, species and individual, for person is the name not of an intention but of a thing. Rather it is a "community of reason" in the sense of "vague individual thing," e.g., "some human being." Why vague? Because a designated individual thing would be called not "person" but a proper name, e.g., Socrates. Person is vague or indesignate individual thing, i.e., the common nature in the determinate mode of existence of particular things. However, there is a final precision to be made, in that a distinction has to be drawn even between indesignate individual thing, e.g., some human being, and person, for the former signifies an individual thing on the part of its nature with the mode of existence of particular things, while the latter signifies a thing subsisting in its nature.

---

6   Cf. *Summa theologiae* I, 30, 4.

This shows the great difficulty that metaphysics in the Aristotelian mould will have in handling the concept of person. Because it denotes a being precisely in its unique and incommunicable subsistence, it presents the being in its mystery, even its unintelligibility. Despite the fact that it is a universal, metaphysics is not at ease with it, and tends to shift its designation, almost imperceptibly, to the point of equating it with the more abstract concept, nature, i.e., a nature in the mode of existence of particular things; but, as Aquinas points out, this is not exactly what is meant by "person."

The sense of the mystery of person is present also in modern thinking, where, as has been remarked, the emphasis moves from subsistence to spirituality. For W. Pannenberg person is characterized by inscrutability, unavailability: "It is no accident that primitive man, and even today the child, personifies whatever is at the same time important to him and not thoroughly known, and so has a hidden inner dimension. Whatever is at least in principle entirely available, however, becomes a thing."[7] For M. Müller and A. Halder person is "a contradiction in formal logic," a contradiction "of the absolutely individual (a freedom which can be exercised by none but itself) and the most comprehensively universal (the spiritual)."[8] Particularly where personhood is seen as not given but achieved, as established in relationship over against other persons, and, above all, God (which view also has its roots in Christian antiquity, specifically in Trinitarian speculation), person emerges as a mystery defying precise definition.

Whether considered in the context of ancient or of modern thought, therefore, person remains a baffling and elusive concept, and the categories deriving from its present meaning, though suited perhaps to a purely positive theology, are insufficient on their own for a comprehensive and systematic theology of grace.

In Pannenberg's view, Scholasticism and afterwards Hegel at least situated man as person in the context of the ontological problem in its most general form.[9] Personalism, on the other hand, has not succeeded in comprehending the whole of reality, and has finished up by placing infra-personal and personal being in opposition. From the historical point of view the appearance of Personalism is not difficult to understand. Human beings saw themselves increasingly as victims of

---

7   "Person," RGG 5, 3rd edn. 232.

8   "Person," SM 4, 405a.

9   "Person," RGG 5, 3rd edn. 233-34.

a world in which science and technology were in the ascendant, making them redundant, and causing them to question radically their own dignity and importance. Personalism emerged as the answer to this question. Clearly, however, this is a phase to be overcome. Theology in particular will have the task of understanding the human being anew in their unity with the world, their fellow-humans and God. E. Simons likewise sees personalism as a phase that can contribute to a more comprehensive future philosophy, but only if it resists the temptation to erect itself into an absolute, and makes a concerted effort with transcendental philosophy.[10]

This view of Simons we wholeheartedly endorse, and indeed attempt to realize theologically in some measure in this book. Without making exaggerated claims for it, we can at least say of transcendental theology that, following on as it does from transcendental philosophy, it tries to overcome the gap between the human being and the world of objects, and yet at the same time fastens attention on the personal subject in their relationship to God, a relationship which embraces also their fellow-humans, and which is realized in the self-communication of God in grace. This view does not require that we simply discard the efforts of earlier generations to grasp this relationship and its implications. Even if their perspectives and hence also their language were relatively deficient, we do well at times to point to the profound religious truths they were trying to safeguard and express, as we have just done, e.g., in the case of the Scholastic conception of grace as an accident. At other times we will find that we still have things to learn from further developing categories belonging to their systems of thought and compatible with transcendental theology. For example, we can show, by invoking divine formal causality, how the Incarnation and grace are proper to the Son and the Holy Spirit respectively while remaining in a sense works of God in the world and to that extent common to the three divine persons (this we will do in the next chapter).

It will be useful at this early stage of our treatment of the theology of grace, when we are considering the categories in which it is appropriate to conduct the discussion, if something is said about the principal biblical category from which this theology must be elaborated, viz.,

---

10 "Personalism," SM 4, 421b.

covenant.[11] More will be said about this later, but at the outset it will be helpful if the main points of covenant-theology are set down.

Among the Hebrews the word for covenant, *berît*, denoted in its profane sense a contract. Because it was normally not possible to have the more easily enforcible written contracts, great solemnity attached to verbal contracts. The parties to such a covenant were bound by it to a common interest, and even God had his part to play, viz., as witness. Often the services of a mediator were engaged. Chosen by the initiator, the mediator approached the other party, and often was endowed with authority actually to enact the covenant. Once entered upon, a covenant demanded from both partners the appropriate attitude of *hesed*, benignity based on the covenantal bond, therefore favor (*ḥēn*) or grace (both *hesed* and *ḥēn* being translated in the Septuagint as *charis*, which became *gratia* in Latin and "grace" in English), and loyalty, felt inwardly but also manifested in act. Of particular interest are covenants between unequal partners, e.g., between the conqueror and the conquered, the king and the vassal (cf. Ezek 17), for into this category the relationship of God to Israel was understood to fit. In such covenants the initiative comes from the superior party, and the gracious character of the covenant and also the dignification of the inferior party are readily seen as important elements. Under these circumstances *hesed* takes on a slightly different meaning for each partner: for the superior it connotes condescension, even mercy if the inferior partner is revealed as unfaithful; while for the inferior it connotes surrender and a practical readiness to carry out the will of the superior. In the covenantal relationship of God and Israel, *hesed* meant for God his bounteous merciful love (his grace), and for Israel its penance (conversion) and faith.

The Old Testament speaks of covenants between God and the people, with Noah, Abraham and Moses as mediators, but of highest importance in the minds of the Israelites was the last-mentioned, described in Ex 19-24, which was enacted on Mount Sinai and sealed with a blood sacrifice. It was this that transformed the wandering tribes into a nation and gave them a national religion. It is clear from the account that God's choice of the people of Israel was made on his own initiative, out of his love and grace, and independently of their merits. He takes them to himself as his own people, offering his

---

11   Cf. J. Haspecker, "Bund," HTG 2, 197-204; J. McKenzie, "Covenant," *Dictionary of the Bible* (London, 1965) 153-57.

intimacy, protection and leadership; and on their side they are bound to observe his statutes, principal among which is the worship of him alone, the God of the covenant. Worship within the covenant is not so much its fulfillment as the concrete form of the covenantal encounter and fellowship of the people with God.

The prophets, especially Jeremiah and Ezekiel, foretold a new covenant in the eschatological future, as the old one had been broken by the infidelity of the people. Israel would be given up to destruction, and the covenant made with its surviving remnant. The new covenant would transcend the old: it would be eschatological, and it would be more spiritual, concerned more with the attitude of people's hearts than with their external actions (Jer 31:31-34; 32:37-41; Ezek 16:60-63; 34:25-31; 37:15-28).

Deutero-Isaiah develops this idea in two directions: the founder and mediator of the new covenant will be the suffering servant of God (42:6-7; 4:6; 53), and the covenant itself will extend beyond the people of Israel to include all people (55:3-5; 49:6).

In its eschatological character the new covenant became a theme central to Messianism. Connected with this is the idea of the out-pouring of the Spirit of God expected in the end-time (Joel 2:28-32). In any action of God in the world and among humans the Spirit is decisive, for he is God's very power. It is in his Spirit, therefore, that God initiates and carries out his covenant, especially the spiritual es-chatological covenant. It is therefore not surprising that in Isaiah and Deutero-Isaiah the Messiah is presented as the bearer of the Spirit (11:2; 42:1; 44:1, 3; also Hag 2:5 and Ezek 36:26-27).

Also to the prophets, especially to Hosea, we are indebted for the image of the covenant as a marriage between God (the husband) and the people (the bride). It is thought likely that the repeated sentence, "You will be my people, and I will be your God," is a variation of the marriage-formula. In this context the outpouring of the Spirit in the new covenant is readily understood as God's gift to his people, sign of his election and love.

In contrast to the prophetic conception of the covenant, that which is found in the priestly source in the Pentateuch must be mentioned. Here the graciousness of the covenant receives particular emphasis, so that the covenants with Noah and Abraham, in which the divine promises were unilateral, emerge as very important. The covenant with Moses is seen as a further stage of the previous covenants, and no stage beyond it is envisaged for the future. For St. Paul in the New Testament the new covenant is the fulfillment of that made with Abraham, and marks the abrogation of the covenant with Moses. His doctrine subsumes elements of both the priestly and the prophetic theology of the Old Testament.

The appropriate places for showing the completion of these ideas in the New Testament will come later, when we speak of the anointing of the humanity of Jesus with the Holy Spirit and the sending of this Spirit, into the community by Jesus risen from the dead. For the present we merely note that the New Testament presents Jesus as the one on whom the Spirit of God is poured out in fullness (Jn 3:34), so that he is constituted as the Messiah, the one who in his death is to be the founder and mediator of the new, eschatological and universal covenant and the fulfiller of the promises of the old. The new covenant is the covenant of the Spirit (2 Cor 3:6), who is sent by the risen Jesus as his own Spirit (Rom 8:9). The Christian Eucharist, memorial of the sacrificial death of Jesus, becomes the supreme form of the covenantal encounter of God and humans in the Holy Spirit. The new covenant is between God the Father and the new people of God, the Church, which is not an exclusive group but is potentially universal; Jesus is its mediator; and it is enacted and fulfilled in the Holy Spirit. The permeation of nature by grace is evident even in the covenant of God with Noah, in which the object of God's promise is the natural good of the world (Gen 9:8-17). However, far from being an obstacle, this is a help toward understanding the relation of nature and grace, for which the two ideas of creation and covenant provide a biblical theology. Since the covenant is here the biblical way of conceiving the supernatural, its importance for a theology of grace can scarcely be exaggerated.

Our discussion of the Incarnation and grace, then, may justly be termed an exercise in transcendental theology, provided this be understood as comprehending also the worthwhile contributions of Scholasticism and Personalism and as having Scripture (and tradition) as its basis and continuing inspiration. We now proceed, in the next chapter, with the task of examining our subject in the light of the procession model of the Trinity.

5 INCARNATION AND GRACE AS THE SELF-COMMUNICATION OF GOD

In this chapter we make a comparison of the Incarnation and grace in the light of the procession model of the Trinity. This requires that we conceive them as prolongations into the world of the two modalities of the self-communication of God in the Trinity. This is done by interpreting them as instances of divine formal causality. Our observations will take shape largely in the framework of a presentation and assessment of the contributions of M. de la Taille and K. Rahner on this subject.

The application of the category of formal causality to grace can be used to shed light on the biblical conception of grace as "the Gift of the Holy Spirit."[1] This expression does not mean that grace is simply a gift which the Holy Spirit bestows; it means, rather, that the gift is the Holy Spirit himself, the Father being the giver or bestower, and human beings the recipients. This is a basic statement in the theology of grace. That grace is the Gift of the Holy Spirit is stated in the New Testament, both directly (Acts 2:38; 10:45) and in equivalent ways (Jn 3:5-8; 14:23-26; Acts 1:8; 8:14-17; 10:44; 11:16-17; Rom 5:5; 8:9-11, 14-17, 23; 1 Cor 3:16; 6:19; 2 Cor 1:22; 5:5; Gal 3:5; 4:6; Eph 1:13-14; 2:18, 22; Phil 1:19; Tit 3:5; 1 Jn 3:24; 4:13), and affirmed in the teachings of the Eastern Fathers, particularly St. Cyril of Alexandria[2] and the Cappadocians,[3] but the line of development taken by the doctrine of grace in Western theology from Augustine and particularly among the Scholastics closed the eyes of the West to the possibility of understanding grace in this way.

Despite the balance of Augustine's own doctrine of grace, the Pelagian, and subsequently the Semi-Pelagian, controversy, in which he became embroiled as the principal defender of orthodoxy, set Western doctrine and theology on a narrow path, the investigation of

---

1   Cf. D. Coffey, "The Gift of the Holy Spirit."

2   Cf. Ch. Baumgartner, *La Grâce du Christ* (Tournai, 1963) 52-54; H. Rondet, *The Grace of Christ* (Westminster, Md., 1966) 80-84.

3   Cf. Baumgartner 55-56; Rondet 77-79.

the need of human beings for grace to keep the law of God and arrive at final salvation. Although it was always realized that grace was God's gift, once given it became in Western thinking a human possession, enabling its possessors to do certain things. This concentration on grace as a human possession led to the development of the Scholastic concept of "created grace." Admittedly this was seen as complemented by "uncreated grace," the indwelling Trinity, but it remains true to say that when the Scholastics said simply "grace" they meant "created grace." Moreover the very distinction of created and uncreated grace led to a certain disjunction between them, in the sense that after the Council of Trent their co-presence in the soul of the just person was seen no longer as necessary but only as factual. Finally, Scholasticism's concentration on created grace received added impetus from Trent's rejection of the Protestant theology of "forensic" justification, i.e., a justification simply imputed by God but without real effect in the soul. Thereafter Catholic theology was to lay great stress on the real change brought about in the soul by grace.

Connected with this was the conviction of the Scholastics that God's action in grace was an exercise not of formal but of efficient causality, and grace itself the product or effect of this exercise. Aquinas witnesses to this when he says, "The soul is the formal cause of the life of the body, and therefore vivifies it without an intermediary form. God, however, vivifies the soul not as formal cause but as efficient cause, and therefore an intermediary form does intervene. For example, a painter makes a wall white by efficient causality and by means of whiteness, but whiteness makes it white without an intermediary form because it whitens by formal causality."[4] The consequence was that grace was regarded purely as a work of God in the world, and as such was considered common to the three divine persons. Hence any possibility of conceiving grace as a work in some way proper to the Holy Spirit, comparable to the Incarnation as proper to the Son, was removed. The remarkable thing was that the category of efficient causality was adhered to so firmly and for so long despite the fact that faith in the Incarnation as being of the Son alone and not of all three divine persons posed so radical a challenge to it. It should be noted, however, that Scholasticism's commitment to efficient causality and to the idea that grace was a work of God in the world helped it dispose of the contention of Peter Lombard that love differed from faith and hope in

---

4   *De veritate* 27, 1 ad 1.

that there was no infused virtue of love, as the Holy Spirit himself and alone inspired love immediately in the just person. (Lombard's theory, of course, can be refuted on other grounds as well.)

The concept of the Holy Spirit in grace as a "form" had been proposed by St. Basil,[5] and from time to time was resurrected in the West, but had no impact on Scholasticism or neo-Scholasticism. For Aquinas the question about formal causality of God in the world was not whether it was exercised by any particular divine person or persons but whether it was exercised by the Godhead as such. As we have seen, even put in this way the question was answered in the negative in regard to grace. However, in the order of operation as distinct from being he admitted divine formal causality in regard to the beatific vision, as the following quotation shows: "Whatever is raised above its nature must be disposed by a disposition above its nature. Thus, e.g., if air is to receive the form of fire, it must be disposed by a disposition to such a form. But since a created intellect sees God in his essence, the very essence of God becomes the intelligible form of the intellect."[6] What Aquinas restricted to the beatific vision two twentieth-century theologians, working independently, de la Taille with his "created actuation by uncreated Act,"[7] and Rahner with his "quasi-formal causality,"[8] extended to the Incarnation and grace.

De la Taille presented his theology in terms of the Aristotelian categories of potency and act. The process by which act communicates or unites itself to potency he called "actuation," as distinct from actualization or making-real, which is the task of efficient causality and does not imply a union of being. Normally, when actuation occurs, it takes place wholly within the world, but there is no absolute objection in principle to the actuation of the potencies of created beings by God. Rahner has pointed out, however, that the created potency must be personal, since in all created being only personal being has, by virtue of its spirit, the transcendence or openness to God that allows it to receive God in himself in a true self-communication, i.e., without reducing him to a mere created reflection of himself, which is what happens

---

5   *Liber de spiritu sancto*, 26, 61 (PG 32, 180; *Sources chrétiennes* 17, 225).

6   *Summa theologiae* I, 12, 5.

7   M. de la Taille, "Actuation créée par Acte incréé", *Recherches de science religieuse* 18 (1928) 253-68.

8   Rahner, "Some Implications of the Scholastic Concept of Uncreated Grace," *Theological Investigations* 1, 319-46.

in the exercise by him of purely efficient causality, viz., in the creation.[9] When a potency of a created being is actuated by God, the being will be put in act only to the extent allowed by the potency, which is finite, so that the actuation is created, even though the act actuating the potency is uncreated. However the potency in question, as a potency to be united with God, is not a natural potency of the being. Though a potency of the being, it is a potency to be "raised above its nature," and is therefore a supernatural, or "obediential," potency, a *potentia obedientialis*. Hence it is concluded that it is in principle possible to have, without any suggestion of pantheism, created actuation by uncreated Act, in which is given by divine formal causality an intimate union of God and non-divine personal being. There are three, and only three, instances of created actuation by uncreated Act: the beatific vision, grace and the Incarnation.

Rahner took his point of departure from Aquinas's theology of the beatific vision, which he applied in the first instance to grace. Since first presenting this theology in 1939, he had many opportunities over the years to refine it. In the original essay he spoke of the divine formal causality as "quasi-formal" in order to distinguish it from the formal causality that takes place wholly within the world, where the form in union with matter is not transcendent. The transcendence of God has to be guaranteed even when he has entered into a union with a creature that can be said to be by formal causality. While this is a point worth making, hereafter we shall omit the "quasi," as it lacks any particular significance, being only a reminder that all language about God is analogical. This is admitted by Rahner when he says, "... the *quasi* ... must be prefixed to every application to God of a category in itself terrestrial."[10] In later writings he has re-grouped the three instances noted by de la Taille into two, the first being the Incarnation, and the second grace and the beatific vision, with the last-named pair related as follows: "Grace and beatific vision form a unity, in which grace initiates and has the same formal character as the vision of God, so that grace and glory are two historical phases of the one grace."[11] Rahner here expresses a traditional Christian truth. The New Testament speaks of our present possession of the Holy Spirit in grace as "first

---

9   Cf. Rahner, *The Trinity* 89-90.

10   Rahner, "Some Implications of the Scholastic Concept of Uncreated Grace" 330.

11   "Revelation. II. God's Self-Communication," SM 5, 354b.

fruits" or "earnest" (first installment) (Rom 8:23; 2 Cor 1:22; 5:5; Eph 1:14), which implies that in glory we shall possess him in his fullness; and this is expressed by the Church magisterium in the teaching of Pope Leo XIII,[12] repeated by Pius XII,[13] that the indwelling of the Holy Spirit in grace and the beatific vision differ "only by reason of our condition or state." A further indication is the thesis of J. Alfaro,[14] following a suggestion by Rahner,[15] that in heaven the mediatorship of Christ, by which grace comes to us on earth, is not abolished, but rather is brought to its completion in the beatific vision.

Further, Rahner has linked the instances of divine formal causality, which are identical with the two modalities of the self-communication of God (the Father) in the world, with the two trinitarian processions, seeing them as the respective projections, free and temporal, into the sphere of the non-divine, of what happens necessarily and eternally within the Trinity.[16] Thus the Incarnation is the free and temporal moment of the generation of the Son, and grace/beatific vision the free and temporal moment of the breathing-forth of the Holy Spirit. While we stress the freedom of God in communicating himself in and to the world, we must point out with Rahner that once this free decision is taken (if we may speak thus anthropomorphically), the manner of its execution is not free, but determined by the necessary consistency of God, according to which, if the persons are to retain their properties, God (the Father) must communicate himself to the world as he does in the Trinity, viz., in the communication of the Son and the communication of the Holy Spirit. (We have already shown that a communication of the Father to the world, i.e., in which he would be received as Father, is in principle impossible.)

It has been shown in Part One that within the Trinity there is an intrinsic order of the two moments, the generation of the Son and the breathing-forth of the Holy Spirit, that comprise the single operation of God. This means that in the Trinity the connection between

---

12   *Divinum Illud*, ASS 29, 653.

13   *Mystici Corporis*, AAS 35, 232.

14   Cf. J. Alfaro, "Cristo Glorioso, Revelador del Padre," *Gregorianum* 39 (1958) 222-70.

15   Cf. K. Rahner, "The Eternal Significance of the Humanity of Jesus for our Relationship with God," *Theological Investigations* 3 (London, 1967) 44.

16   Cf. Rahner, *The Trinity* 101-03.

the communication of the Son and the communication of the Holy Spirit, the two modalities in which the self-communication of the Father takes place, is not just factual but necessary. Since the free self-communication of God to the world, if it is to be given at all, has to be given in projections of these modalities into the world, the connection between these projections once given must likewise be not just factual but necessary. Therefore the mission of the Son in the Incarnation (Jesus Christ) and the mission of the Holy Spirit in grace (the Church) may not be regarded as connected simply by temporal succession, but the former must be recognized to be directed by its inner dynamism to the latter. Here we have a good example of how the application of a trinitarian model to the divine economy yields not new factual knowledge but new intelligibility.

A shortcoming of the theology of de la Taille is that the question of who precisely is the agent in grace, whether God, the Holy Spirit, or each of the three divine persons, was not discussed by him. Rahner, though he presents grace as the projection into the world of the second modality of the self-communication of God, and therefore as the communication of the Holy Spirit, uses language that could be construed inconsistently with this when he says, e.g., that "each one of the three divine persons communicates himself to man in gratuitous grace"[17] and refers to grace as "these three self–communications."[18] Inconsistency would arise if "self-communication" were meant univocally in these instances, but not if it were meant analogically. For basically it is only the Father who communicates himself; the Son and the Holy Spirit are communicated by him, though in different ways. However, there is also a secondary sense, in which the Son and the Holy Spirit must also be said to communicate themselves, because they come not unwillingly or passively, but willingly and actively.

The importance of the analogous shifts between a primary and a secondary sense of self-communication and between different ways in which divine persons are communicated becomes evident in Rahner's observation that wherever there exists among the persons a real univocal correspondence, there is absolute numerical identity.[19] If such a correspondence exists in relation to what is in some sense a work of God in the world, then we conclude that it is a work of God in his

---

17   Ibid. 34.

18   Ibid. 35.

19   Ibid. 11-12, note 6.

unity, a work of the divine essence as such rather than of the persons as such, and therefore a work of efficient rather than formal causality. It is *merely* a work of God in the world. Since, as we have shown, formal causality includes efficient causality, a work of divine formal causality will also be a work of God in the world, but not merely such a work, for it is also a self-communication of God. As such, it draws a worldly reality into the Trinity, placing it in union, therefore, with either the Son or the Holy Spirit, and making it receptive of the self-communication of the Father. It is therefore—in a sense we will soon have to qualify—a work of the Son alone or of the Holy Spirit alone. In saying that "each one of the three divine persons communicates himself to man in gratuitous grace" or referring to grace as "these three self-communications," Rahner runs the risk, contrary to his intention, of reducing grace to a work of merely efficient causality, thus making it impossible to maintain that over and above being a work of God in the world—and at that level common to the three divine persons—it is the communication of the Holy Spirit alone.

In Rahner's perspective the principal difference between the two communications is that one is of the Son and the other of the Holy Spirit. As the divine persons received into the world—in which alone the category of causality applies—they alone exercise divine formal causality in its regard. The analogously different ways in which they do this constitute a secondary difference between them. It resides in the fact that whereas in the Incarnation the Son establishes a *substantial* (hypostatic) union between himself and humanity (in the form of a single human nature), in grace the Holy Spirit effects only an *accidental* union between himself and humanity (now in the form of many human persons). The latter union, moreover, brings about a further accidental union, viz., between believers and the Son, because the Holy Spirit as Spirit of filiation incorporates them as adopted sons and daughters into Christ, the only-begotten Son of God. The secondary difference between the two divine self-communications can therefore be expressed as that which obtains between the two respective modes of divine filiation in the world.

The qualification we must make to the statement that the two modes of the self-communication of God are respectively communications of the Son alone and of the Holy Spirit alone is that it is made only in the perspective of the procession model of the Trinity and of descending theology. But it also needs to be made in the perspective of the return model and of ascending theology; and there it becomes evident that each is a communication of *both* the Son and the Holy Spirit. For the Incarnation appears as the most radical possible (i.e., creative) communication of the Holy Spirit, Spirit of Sonship, who brings about a hypostatic union of the humanity thus created with the pre-existent Son; and grace is the union, effected by the same Spirit, of re-created human beings with the same Son, so that they are rendered adopted sons and daughters of the Father. The latter double union was evident, as we have just seen, even in the first perspective; but in the Incarnation, viewed in this way, the role of the Holy Spirit remained hidden, to emerge into the light only in the second perspective. In this perspective the secondary difference that we discerned above between the two modes of self-communication, viz., as that between a substantial identification with the Son (in the case of the first) and an accidental identification with him (in the case of the second), is elevated to primary status. Likewise, as will be explained soon, the created grace of the Incarnation, the "grace of union," is a substantial grace, while the "grace of grace" (if such an expression may be permitted) is an accidental grace. In all this it needs to be remembered that each of the two perspectives is valid and that they are complementary. The first, which is the perspective adopted for this chapter, looks to the Fourth Gospel and to subsequent Church teaching and theology, while the second looks to the Synoptic gospels, and especially to Luke. Hence we may continue in this chapter to speak of the first mode of self-communication as the communication of the Son alone and of the second as the communication of the Spirit alone, corresponding to the undoubtedly distinct processions of the Son and the Holy Spirit in the Trinity, but always with this qualification in mind.

According to Scripture, the Holy Spirit is communicated to the world not only by the Father but by the Son. It may be objected that it is not possible for the Son to communicate the Holy Spirit to the world, since the humanity of Christ in its finiteness is incapable of being a true source of the Holy Spirit. Underlying this objection, however, is a lack of appreciation of the uniqueness of the sacred humanity. Two considerations in particular apply here. First, as will be explained more in chapter seven, the created grace of Christ is not a quantitative fullness of accidental (sanctifying) grace but a unique substantial grace whereby Jesus is the Son of God in his humanity and not only in his divinity.[20] What is being said here is no monophysitic claim that the humanity of Christ disappears into the divinity, but that the created substantial grace of which we speak is to be identified as the "grace of union," both caused by, and disposing to, the hypostatic union. The very uniqueness of this grace renders it impossible to predict whether the Son qua incarnate can be a true source of the Holy Spirit, and in this matter, therefore, we can only look to Scripture, which teaches that after his death and resurrection Christ sends the Holy Spirit precisely as his own (the "Spirit of Christ"). In so teaching, it opens the way to the assertion that the incarnate Son *is* the source of the Holy Spirit, with the latter as the Spirit of Christ.

Second, though through the grace of the Incarnation given him at his conception Jesus was Son of God from the first moment of his human existence, this grace remained to be realized in him in his human history. The intensely historical character of this grace should to be neither overlooked nor underestimated. In the sense that his divinity was a function of his humanity, it was only when this humanity was fully realized, through his free obedience to the Father throughout his life and particularly in his death, that the grace of the Incarnation was fully realized in him. And hence it was only through his death and resurrection that he became, along with the Father, the source of the outpoured Spirit. Here, then, is a theological explanation of the statement of Scripture that the outpouring of the Spirit had to await the death of Jesus (cf. Jn 16:7; 7:39).

That only the Son is incarnate in Jesus Christ does not mean that the latter is not united to the Father and the Holy Spirit. To use the expression from the economic Trinity corresponding to perichoresis in the immanent Trinity, he is united to the Father and the Holy Spirit by virtue of trinitarian communion. However, it may also be said that in an analogous sense the Holy Spirit too is "incarnate" in Christ.[21] By this I mean that as the Son he possesses the Spirit as his own though he is not himself the Spirit. If this be granted, Christ is united only to the Father by trinitarian communion, for he *is* the Son and he *possesses* the Holy Spirit as his own. In grace, we too are united only to the Father by trinitarian communion, for we *are* sons (and daughters)

---

20   Here I anticipate a later development in my theology. See my article, "The Theandric Nature of Christ," *Theological Studies* 60 (1999) 405-31.

21   See my subsequent article, "The 'Incarnation' of the Holy Spirit in Christ," *Theological Studies* 45 (1984) 466-80.

and we *possess* the Holy Spirit as Spirit of the Son. It is therefore not the case that our union with the Holy Spirit is merely appropriated to him, i.e., said to pertain to him alone because it is fitting to say that the divine person who is the bond of the Father and the Son in the Trinity is the bond of God and humans. The indwelling is proper to the Holy Spirit in that he alone is given to us in "immediate immediacy." [22]

It will be useful at this point to modify somewhat Rahner's conception of grace and beatific vision as forming a unity. As we remarked above, this idea is basically correct and expressive of a Christian truth. However, it needs to be made more precise, since Scripture presents the vision of God in heaven as the completion not of grace but of faith (cf. 2 Cor 5:7). Of course, in Scholastic theology grace is seen as an ontological reality, and the act of faith, i.e., faith that is "living" or "informed by love," as a psychological reality flowing from it, so that this faith is an operation, or manifestation, of grace. In the light of this the truth contained in Rahner's statement can be seen. Grace is brought to completion in the sense that faith, its operation in this life, is transformed (through the "light of glory") into vision, a higher, indeed unsurpassable, operation. Considered strictly in itself, however, grace remains the same, whether understood in the Scholastic perspective of created grace or in the perspective adopted here, viz., of the Gift of the Holy Spirit, where it is actually human beings who are brought to completion, through the dynamic way in which they possess the Holy Spirit, i.e., by faith in this life and by vision (of the Father) in the next.

It follows from this that it is not correct to erect the beatific vision into a separate instance of divine formal causality, as did de la Taille, and to a lesser extent, Rahner. It is true that in Scholasticism the beatific vision is distinct from the Incarnation and grace as operation is distinct from being; but on the other hand operation is the operation of being, and so does not call for a distinct explanation. It is the prerogative, indeed the proper activity, of the Son to see the Father in heaven (cf. Jn 1:18), and so the beatific vision is sufficiently explained by the divine filiation, in the first place as possessed uniquely by Jesus, and then as possessed by human beings through his mediation. Admittedly, this vision is held back in this life by the veil of faith, but

---

22 To invoke another later development in my theology. See my *"Did You Receive the Holy Spirit When You Believed?" Some Basic Questions in Pneumatology* (Milwaukee, Wisc.: Marquette University Press, 2005) 37-38.

according to Scripture this by no means invalidates the divine filiation of humans living on earth. It is true that Aquinas could say that in the beatific vision God becomes "the intelligible form of the intellect," but this is only because those who are granted the beatific vision are already sons and daughters of God in the ontological order by grace and hence also in the psychological order by faith. The beatific vision, then, is the eschatological determination, in the field of operation, of *both* ways in which the ontological self-communication of God or divine filiation is given in the present age, viz., Incarnation and grace.

The question arises as to how far the analogy of formal causality can be pressed in relation to the Incarnation and grace. Can it be asked, e.g., whether the Son and the Holy Spirit in their respective communications act as substantial or as accidental form? This question, of course, was not asked in Scholasticism, since the recognition of the Incarnation and grace as instances of formal causality came so late, but we can say what the answer would be, viz., that in the Incarnation the Son acts as substantial form, and in grace the Holy Spirit acts as accidental form. This statement we now proceed to demonstrate and to assess.

In Scholastic philosophy the substantial form of the human being is the soul. Jesus had a human soul, which was therefore his substantial form as a human. However, when it is said that the Son acts as substantial form in relation to the humanity of Jesus, it is not this that is meant. The discussion is not at the level of the composition of Jesus' human essence; and it is not maintained that the Son supplies the function of the human soul as substantial form in relation to the body, which in any case would be Apollinarianism. Nor is the discussion at the level of the composition of Jesus' human being; and it is not maintained that the Son supplies the function of the human existence in relation to the human essence. Neo-Thomists hold that this would be a form of Docetism, and that it was the final and better opinion of Aquinas that Jesus had a proper, though secondary, human existence without prejudice to the fact that his sole person (in the Chalcedonian sense) was the divine Son.[23] Nor is it maintained that the sole function of the Son is to actuate Jesus' human essence to a proportionate

---

23　This is the doctrine of the disputed *Quaestio de unione Verbi Incarnati*, whose authenticity has been strongly defended by Pelster and others. Cf. T. Clarke, "Some Aspects of Current Christology", *The Encounter with God* (ed. J. O'Neill) (New York, 1960) 37.

human existence. The discussion is at the level of the composition of the entire being of Jesus, in which his humanity (in the Chalcedonian sense, which is not to be simply equated with his human essence in the Scholastic sense), therefore his body, soul, human essence, and, if need be, human existence, subsists as that of the Son of God. When the Son gives this subsistence to the humanity of Jesus, he may be called substantial form in a special and supernatural sense, since he is so communicated to the humanity that the latter is united to him in oneness of person.

The Scholastic theology of grace held that created habitual grace was an accidental form. It is clear, therefore, that once it is admitted that the real form in grace is uncreated grace, the latter would be recognized to be the accidental form in question, and that created grace would be recognized to be simply an accident, i.e., created actuation belonging to the order of accident. In the context of Scholasticism there would be no alternative to saying that uncreated grace is precisely an accidental form, since this would be the only way of safeguarding the distinction of persons between God (the Holy Spirit) and the human being in grace. Grace was a participation in God, and if the human being was to retain their human personhood in grace, they could participate in God only in an accidental way; if they participated in a substantial way, there would have to be a hypostatic union of the human and the Holy Spirit in grace. Hence to say that in grace the Holy Spirit acts as accidental form is to say nothing about the Holy Spirit in himself: it is merely a statement about the way in which he is received by human beings. Further, to say that grace was an accidental form was to allow the possibility of human beings' existing without grace at all, which is the condition of human beings in personal sin and also their original condition.

It is but a short step from the position reached above to transcendental theology, for if the humanity of Jesus possessed the potency to be united in person with the divine Son, humanity as such must possess the same potency, since the humanity of Jesus was the same as that of all humans except in regard to sin. What we have, therefore, in Jesus is the highest possible actuation of the potency of human nature in its most essential characteristic, viz., openness to God. Also, when it is said that grace is an accidental form, it must be remembered that the word "accidental" is used here in the metaphysical sense, which simply preserves the distinction of the divine and the human person in grace, and not in the logical sense, which would make grace extraneous to essential human being. The concept of uncreated grace as accidental form in no way prevents created grace from being a determination of the human precisely in this openness that they have toward God. Transcendental theology, then, has no quarrel with the concept of the Holy Spirit as accidental form in grace, even if that is not the language that it would use itself. Descending Christology and its implied theology of grace are unable to say why precisely the highest possible actuation of human nature results in union with the Son while lesser actuations, viz., in grace, result in union with the Holy Spirit. We have already intimated an answer to this question, but we defer further treatment of it until we have approached the matter from the standpoint of ascending Christology.

It may be asked why it is that the divinity of Christ requires that the Son act as substantial form in regard to him from the very beginning of his human life, and not initially as accidental form, as the Holy Spirit does in regard to ordinary humans in grace. If transcendental theology is correct in seeing the Incarnation as the highest possible determination of humanity by grace, could not Jesus, in other words, have begun life as a human being in every respect like others and so surpassed them in the obedience of his life and death that under grace he achieved unity of person with God as distinct from simple union of persons as in the case of others?

We shall not be in a position to answer this question adequately until the end of Part Three, but already we can give a reasonably satisfactory answer. First, from the standpoint of faith it must be said that the suggestion is a form of adoptionism, which is contradicted by those parts of the New Testament that insist that Jesus was one in person with the divine Son from the first moment of his earthly life.

Secondly, from the standpoint of theology it must be said that if a human's union with God in grace rests on the basis of a purely human personhood (as it does in the case of ordinary humans), this union will have to be achieved through human co-operation with grace. This means that it is impossible that any determination thus brought about be such as to result in unity of person with God. This is because, however great the determination, it will remain a determination of a qualitative reality on the side of its finiteness, and therefore will itself be finite. This can be illustrated from mathematics. If one begins with a finite number, no matter how much it be added to, or multiplied by, other finite numbers, the result will still be a finite number, even if a very large one.

Yet we must take seriously the statement of transcendental theology that humanity is openness to God, and admit the possibility of an unsurpassably high determination of humanity by grace which consists in unity of person with God. This, however, is only possible where this determination is given from the very start, by the grace of God independently of all human cooperation. Even though the human is rightly defined as openness to God, the gap between humans and God is infinite and is bridged in this way only through the unique prevenient grace of God, and not through a grace requiring human cooperation in order to be effective. Divinity, then, can never be achieved *by* humanity; it can only be achieved (or realized) *in* humanity.

This is what the grace of the Incarnation is. Some might think that this makes a mockery of the genuine humanity and human experience of Jesus, but in fact this is not the case. The humanity thus determined in advance by grace remains still to develop and have its human history precisely as humanity, which it still is and always remains. It is not privileged, in the sense of enjoying short cuts to fulfillment not granted to others. As this humanity expands and develops in the course of its history as a result of the free obedience of Jesus to the claims of his unique grace, it becomes an ever more suited medium for the realization of the grace in which it was founded; and in its completion and perfection in death it achieves its highest point and thus becomes the perfect medium. Although Jesus did not achieve divinity in cooperation with grace, he did as a human freely cooperate with his unique grace, and it was this cooperation that enabled the unsurpassable realization of divinity in him. Thus we can see why the divinity of Christ required that the Son act in regard to him as substantial form from the very beginning of his human existence, and not as accidental form, as does the Holy Spirit in regard to other humans in grace. To put it another way, we see the essential difference that must be postulated between Jesus and even the greatest of the saints. Finally, we must point out that the position presented here offers a reconciliation of the apparently divergent claims of "Incarnation" Christology and "resurrection" Christology in understanding the union of the man Jesus with God.

While conceding that divine formal causality gives a reasonable account of the Incarnation, Mühlen thinks that it cannot be used in regard to grace, since in grace there is no union of being comparable to the hypostatic union.[24] There is, however, no doubt that Scripture teaches that grace is a union of God and humans, indeed of the Holy Spirit and humans. In this union the Holy Spirit is truly communicated, i.e., imparted in himself and not in a reduced form or image. Further, as communicated, the Holy Spirit, of and in himself, brings human beings to a new perfection. They are changed from slaves of sin to sons and daughters of God, and hence enabled to act as sons and daughters, i.e., to believe and hope in, and to love, God, and eventually to "see" him in heaven. The elements required for formal causality are verified here for the Holy Spirit in grace. The union of a human and God in grace does not have to be precisely a hypostatic union in order to be a genuine union of being. We have shown above that Scholasticism can be developed to the point of stating that the difference between the Incarnation and grace is that in the former the Son acts as substantial form in relation to the sacred humanity, while in the latter the Holy Spirit acts as accidental form in relation to humans receiving grace. The Holy Spirit is the act, in relation to which the potency basically is the human person, more precisely the human in their spirituality, and more precisely still, the human in the last disposition of this spirituality, viz., love of God, for union with God in grace. Acting as accidental form, the Holy Spirit establishes a union between the being of God and the being of humans, even if not at the level of substance or personal identity as in the case of the other modality of this self-communication, the Incarnation. Apparently, Mühlen's objection overlooks the fact that accidental form as well as substantial form brings about union of being.

It will be clear from what has been said above that once it is admitted that it is useful to understand the Incarnation and grace according to the model of formal causality, the question as to whether the relevant divine persons, the Son and the Holy Spirit respectively, act as substantial or as accidental form cannot be avoided; and from the discussion it will also be clear that the working out of an answer to this question provides a worthwhile clarification of certain aspects of the theology of grace.

We have seen that if the self-communication of God (the Father) to the world is to take place at all, it must be by the communication of the Son and of the Holy Spirit, that the world can receive this

---

24 Mühlen, *Der Heilige Geist als Person* 268.

self-communication only by medium of personal beings, and that, in the language of formal causality, it can be received in only two ways, i.e., as substantial form and as accidental form. We know also the facts that the Son as substantial form entered into hypostatic union with the humanity of Jesus, and that the Holy Spirit as accidental form is received by humans in grace. We now ask whether there is a necessity governing these facts, or whether they are *merely* facts, which by God's will could have been the other way round, so that the Holy Spirit would have been incarnate in Jesus, and the Son be received by humans as grace. Our answer to this is that these facts are governed by necessity, in the sense that, given God's free decision to communicate himself to the world, this had to be done in the ways in which it is actually given. We can now substantiate this answer, though we must await the end of Part Three in order to do it fully.

As we have seen, within the Trinity the Son proceeds as the self-knowledge of the Father, and the Holy Spirit as the bond of love between the Father and the Son. Because of the necessary consistency of God, when the Father communicates himself to the world by projections of the ways in which he communicates himself in the Trinity, the Son and the Holy Spirit as thus communicated to the world must retain their respective identities as given in the Trinity. Therefore the Son must be communicated as the revelation of the Father to humans, and the Holy Spirit must be communicated as the bond of love between the Father and his children, sons and daughters in the Son. We now consider each of these modalities separately.

Jesus is presented in the New Testament as the complete revelation of God (the Father) to the world. This is done by means of the Semitic category of eschatology, in which Jesus is said to bring in his person the ultimate reign of God over human beings. As is evident from the Old Testament, partial and provisional revelations of God can be made through ordinary humans, e.g., the prophets, but the definitive revelation of God can be made only through God himself.[25] Only Emmanuel (God with us) can reveal and offer the whole reality of God to humans. This implies that the medium of revelation must exist in radical unity of being with God revealing, who is the divine Word or Son, which is to say that the medium must actually *be* the Son. This requires a hypostatic union, in which the Son is communicated

---

25   Cf. J. McIntyre, *The Shape of Christology* (London, 1966) 144-71; W. Pannenberg, *Jesus - God and Man* (London, 1968) 129-30, 168.

as substantial form, in the sense explained above, to the medium, who, as we have said, has to be created personal being, therefore human. Moreover the definitiveness of this revelation requires uniqueness and unrepeatability in this hypostatic union or Incarnation. If it were repeatable, in principle the revelation made through it would not be definitive. The hypostatic union, therefore, must be between the Son and a single human being. And because this human being must exist at every moment of their life in unity of person with the Son, their humanity is called (in the Chalcedonian framework) a nature and not a person. We conclude, therefore, that the hypostatic union must be between the Son and a single human nature.

As the spirit of a human is revealed sacramentally in their body, so the full reality of God is revealed sacramentally in the humanity of Jesus, to which the Son is united in unity of person. (Interestingly, the comparison of the hypostatic union to the union of body and soul in the human being had been made by Cyril of Alexandria, within, of course, the Platonic framework, in which body and soul were distinct essences.[26]) Thus united, the humanity of Jesus becomes the sacrament of God, in which God is revealed and offered to humans. As we have indicated, the union takes place in the soul of Jesus, and is sacramentalized, i.e., revealed and offered, in his bodily words and actions. Indeed, since transcendental theology tells us that the divinity of Jesus is a determination of his human spirit, the sacrament of God is precisely the body of Jesus. Origen, then, was right in seeing the human soul of Jesus as the link of divinity and bodiliness in him, though no one today would explain the manner of this in the simple way that he did.[27] In this union the Father is made visible and offered to humans, though not, as Origen was careful to point out, in himself, but in the Son.[28] The accessibility, the intimate nearness of God to humans in Jesus is conveyed strikingly in the two regulative ideas in the preaching of Jesus, the Fatherhood and the Kingdom (the reign) of God, realized uniquely in himself and offered to others in him.

As to the second modality of the self-communication of God to the world, the nature of the communication of the Holy Spirit to humans must be understood in the light of his function in the Trinity, where,

---

26   Cf. *Quod unus sit Christus* (PG 75, 1292; *Sources chrétiennes* 97, 374-377); *Epistola 46* (PG 77, 241).

27   Cf. *De principiis* 2, 6 (PG 11, 209-15).

28   Cf. *Contra Celsum* 7, 43 (PG 11, 1483; *Sources chrétiennes* 150, 114-17).

in as much as he proceeds by love from the Father and the Son, he is the bond between them. As bond, the Holy Spirit must preserve the distinction of the Father and the Son whom he unites; nor may he be identified with either of them; but each must simply possess him as his own, or their mutual, Spirit. In the revelation of the Trinity also, in the Incarnation, the Holy Spirit is the bond of the Father and the man Jesus, Son of God incarnate. That this is so is evidenced by such texts of Scripture as Mk 1:10,12 and parallels; Mt 1:18; Lk 4:1, 14, 18, 10, 21; Jn 3:34, Rom 1:4; 8:11 and Heb 9:14, though the manner in which it is so remains to be explained. It is important to note that the Holy Spirit could not be the bond of God and the man Jesus if he were united in person to the latter. Also in the case of Jesus, therefore, the Holy Spirit may only be possessed. Jesus could not actually *be* the Holy Spirit incarnate. All the more more, then, in the operation of the Trinity, where the Holy Spirit must continue to be the bond of persons, of the sons and daughters (in the Son) with the Father, and thus also of these brothers and sisters with each other in the Church, which is thus brought into being, may the Holy Spirit only be *possessed by* humans in grace. If (*per impossibile*) he were incarnate in them, he would duplicate the function of the Son. This would compromise the consistency of God, which, however, we know to be necessary.

As it is, the first modality of the self-communication of God to the world is ordered to the second, so that when both are accomplished, God's purpose for humans is achieved. The Son was sent by the Father that men and women might be gathered into his Sonship by the power of the Holy Spirit sent by him. Rahner says that the self-communication of God to the world finds in the Incarnation "its peak and irreversible finality."[29] There is a sense in which this is profoundly true, but it is also true that the matter may be regarded from a different point of view. While the Incarnation is a unique instance of the self-communication of God, it is not given as an absolute ultimate, but is directed beyond itself as the means by which God's absolutely ultimate purpose, the bestowal of divine filiation on humans in an eschatological outpouring of the Holy Spirit (cf. Acts 2:17; Joel 2:28), is realized. The Letter to the Ephesians expresses the fact of Jesus' ordainment to others when it says that "he (the Father) chose us in him (Christ) before the foundation of the world" (1:4), "to be his adopted children through Jesus Christ, according to the purpose of his will"

---

29   *The Trinity* 90.

(1:5). And Jesus himself shows that he understands and accepts his allotted place in God's design when he says that "the Son of Man came not to be served but to serve" (Mk 10:45). It is only in the totality of his other-directedness that the Lordship of Christ in the Church is rightly understood.

Hence a situation feared by the Church magisterium, the rise of a theology that sees grace as a hypostatic union of the Holy Spirit with humans, though always a possibility of fact, is an impossibility from the strictly theological point of view. The human being who receives the Holy Spirit cannot be or become the Holy Spirit, but may only have or possess him. Thus we see that the two basic verbs "to be" and "to have" exhaust the possibilities of the ways in which humans can be united (by divine formal causality) to divine persons, and that "to be," corresponding to substantial form, pertains of necessity to the Incarnation of the Son, while "to have," corresponding to accidental form, pertains of necessity to the Gift of the Holy Spirit in grace. While the Son may be communicated only to a single human nature, the Holy Spirit may, and must, be communicated to many human persons in the Church. Thus we are brought to the comprehensive conclusion that the two ways in which the self-communication of God to the world is actually given, the communication of the Son in the Incarnation and the communication of the Holy Spirit in grace, are not merely facts that could have been different, but, given the free decision of God to communicate himself to the world, are governed by a necessity that is rooted in the nature of God as he is in himself.

In this chapter, in considering the Incarnation and grace as projections into the world, by divine formal causality, of the self-communication of God in the Trinity, we have concentrated on God's side of the action. In the next chapter we complete our consideration by focusing attention on the human side, the receiving end, of the action, and take up the question of the relation of divine filiation and faith, in Jesus and in ordinary humans.

6 DIVINE FILIATION AND FAITH

In the last chapter we pointed out that the beatific vision should not be considered either as a distinct instance of the self-communication of God to human beings as in the theology of de la Taille, or as the completion only of grace as in the theology of Rahner. The beatific vision is the completion of faith; and faith is the dynamic and psychological aspect of divine filiation; and divine filiation is the ontological object and result of both the Incarnation and grace, constituting in the former the paradigm for the latter. Clearly the supernatural union of God and humans has to be understood, from their side, as effective at both levels of their being, the ontological and the psychological. Hence Aquinas does us a service in reminding us that the divine indwelling, which is the supernatural presence of God to humans conceived ontologically (but from God's side), must be understood (from the human side), also in terms of humans' spiritual and supernatural actions in regard to God. This Aquinas does when he tells us that God dwells in the just person "as the known in the knower and the loved in the lover." We may restate this by saying that God dwells in humans in this life according to their faith and in the next according to their (spiritual) vision.

This makes it necessary for us to discuss first of all the question of the faith of the man Jesus. It is not necessary to show here that during his earthly life Jesus did not possess the beatific vision, or that he did possess the virtue of faith, as this has been done adequately by others.[1] The dogmatic content of the previously held theologumenon of the possession of the beatific vision by Jesus during his earthly life is now seen as implied in the doctrine of the Incarnation itself, i.e., as a unique supernatural union of God and a human being, requiring, therefore, to be in some way experienced psychologically as well as to be given ontologically. Similarly, the dogmatic content of the corresponding

---

1 For the beatific vision cf. E. Gutwenger, *Bewusstsein und Wissen Christi* (Innsbruck, 1960), and K. Rahner, "Dogmatic Reflections on the Knowledge and Self-Consciousness of Christ", *Theological Investigations* 5, 193-215, especially 220-10. For faith cf. P. Schoonenberg, *The Christ* (London, 1972) 146-152.

theologumenon of the absence of faith in Jesus is the distinction of Jesus from other humans, which can be seen as guaranteed by the difference of his faith from that of others, for as he differed from them in filiation, so he differed from them in faith. This difference lies in the fact that for Jesus faith in God involved also belief in himself, as one graced with a unique and unsurpassable intimacy with God and hence the bearer of a unique mission to his fellow-humans, "pioneer of their salvation" (Heb 2:12), owing unswerving fidelity to that mission; whereas for others a fully articulated (therefore Christian) faith involves acceptance of another, viz., Christ, as mediator of their salvation. This important difference being allowed for, however, we can go on to say that basically faith for Jesus was the same as for others, i.e., steadfast adherence to God and his will in the face of opposing difficulties and temptations. Jesus, then, is not just the object, but the supreme model, of faith (cf. Heb 12:2); and for him, as for others, the veil of faith gives way at death to the vision of the Father. Since faith is the activity and manifestation of divine filiation proper to this life, in what follows we speak of faith in preference to vision. Nothing is lost hereby, since vision is simply the completion of faith.

We have said above that in Scripture the word "faith" generally denotes steadfast adherence to God and his will in the face of opposing difficulties and temptations. Sometimes, however, the word is used in the context of the darkness in which humans live out their obedience in this life in contrast to the light that will be given them in the next, and in this sense faith is distinguished from "sight" or "vision" (2 Cor 5:7). Elsewhere faith is distinguished from hope (1 Pet 1:21), from love (Gal 5:6; Eph 6:23; 1 Thess 3:6; 5:8; 1 Tim 1:14; 2:15; 4:12; 6:11; 2 Tm 1:13; 2:22; Tit 2:2; 3:15; Rev 2:19), and from hope and love together (1 Cor 13:13; 1 Thess 1:3); but it would be a mistake to see the adequate distinctions of later theology between faith, hope and love as already simply given in the biblical distinctions, though doubtless their basis is there. The texts cited above show that hope is faith directed to the future action of God in Christ, and that love includes, with love of (faith in) God, love of neighbor in obedience to Jesus' double commandment (Mk 12:28-31). This love of neighbor, moreover, finds expression in action and especially in sharing one's own faith with him (Philem 1:5-6). In Scripture, then, "faith" sums up the entire attitude of subjection, obedience, trust and love of the religious person toward God. Except where we clearly indicate otherwise, this is the sense in which we shall use the word in this book.

We now undertake the task of relating divine filiation and faith, first in Jesus and then in others, and of making, on this basis, a further comparison of the Incarnation and grace. We take up the question of Jesus' divine Sonship and faith first of all on the ontological level. With Jesus there could never be, as with others, a divine filiation that comes into existence on the foundation of an already established human personhood, a filiation that begins with the formation of faith. From the first moment of his human existence Jesus was united in person to the divine Son. Clearly, then, his divine Sonship did not simply result from his faith, but his faith flowed from his Sonship as its psychological and experiential expression. Nevertheless, there is an important sense in which the divine Sonship of Jesus may be said to have resulted from his faith, and this sense we must now explain. If, as transcendental theology maintains, this Sonship was realized precisely in the humanity of Jesus, as its highest possible determination, it was only to the extent that his humanity was developed that the divine Sonship was realized in it, for humanity is to be conceived not as a static given but rather as spirit in matter, which grows in being through its personal history, which embraces not only life but also death. Only when his humanity, therefore, is completed in death can this Sonship be fully realized in it. This does not mean that Jesus became Son of God only through his death, though the earliest New Testament witness in its simplicity did not hesitate to express the matter just so, as we shall later see in detail. Rather, as later New Testament witness was careful to point out, Jesus was unique Son of God from the first moment of his human existence; but (to attempt to express by analogy something which by definition is unique) this divine Sonship continually filled the space created for it in the humanity of Jesus through the development of that humanity. And this development took place not just through passive submission to fate, but through the positive activity of Jesus, which in this regard must be seen as his virtue and ultimately as his faith. From one point of view, then, indeed the ultimate one, the faith of Jesus must be seen as flowing from his divine Sonship, since this was always the ontological base of his activity; but it is also true, and important to note, that this divine Sonship was realized in him only through the exercise of faith by him.

Our question is affected by two factors, both at the psychological level, viz., the knowledge and the virtue of Jesus. Of the former it is only necessary to say that the absence of the beatific vision from Jesus' earthly life created in him room for the exercise of faith, which can exist only in the sphere of darkness experienced by all humans in their relationship to God in this life. We pass on immediately to consider the second factor mentioned above, the virtue of Jesus, or, in negative terms, his sinlessness and indeed his incapacity for sin. This is relevant, because, if the faith of Jesus was genuine, it had to be exercised in freedom, yet it is precisely the freedom of Jesus that is called into question by a declaration of his sinlessness and incapacity for sin. That Jesus was in fact without sin is the testimony of the New Testament writers (Jn 8:46; 2 Cor 5:21; Heb 4:15; 1 Pet 2:22; 1 Jn 3:5), and reflects, probably, at least as much an a priori conviction of faith about his unity with God as a judgment passed a posteriori on his actual life. Thus we have passed already from a mere factual sinlessness to incapacity for sin in Jesus. We would say that this incapacity is a corollary of his divine personhood: it is impossible for the Son of God to sin. Theology cannot be satisfied with a simple declaration of the sinlessness of Jesus, but on account of his divinity must insist also on his incapacity for sin.

The New Testament presents Jesus as threatened by temptation and perfected in temptation overcome. Thus the faith of Jesus is seen to be genuine, since faith exists not in a vacuum but in the overcoming of difficulties. The Gospels give accounts of temptations of Jesus in the wilderness (Mk 1:12-13 and parallels) and Gethsemane (Mk 14:32-42 and parallels) as testings of his Messianic spirit by the spirit of evil. These bear on Jesus' inner experience, but only indirectly, in that evil would have prevailed had Jesus been persuaded to settle for a political interpretation of his Messianic office, which would, however, have entailed on his part a defection from faith. Jesus' refusal to do this and his determination, in regard to his office, to persist in God's will despite, even in, the magnitude of its demands constitute a re-affirmation of his faith. The Gospels (Mk 15:34; Mt 27:46) also present the death of Jesus as his supreme act of faith, in that for him, as for all people, death is the supreme test, surmounted only by a proportionate affirmation, which is, therefore, the summing-up of a whole life of faith.[2]

---

2   Cf. K. Rahner, *On the Theology of Death* (Edinburgh, 1961), L. Boros, *The Moment of Truth: Mysterium Mortis* (London, 1965).

In addition, the Letter to the Hebrews speaks plainly of Jesus' temptations (2:18; 5:7-10), even going so far as to say that he was tempted in every respect as we are (4:15).

To discuss the question of temptation in the life of Jesus it is necessary for us to say a few words at this point on the subject of concupiscence, though we shall return to it more fully in Part Five, when we consider its place in the lives of ordinary people.

In the divine economy in which we live, characterized as it is by the sin of humans and the redeeming grace of God, concupiscence exists as desire that springs from humans' sinful state and leads them to personal sin (cf. DS 1515). If grace prevails, it is not because it abolishes concupiscence or exempts them from it. This is so because concupiscence is in itself natural, in that it consists in the inability of the human being as such to express adequately their person, i.e., what they desire to become, in their nature, i.e., what they are given, an inability that they experience as much in regard to their good actions as to their bad.[3] The ultimate reason for the naturalness of concupiscence in humans is that spirit necessarily encounters resistance in expressing itself in the otherness of matter. Therefore a human could not simply be exempted from concupiscence without also being exempted from being human; and concupiscence is sinful not in itself but only because of the actual order, of sin and grace, that obtains. Therefore the tradition of the "integrity" of Jesus, i.e., his freedom from concupiscence, means not that he was exempted from concupiscence, but that in him concupiscence existed only as already mastered, or as becoming mastered, by grace.

The grace that bestowed this integrity on Jesus was the Incarnation itself, considered both ontologically, as fact, and psychologically, as motivation and power. Evidence for the former are the New Testament statements of the sinlessness of Jesus, and for the latter the clarity and vigor, evidenced in the New Testament, with which he related all moral choices to the reign of God. With ordinary humans long fidelity to grace produces a degree of integrity, the beginning of what is completed in the eschaton, and this phenomenon is clearer still in the saints. Hence it is not remarkable that the Incarnation, the supreme grace, should have produced complete integrity in Jesus. The relative

---

3   Cf. K. Rahner, "The Theological Concept of Concupiscence", *Theological Investigations* 1, 347-382; L. Scheffczyk, "Concupiscence", SM 1, 403b-405a; J.B. Metz, "Konkupiszenz", HTG 1, 843-51.

integrity of the saints did not exempt them from temptation, particularly from temptation against faith. In staking their lives so completely on faith, they exposed themselves to heightened temptations against it, and their lives show that they often underwent temptations against faith that ordinary people never experience. Despite his uniqueness, Jesus can be compared to them in this. We have already pointed out that while the New Testament says that he was tempted in every way that we are, it places particular emphasis on his temptations against faith.

Virtue does not exist in a vacuum, but establishes itself in the face of temptation, which is to say, in the face of concupiscence. (The other view, that virtue can exist simply despite temptation, is a less profound account of the reality.) Hence the integrity of Jesus cannot mean that he did not experience temptation. In any case, the New Testament, as we have seen, clearly says that he did. Rather, his integrity means that the grace of the Incarnation enabled him to express his person in the acts of virtue, of faith and the moral virtues, that were called into being in the mastering of concupiscence, so that there was left in him no remainder of nature in resistance to his self-disposition. It is true, of course, and important to note, that these virtues flowed from his divine Sonship, but there is no contradiction between this and saying that they were established in the mastering of concupiscence. Indeed it was precisely thus that the divine Sonship was progressively realized in him, as explained above.

Jesus' incapacity for sin was a corollary of his divine personhood, and was therefore an ontological incapacity. If, however, Jesus' temptations, which were experienced in his human nature, were genuine and not feigned, they must have presented themselves to him as real threats to his unity with God. A human is able to sin, and therefore on the level of the humanity of Jesus we recognize in him only factual sinlessness and with it the psychological capacity for sin. We must now look into this matter more closely.

As the hypostatic union was experienced consciously by the humanity of Jesus, it must have communicated to him an extreme revulsion from sin. It is difficult to see, therefore, how evil could have had any attraction for him at all. However, it must be remembered firstly that the attraction of evil in concupiscence is spontaneous, not reflexive. Hence contrary motivation does not simply remove concupiscence, but only holds it in check and enables the person to come to expression in the face of the concupiscence of their nature. This is always a difficult achievement, and not less so when motivation is strong. Indeed, only in a person with the gift of integrity, where motivation is at its strongest, is the full opposing force of concupiscence experienced, since only there is concupiscence fully mastered by the free act, and only there does person come fully to expression in the limits of nature. Despite this, with Jesus, continued moral progress was possible (cf. Lk 2:52), because these limits were constantly being expanded in his personal history. His motivation, which was stronger than that of other humans, is here spoken of in negative terms, as his revulsion from sin, but we may express it also positively, as his desire to promote the reign of God. It is in the power of this motivation at work in Jesus, enabling the expression and realization of his divine person as fully as possible in human nature, that his integrity is manifest to us. It is to be understood as a gift deriving from his unique grace, the Incarnation.

It must, however, be acknowledged that there is more to the power of concupiscence than a simply spontaneous and non-rational inclination toward evil. When we said above that concupiscence was non-reflexive, we meant that its *origin* is non-reflexive. But in order to become a real force in a human being it must immediately find a rational justification. This accounts for the "darkening of the intellect" and the "weakening of the will" attributed to concupiscence. It must invest the contemplated action with a species of rationality. With ordinary people this species is the advantage that a short-term benefit can have over ultimate values. It is precisely here that it is difficult to see how Jesus, with his unique intimacy with the Father, could have been so attracted. However, as T.S. Eliot has persuasively shown in the speech of the Fourth Tempter in *Murder in the Cathedral,* the more intimate a person is with God the more alluring and feasible does the prospect become of usurping his place. Both a priori and a posteriori (from the New Testament evidence) we can say that the temptations of Jesus against faith took the two extreme forms, toward giving up faith altogether in despair, and toward putting himself in the place of the Father. Each of these has a species of rationality. These were the temptations which, with the help of grace but also in the darkness of faith, he had to overcome.

Jesus' ontological incapacity for sin assured his sinlessness in advance and in principle, but did not thereby destroy his human freedom. We can say this with confidence, basically because we know that the sovereignty of God in grace never jeopardizes the freedom of a human being. Though we must defer the discussion of this as a problem, we may invoke it now as a fact, and point out that in Jesus we have only a particular, even if the most acute, instance of the general problem. In any given event where a person is victorious over temptation, the victory is attributed to God in his efficacious grace, without detracting from the freedom of the person. And when a person remains free of sin "for a long time," this too is attributed to God without prejudice to the freedom of the person. The difference in the case of Jesus is the uniqueness of his grace, the Incarnation, which can be expressed by the fact that it ensures victory over temptation not just in particular events, or for a long time, but for the whole of his life. For Jesus, however, as for us, every temptation presented itself as a new threat to his unity with God, but in his case was overcome by an act that was at the same time free and human, and impregnated at every level with grace, the grace of the Incarnation.

We summarize our treatment of the relation of divine filiation and faith in Jesus by saying that to him was given a unique grace, the Incarnation, which established in him a unique divine Sonship, which both came to expression in and was realized through his faith, which was established in the common freedom and darkness experienced by humans in this life, and also in the full mastering of concupiscence, so that in him the unique Son of God was expressed, revealed and realized as fully as possible in the limits of humanity. We have already shown that the completeness of the revelation made in Jesus requires precisely a hypostatic union of the divine Son with the humanity of Jesus. We can now add as a final observation on this point that this very completeness requires that the grace of the hypostatic union include the gift of integrity, as otherwise the humanity would not be totally given over as the medium of the divinity.

Turning now to ordinary humans, we find a rather different relationship of divine filiation and faith. Here the filiation, is formed in consequence of the human response of faith, yet at the same time, paradoxically, the response is dependent on the forming of divine filiation, i.e., on the ontological result of the action of grace. The last statement is necessary for the avoidance of Pelagianism. Scholasticism too excludes Pelagianism when it insists that (living) faith, as both habit and act, results from the possession of habitual, or sanctifying, grace.

The doctrine of *fides informis* and *fides formata* (cf. DS 1544, 1578), i.e., faith respectively uninformed and informed by love, or respectively "dead" and "living" faith, shows the existence of a threshold above which faith exists as complete dedication to God, and below which it is less than this, but can be taking shape, gathering strength in tending toward that condition. Correspondingly, at this threshold divine filiation is constituted, or, as the Scholastics would say, *in facto esse* (in attained existence), and below it it is not constituted, but can be in the process of being formed, or, to use again a Scholastic expression, *in fieri* (in becoming). In the patristic age the spiritual life of humans below this threshold was linked with the catechumenate, and their spiritual life above it with Church membership, the threshold itself being understood to be marked by baptism. However, while there is a certain truth in this, viz., the assertion of a necessary link between one's private and communal spiritual life, in fact the threshold can be crossed in either direction, i.e., by full faith and by sin, both before and after baptism. The objection of circularity, to which the statement of the mutual inter-dependence of faith and divine filiation in humans is open, was already met adequately enough by Scholasticism within its own context of thought, and with only slight adjustment we may take over its answer into our own context. The following quotation from the *Summa theologiae* gives Aquinas's final thoughts on the subject. "By the order of nature, the disposition of the subject precedes the reception of the form, but follows the agent's action through which, also, the subject is disposed. And therefore by the order of nature the movement of the free will precedes the *gaining* of grace, but follows the *inpouring* of grace" (italics mine).[4] Here Aquinas sees two different orderings, which, since they are made from different standpoints, are not contradictory or incompatible. From the standpoint of the human, their conversion to God precedes their acquisition of grace, which is, of course, conceived as created habitual grace. This conversion disposes them for grace, but it is not conceived in Semipelagian fashion as emanating from them, exclusively, even though it is clearly their own act: it is conceived also as a disposition brought about by God without prejudice to their freedom so that the created form of habitual grace can be infused. In speaking thus, we have already adopted the standpoint of God, from which he is seen to move humans by the bestowal of grace so that they move in the act of conversion. It

---

4   *Summa theologiae* I-II, 113, 8 ad 2.

must not be thought that Aquinas here, uncharacteristically, regards grace as uncreated, identical with God. He adopts the model, mover-moved, only because the more congenial one of the operative habit and its act in dependence on the ontological habit is not available to him as long as the human remains unpossessed of the ontological habit of grace. When the human does possess this habit, Aquinas unhesitatingly adopts the being-act model as the explanation of their ongoing faith, hope and love. With our concept of unformed and formed divine filiation and faith (comparable to the later Scholastic concept of *habitus in fieri*, habits in formation), we do not need to abide by this limitation when we translate Aquinas's thought into our context. We can say that from the standpoint of the human, divine filiation is brought about by the movement of faith as self-disposition, but that from the standpoint of God this same movement is the disposition of the human by God. The human's faith, then, is both their own and God's doing. We here simply re-state as fact what we shall later discuss as a problem, the compatibility of the sovereignty of God and the freedom of the human. As the human's act, faith is what Aquinas calls the gaining of grace, and what we prefer to call the acceptance (in an active sense) of grace; as God's act, it is what Aquinas calls the inpouring, and it is what we call the bestowal, of grace. The human's acceptance corresponds to God's offer, of grace. And so we have the very important distinction of the offer and the bestowal of grace. Corresponding to it in the Trinity are, respectively, the procession and the bestowal of the Holy Spirit. Grace is the Father's Gift of the Holy Spirit, the Spirit of filiation, who forms willing humans into children of God. From the standpoint of the acceptance of grace, faith brings about divine filiation; from the standpoint of the bestowal of grace, faith flows from the bestowed divine filiation.

It is, of course, always possible for the human to refuse the offer of the Gift of the Holy Spirit, and when they do they must bear the responsibility for their refusal. We repeat: human freedom, on which responsibility depends, is not annihilated by grace.

These things being said, we should not be misinterpreted when we say that for ordinary humans, i.e., other than Jesus, the gaining of divine filiation depends on their faith. It could not be otherwise. If a human is not a child of God already at the deepest level of their being, the only possibility for them in relation to divine filiation is that they *become* a child of God, i.e., that God *make* them his children, by regeneration, at a less profound level, at which the identity of their exclusively human personhood is preserved. But it is impossible that God do this against or independently of the person's will, as this would abuse their freedom, and destroy their humanity. It follows that God can regenerate a human person as his son or daughter only in cooperation with their free response, which is faith. Here, then, we have an important contrast with Jesus, for whom basically faith flowed from divine Sonship. At the same time the ordinary believer can also be likened to Jesus in this matter, since, as we have pointed out, the faith of the former may also be seen as flowing from his filiation.

Further, if for ordinary people divine filiation depends on faith; and faith, even above the threshold at which it becomes formed, can be more or less intense: it follows that the divine filiation of humans is capable of varying intensity even above the threshold of formation. Here again a contrast with Jesus is to be drawn, since for him divine Sonship at the level of human realization was capable only of increase in the sense explained above. In Scholastic terms the difference between Jesus and other humans in this respect can be expressed by linking the divine Sonship of Jesus primarily with being and that of others with operation, and then recognizing that this operation (of faith) presupposes in them a basis in being, which is then contrasted with that of Jesus as accident to substance.

Jesus had no human existence prior to his divine Sonship, but other humans do have such an existence, and it is one that is marred by sin, either original or personal. The faith of such a person, therefore, by which they pass from sinner to child of God, must include penance, or change of heart. And just as a human acquires their new state of filiation through their own acts (under grace), so also they may lose it by their own acts, i.e., by sin, which causes them to relapse to their former state. This sin can be such as to push their faith below the threshold of formation, or it can be such as to extinguish it altogether. The further discussion of this matter, however, we defer to later. Here too we have a contrast with Jesus, who was sinless and incapable of sin, and whose divine Sonship could not be lost or marred in any way.

It is, of course, realized that since in infant baptism the divine filiation conferred in the sacrament precedes the exercise of faith, infant baptism can be brought forward as an objection to our statement that in ordinary believers divine filiation depends on faith. However, while infant baptism is justified by the constant practice and tradition of the

Church, it is recognized to present a problem of theology in that faith is realized to be a prerequisite for reception of the sacrament of faith. Since our exposition only draws attention to the reason for which infant baptism is already recognized to present a problem for theology, infant baptism cannot be pressed as an objection against the validity of what we have said. It is important to note that the traditional solution offered for this problem (on which we cannot comment further, as it would lead us too far from our subject) admits the necessity of faith even in infants to be baptised, when it says that faith is supplied for them by the Church. Christian faith must be understood as, in itself, an adult matter, a matter of free decision, and this is so even for adults who were baptised as infants. On attaining maturity, they cannot escape making a personal decision either affirming or rejecting the faith in which they were baptized. Hence, while infant baptism is *normal practice* in the Church, from the strictly *theological* point of view it is an *exception*, and so cannot constitute a valid ground of objection to statements describing a theologically normal situation.

In summary, the divine Sonship of Jesus is basically given, and then expressed (and revealed) in his faith, which, however, is established in the face of temptation; at the same time, by this means, his divine Sonship is realized in his humanity. The divine filiation of ordinary people, on the other hand, is basically brought about through their faith, which likewise is established in the face of temptation; and at the same time it is expressed in their faith.

The nature of humans is so constructed that in them it is in dependence on matter (the body) that spirit is both active and receptive. Hence communication between one human person and another, which is the meeting of spirits, or dialogue, and as such comprises bestowal of self, reception of the other and response to the other, requires the medium of matter. From this mediating function of matter it follows that human communication is necessarily sacramental. Here we have a model for the self-communication of God to humans. The pure spirituality of God does not require, indeed does not allow, the self-communication of God in the Trinity to be sacramental. There it can only be immediate and direct. But when God communicates himself to humans in their otherness from him, the nature of the recipients places its limitations on the communication, so that so far as the recipients are concerned it has to be sacramental. However, even though Jesus was a human, this was not the case with him, since of all humans he alone was not other than God, but was one in person with the Son, to whom the Father communicated himself without any medium. But if God is to communicate himself to ordinary humans, it must be by a grace which, while transforming the whole person, leaves intact their inner core or person in its otherness from God. This core, then, can be reached by God only (as it were) from outside, which, given the structure of human nature, can be done only in a sacramental communication, which may justly be called an encounter, since it is an event in which God is truly met as making a claim on the person for their faith. If a person responds in faith, the Father regenerates them in grace as his child. Ordinary humans experience both the offer and the bestowal of grace by God in the sacramental encounter. Since, however, the Sonship of Jesus was not acquired sacramentally, there was no offer of grace to him, but only the bestowal that constituted him Son of God in human existence.

The sacraments through which God in his particular providence claims from humans the response of faith are greatly varied, for God can use the multifarious events (interpersonal encounters and also humbler experiences, which, however, necessarily derive their meaning from the interpersonal ones[5]) of secular life as ways of summoning humans to faith.

These events determine and limit the self-revelation of the Father that takes place in them. Since in the Trinity the full expression of the Father is the divine Word, these secular sacraments, as partial self-revelations of God, constitute humble reflections of the divine Word, who is thus shown to be present and active in them. This statement is supported by the patristic tradition which attributed to the divine Word the theophanies of the Old Testament.[6] In a secular sacrament a human is engaged by the Holy Spirit sent by the Father through the Son present in the sacrament. Because of the limitation of the sacrament a consequent limitation is placed on the articulation, though not necessarily on the degree of commitment, of the person's response. This response, if it is positive, is a genuine, though hidden, faith, since it is made to grace, the Father's Gift of the Holy Spirit, offered in his

---

5   Cf. K. Rahner, "Reflections on the Unity of the Love of Neighbor and the Love of God," *Theological Investigations* 6, 239-41.

6   For Justin, Theophilus of Antioch, Irenaeus, Clement of Alexandria and Origen, cf., respectively, pp. 91, 93-94, 100, 108 and 116, of R. Latourelle, *Theology of Revelation* (Staten Island, N.Y., 1966).

sacramental self-revelation, and since in the acceptance of the sacrament it embraces the Father, though only under the symbol of whatever transcendental value it conveys.

Among the many sacraments in which God reveals and offers himself, the glorified Christ, i.e., as present in the Church in its ministry of word and sacrament, occupies the first place, because in him God is revealed and offered in an unsurpassable way. This is so because Christ is no mere reflection of the divine Word, as are secular sacraments, but is this Word incarnate, and so constitutes, as we have shown, the full revelation of the Father. The Holy Spirit, therefore, who engages humans in this as in all sacraments, and in whom the Father regenerates the human as his child, and who therefore becomes the bond of the new child and the Father, is sent by the Father through the Son (per filium) not as merely reflected in the sacrament, but as so at one (in person) with the sacrament of the sacred humanity that in it, and therefore by his *human* will, the Son is the sender of the Holy Spirit from and *with* the Father (filioque, cf. Jn 15:26). This greatest of sacraments is offered to Christians only at certain times (and most particularly in the Eucharist), though, of course, its effects remain with them always and determine their whole lives. With other humans, they experience also the range of secular sacraments, which, however, they spontaneously refer to their full sacramental encounter with God in Christ. We have here merely touched on the question of the faith of non-Christians, to which we shall return later.

We now offer a further comment on the contrast of the divine filiation of ordinary humans as acquired sacramentally with that of Jesus as acquired non-sacramentally. The immediate reason for this is that the divine filiation of humans depends on their acceptance of the offer of grace, i.e., on their faith, while with Jesus there was no offer, and therefore no acceptance, but simply the bestowal of grace that constituted him Son of God in human existence, so that for him faith flowed from his Sonship. This was so because in the Incarnation, and ultimately in the Trinity itself, the Holy Spirit was the bond between the Father and the Son. By virtue of the perichoresis, Father and Son are immediately present to each other and therefore no medium is necessary or even possible. Between the adopted children and the Father, however, the Holy Spirit is the bond certainly, but more than a bond, a medium. This is required by the basic otherness of the human being in their person from God. While the person of Jesus, because of his identity with the Son, was homoousios with the Father, ordinary humans in their persons are not. The necessity of a medium in the case of ordinary humans explains the sacramental character of their filiation, as the non-necessity, indeed the impossibility, of a medium in the case of Jesus explains the non-sacramental character of his.

Of course, the faith of Jesus was still established, as is ours, in the events of life. However, it cannot be said that in these the Father revealed and offered himself to Jesus as he does to us. For Jesus these events were opportunities for his ontological divine Sonship to become realized at the level of genuine historical human experience, i.e., as a lived faith. This is seen in the New Testament in Jesus' perception of his unique relationship to the Father, his obedient acceptance of his mission to men and women implied in that relationship, and his persevering faithfulness in the overcoming of temptation. We should note, finally, that there is a sense in which the faith of Jesus was sacramental even though not acquired sacramentally: it was articulated sacramentally, i.e., in the events of his life, which took place in the framework of his whole inherited religious culture. These events, then, served him both as means of establishing his faith and as symbols for articulating it.

We summarize these considerations by saying that whereas in Jesus faith flowed from his divine Sonship, in ordinary believers their divine filiation results from their faith. And while the Sonship of Jesus was simply bestowed on him, theirs, being acquired sacramentally in penance and faith, can be reduced or even totally lost through sin. Thus, on the basis of the relation of divine filiation and faith, we have been able to make a further useful comparison of the Incarnation and grace, the two modalities of the self-communication of God the Father to humans in continuation of the same self-communication in the Trinity.

In this part of our book we have been at pains to show that in the Incarnation and grace humans are drawn by God into his own life to receive the self-communication of the Father to the Son and the Holy Spirit, respectively, that takes place in the Trinity. There this self-communication is brought about by principiality, but in humans it is brought about by divine formal causality. In the Incarnation and grace respectively the action of God in regard to humans is single, but in it two contrasting moments, the one centrifugal, the other centripetal, are to be distinguished. Initially the human has to be considered in their simple otherness from God. God therefore has to reach out to them in a centrifugal action. From this point of view God's action can be conceived as one of efficient causality, common to the three divine persons. Thus we say that the sacred humanity and created grace are the work of the three divine persons, each, however, acting in his own property. But in thus making contact, God communicates himself to humans, which is possible on their side because of the spiritual component of their nature, in which is rooted their supernatural potency to be thus united to God. The (logically) second moment of God's action is centripetal and assimilative. God draws the human into the ambit of his own personal life. While the human remains always other than God, they are now not *simply* other, for God communicates himself to them, so that in the Incarnation Jesus is other than God only in his human nature, being one (homoousios) with him by virtue of his person, which is that of the divine Son, and in grace humans are other than God in their persons, but are one with him in their possession of his Spirit, who as Spirit of filiation gives them a new and divine mode of being, adoptive divine filiation. In its totality the action of God in the Incarnation and grace respectively can be conceived as one of formal causality, in which is included efficient causality as its postulated basis and condition of possibility. By divine formal causality the Son alone in the Incarnation, and the Holy Spirit alone in grace, are communicated to humans. The divine indwelling by grace is that of the three divine persons, but the Father and the Son are present by virtue of the perichoresis, on the basis of the special presence of the Holy Spirit. Grace may be defined quite simply as the Gift of the Holy Spirit.

Since the concept of divine formal causality was first introduced to furnish a new theology of the supernatural, specifically of the Incarnation, grace and the beatific vision, a number of theologians have remained unconvinced, either of its validity as a theological concept in general or of its applicability to grace in particular. For our part, we do not want to exaggerate the importance of the theology of divine formal causality. It remains a model chosen from the world, subject to the limitations of all theological models, and requiring due care and moderation in its use. Without, however, having set out to meet all the objections expressly, we did in fact answer the more important of them in the course of our positive exposition, in which the theology of divine formal causality was integrated into the more comprehensive theology of the self-communication of God. Thus, while admitting the relative inadequacy of the concept to convey the supremely personal nature of God's relations to humans, we have justified its general use, shown its applicability to grace, and presented its positive advantages. Among these is its capacity to show why precisely the Son became incarnate and why precisely the Holy Spirit is given in grace. While inadequate, it is demonstrably less so than the concepts in which the Scholastic theology of grace was elaborated. Its main task is to provide a framework in which Scripture and Tradition are allowed to speak without the kind of obstruction that occurs, e.g. when theologians, influenced by the theology of divine efficient causality, reduce statements about individual divine persons to mere appropriations. Further, it allows that part of the theology of the self-communication of God that has to do with the world to be expressed in terms intelligible and acceptable in the Scholastic tradition. This theology can be then re-expressed in personal categories, particularly within the biblical context of covenant, and also in terms of transcendental theology. At the same time the self-communication of God that takes place in the world can be linked with that which takes place in the Trinity, so that some understanding is reached of the profound unity in diversity of God both in himself and in his dealings with humans.

In regard to the Incarnation it is clear that a theology of the self-communication of God necessarily implies a "descending" before an "ascending" Christology. However, our work here has now brought us to the point where it is indicated that we should move from descending to ascending Christology and follow up the implications of this for the theology of grace. If the Incarnation and grace are to be seen as the modalities of the self-communication of God to humans, this implies, as is pointed out by transcendental theology, that in their very being humans must be open to this communication. The Incarnation and grace are determinations precisely of humanity. Having explored the implications of communication from above, through the method of descending Christology, we now adopt, in Parts Three and Four, the method of ascending Christology and focus attention on the human and the transformation of their being brought about by the self-communication of God. We shall see that the appropriate Trinitarian model to guide us in the execution of this task is the return model, which was acquired in Chapter Two.

PART III

THEOLOGY OF THE INCARNATION AND GRACE IN THE LIGHT OF THE RETURN MODEL

I. THE ANOINTING OF JESUS WITH THE HOLY SPIRIT

7 ASSESSMENT OF THE ANOINTING THEOLOGY OF SCHEEBEN AND MÜHLEN

Up to now we have considered the Incarnation and grace in the light of the procession model, i.e., as, respectively, communications, by the Father, of the Son to the humanity of Jesus, and of the Holy Spirit to other human beings. In this perspective, which is that of descending Christology, they are seen as constituted, or *in facto esse*, to use the Scholastic expression. We now wish to consider them in the light of the return model, which will require us to adopt the standpoint of ascending Christology and see them in their formation, or *in fieri*, to use Scholastic language once again. In this perspective both will emerge as communications, by the Father, of the Holy Spirit, to humans. To this statement so bluntly made a number of qualifications need to be added, and this we shall do in the course of our study. We shall be satisfied now with briefly making two points. First, our thesis does not reduce the Incarnation to an instance of grace that is merely more intense than that of other people. Secondly, there is no incompatibility between the two phases, of formation and constitution, as described above. This is because the Holy Spirit is the Spirit precisely of filiation (cf. Rom 8:15). As such, he constitutes both Jesus and other humans children of God, even if divine filiation changes greatly (though not totally) in meaning and content from the former instance to the latter. The Father makes the man Jesus his Son, one in person with his eternal Son, by bestowing the Holy Spirit on him in a uniquely radical way. This makes Jesus the very paradigm of divine filiation. The Father makes other humans his children also, but in a much humbler way, viz., as sons and daughters *in* the Son, by bestowing on them the same Spirit, who is offered to them in the sacrament of Christ. The difference between the two instances may be stated succinctly as follows. The Father bestowed the Holy Spirit on the humanity of Jesus in an act by which at the same time that humanity was created, sanctified and united in person to the divine Son. He bestows the Holy Spirit on others in an act which finds them already constituted as human persons (sinners, however), but which with their cooperation sanctifies them and unites them to

Christ the divine Son as sons and daughters in the Son, in the sense that they now possess the same Spirit who made him unique Son of God in humanity.

This thesis is readily assimilated by transcendental theology, which sees the Incarnation and grace as determinations, by God, of humanity in its openness to him, the Incarnation being the uniquely highest such determination. If in each case it is the Holy Spirit as Spirit of filiation, who is communicated by God (the Father), it is clear that the uniquely highest form of this determination will be that in which the humanity becomes one in person with the divine Son, while lesser determinations will not be such as to rule out independent human personhood, and so will remain unions of human persons with the Holy Spirit, sons and daughters in the Son. Thus would be supplied the answer to the question which we had to leave unanswered in the last part, as to why precisely the uniquely highest determination of humanity necessarily resulted in union with the Son, while lesser determinations bring about union with the Holy Spirit.

All this, it is realized, will have to be established and explained in detail. We hope, however, that already it is clear that in formation the Incarnation and grace can both be communications of the Holy Spirit, while in constitution the former is the communication of the Son, and the latter the communication of the Holy Spirit.

We remarked that to consider the Incarnation in formation was to consider it from the standpoint of ascending Christology, while to consider it in constitution was to do so from the standpoint of descending Christology. This is because in the formation of the Incarnation that which changes is not God (who cannot change) but the human nature, which at its creation is determined and elevated to become the humanity of the Son of God. This elevation clearly pertains to ascending Christology. In the Incarnation as constituted it is the Son who is united with the human nature. For the Son this is an "emptying" (cf. Phil 2:7), which belongs to descending Christology.

Obviously, the Christological part of our thesis will require careful presentation, and to this end this part of the book is devoted. The next part will be given over to the second half of the thesis, concerning the grace of ordinary humans. In this part we shall show the development of our Christological thesis in the history of theology by following the evolution of the biblical and patristic theme of the anointing of the humanity of Jesus by the Father with the Holy Spirit. This can be done conveniently by reference to the work of two men, Matthias Scheeben (1835-1888) and Heribert Mühlen (1927-2006). In this chapter we shall first present Scheeben's position without criticism, and then Mühlen's position, which contains a critique of Scheeben. We shall then criticize the positions of them both, enunciating our own position in the process; and then in the next chapter we shall present our position directly from the sources and in detail to the extent that this remains to be done.

The object of the exercise is to unify the doctrine of grace at the deepest possible level. This we will have done if we succeed in showing that all grace is the Gift of the Holy Spirit, not just for others but for Jesus as well. We must, however, immediately correct the perspective in which this last statement is made. All grace for human beings is the Gift of the Holy Spirit precisely *because* that is what it is for their paradigm, Jesus. We now embark on the task of this part of our work, to establish that the fullness of this Gift is in fact the grace given to Jesus Christ.

Scheeben's theology of the anointing of the humanity of Jesus is found in two places in his works, in *Die Mysterien des Christentums* (*The Mysteries of Christianity*)[1] and in Book Five ("The Redemption") of the *Handbuch der Katholischen Dogmatik* (*Manual of Catholic Dogmatic Theology*).[2] We take up the *Mysterien* first. The relevant part is a reflection on the anointing of Jesus based on Scripture and the Fathers, though no reference is made in the text to any statement from either source. The argument is based *on* the sources without being elaborated *from* them. However, source material is indicated in two footnotes, the first of which, supplied by the editor (and therefore not commented on here), gives biblical references, and the second of which, from the author, gives three patristic texts. These are as follows:

1. Gregory of Nazianzus, *Oratio Xa:* " ... the Father of the genuine and real Christ, whom he anointed with the oil of gladness above his companions, anointing the humanity with divinity so as to make the two of them one."[3]

---

1   M. Scheeben, *Die Mysterien des Christentums* (Gesammelte Schriften 2) (Freiburg im Br., 1958). Cf. English translation, *The Mysteries of Christianity* (St. Louis, 1951) 331-34.

2   M. Scheeben, *Handbuch der Katholischen Dogmatik* (Gesammelte Schriften 6/1) (Freiburg im Br., 1954) 222 (176-84).

3   PG 35, 832.

2. John Damascene, *De fide orthodoxa III*: "Christ we say to be the name of the person, not used with a single designation, but indicating the two natures. For he anointed himself: anointing as God the body with his divinity, but being anointed as a human, for he is both the one and the other. The divinity is the ointment of the humanity."[4]

3. John Damascene, *De fide orthodoxa IV*: "Accordingly was born of her the Son of God incarnate, not a God-bearing human, but God incarnate, anointed not like a prophet, with power, but with the presence of the whole of the anointer, so that the anointer became human and the anointed became God, not by change of nature, but by union according to person. For he was both the anointer and the anointed, as God anointing himself as a human."[5]

Scheeben's doctrine here comprises two points. The first is that the Incarnation is constituted by the anointing of the sacred humanity by the divine Word or Son. God the Father is recognized to be the agent of the anointing only in the sense that he is the principle of the Son. And the fact that the Fathers sometimes (elsewhere) say that Christ is anointed by the Holy Spirit is explained as meaning that he is anointed "by personal union with the principle of the Holy Spirit,"[6] i.e., the Son. This idea is expanded in a footnote. Christ is anointed by the Holy Spirit not in himself (the Spirit), but rather as "the source from which he (the Spirit) issues, but including, besides this source, all its wealth and its overflow."[7] When the Fathers ascribe the Incarnation to the Holy Spirit, this is mere appropriation.

The second point is the suitability of the word "Christ" ("Anointed") to express the reality and significance of the person Jesus Christ. The name "Jesus" indicates the function that this person was to exercise, but the name "Christ" (significantly called by Scheeben a name and not a title) indicates his "inner being and constitution."[8] This is because "Christ" denotes the unifying of divinity and humanity in him, an action that is not a mere deputation to office but the constitution of Jesus as "the true God-man,"[9] "a divine-human being."[10]

---

4   PG 94, 989.

5   Ibid. 1160-61.

6   Scheeben, *Mysteries* 333.

7   Ibid. 332, note 7.

8   Ibid. 333.

9   Ibid. 332.

10   Ibid. 333.

We turn now to the *Dogmatik*. Here the doctrine of the anointing of Christ is the same as in the *Mysterien*, but it is expressed more fully. Scheeben presents his case for the suitability of the name (as he calls it) "Christ" ("Anointed") to express the inner reality of the person of the God-man. The Incarnation is depicted as the anointing of the sacred humanity by the divine Son. As in the *Mysterien*, the argument is not elaborated directly from the sources. The few references to Scripture are not significant. As regards patristic references, a few are made indirectly. Of those actually quoted (with which alone we shall concern ourselves), two are the same as the first two in the *Mysterien*. There are two more, which we now give:

1. Gregory of Nazianzus, *Oratio XLVa:* "He is perfect not only because of the divinity, than which nothing is more perfect, but also because what he assumed was anointed with divinity, and made the same as that which anointed, that is, to speak boldly, the same as God."[11]

2. Peter Chrysologus, *Sermo XL:* "When the Son of God, with the whole ointment of the divinity, poured himself, like dew on the fleece, into our flesh, he was named, from the ointment, Christ, and he, who by God was poured over and in, so that man and God might be one God, remains the sole originator of that name."[12]

It is clear that Scheeben has quoted these four texts because they appear to support his view that in the Incarnation the sacred humanity is anointed by the divine Word or Son. However, he recognizes that the Fathers speak of this anointing also in other ways. He rationalizes these by attempting to harmonize them with his basic position. Thus he says that when the Fathers say that the sacred humanity is anointed "with the divinity," the word "divinity" does not necessarily have an abstract sense, but in this context very often denotes the person of the Word. When they say that Christ is anointed by God the Father, this means that the Father "brings it about through the eternal generation that the Son can anoint his humanity and in it himself with that which he has and is in himself,"[13] and "that the Father together with the Son effects through his will the joining of the ointment with its substrate."[14]

---

11   PG 36, 640-41.

12   PL 52, 367.

13   Scheeben, *Dogmatik* 5, 181.

14   Ibid.

According to Scheeben, when the Fathers say that the sacred humanity is anointed through, with, or in, the Holy Spirit, this does not denote the basic anointing that is identical with the Incarnation. When they say "through" the Holy Spirit, this is an appropriation, in that the Holy Spirit, as proceeding from the Son, is conceived as the mediator between the Son and the humanity in the hypostatic union. When they say "in" or "with" (by) the Holy Spirit, this can be understood to *symbolize* the basic anointing, in that the Holy Spirit anoints the humanity only in so far as he proceeds from the Son, but this anointing should not be conceived as identical in fact with the basic one, of which it is only a corollary.

However, Scheeben concedes, "occasionally" the Fathers mean the basic anointing identical with the Incarnation when they say that Christ is anointed with the Holy Spirit. In these instances, "by Holy Spirit is understood not the person who bears this as his proper name, but the person of the Logos (Word) in so far as he is the principle of the person of the Holy Spirit, and is likewise Spirit and holy in the absolute sense, and precisely in this property forms the ointment of the humanity of Christ and of the man Christ."[15]

We turn now to the treatment of the theme of the anointing of Jesus by Mühlen in his book *Der Heilige Geist als Person*.[16] Mühlen commends Scheeben for having resurrected the patristic theme of the anointing, a theme that found no place in Scholasticism. He points out that for Scheeben there was no distinction between the Incarnation and the anointing. Against this, he observes that Scheeben was incorrect in regarding "Christ" as a proper name. At least in the Synoptics a clear distinction is made between "Jesus" as a proper name and "Christ" as a title of office. It was only later, in the Greek-speaking world, which had no background of Messianic expectation, that the word "Christ" came to be regarded as a name. The Synoptics knew of an anointing of Jesus, but it was an anointing by the Father and with the Holy Spirit, not identical with the Incarnation, but connected with the mission of Jesus, which was a *consequence* of the Incarnation. It was his deputation to office. It is permissible, however, to extend the theology of anointing and say that the Word anointed himself, for the Word is the origin of the Holy Spirit, who thus becomes the ointment. The Word

---

15   Ibid. 182.

16   Heribert Mühlen, *Der Heilige Geist als Person* (Münster: Verlag Aschendorff, 1966) 170-87.

anointed himself *with the Holy Spirit.* It is not necessary to restrict the role of the Holy Spirit in relation to the sacred humanity to an appropriation, viz., that the Holy Spirit is the mediator between the Word and the humanity. The Holy Spirit has a proper function in relation to the humanity, viz., in regard to the created grace of Jesus. Scheeben, therefore, was incorrect in identifying the Incarnation and the anointing. They are distinct mysteries, the Incarnation centering on the person of the God-man, the anointing on his office. The Incarnation is the appearance in salvation-history of the Son, the anointing the appearance of the Holy Spirit. In his theology of grace Scheeben recognized a proper indwelling of the Holy Spirit in the just person. Consistently, he should also have recognized a proper role of the Holy Spirit in relation to Jesus.

Mühlen goes on to reproduce the three patristic texts given by Scheeben in the *Mysterien,* to which he adds a fourth, taken from St.Cyril of Alexandria's commentary on the Epistle to the Hebrews (which we shall quote later). He admits that in the absence of a monograph on the doctrine of the anointing of Christ in the Fathers, he has drawn his conclusions from these four texts alone. He accepts Scheeben's conclusion that the Fathers understood the Incarnation as the anointing of the sacred humanity with the Word, but obliquely criticizes them by saying that this understanding was possible only in a world which, not knowing that "Christ" was the translation of "Messiah," had erected it into a proper name, so that now it signified the whole reality of the God-man.

Mühlen begins the positive presentation of his theology of the anointing of Jesus with a consideration of the relation between the name "Jesus" and the title "Christ." He maintains that the New Testament writers regarded "the Christ" as a predicate of the person Jesus, saying that Jesus was the Christ, and thus equivalently distinguishing between the Incarnation and the anointing. In this they showed a greater appreciation of the reality than did the Fathers when they simply identified "Christ" with "Jesus," thus identifying the anointing with the Incarnation. Invoking Geiselmann, Cullmann and Foerster, Mühlen points to the development of the title "Christ" in the Synoptics and Acts to the point where it becomes a name in the letters of Paul. "Jesus," on the other hand, is simply a name, though it has a significant meaning, "the Lord saves." It indicates a particular human, of whom it is said in faith that he is the Christ. This allows the name

"Jesus" itself to undergo theological development, so that it indicates a particular human no longer simply in his historical existence but in his election by God as the Christ.

"Christ," the title of office, takes its basic meaning from the Old Testament, where those anointed were the king (1 Sam 9:16, 16:3; 1 Kings 1:34), the High Priest (Ex 28:41), and ordinary priests (Ex 30:30, 28:41, 40:15; Lev 7:36, 10:7; Num 3:3). The anointing was a deputation to a particular service of God. Relying on Lys, Mühlen observes that the anointed person is set apart and henceforth belongs to the divine sphere (without, of course, ceasing to belong to the human sphere). He is constituted a mediator between God and humanity. These anointings were done with oil. However, the Old Testament speaks also of an "anointing" not done with oil, a deputation to office not signified by a material anointing, viz., the anointing of the prophet (I Kings 19:16). Whether done with oil or not, says Lys, anointing brings about in the anointed person the presence of the Spirit of God, which empowers them to do the work to which they are deputed.

Relying on Ignace de la Potterie, Mühlen understands the anointing of Jesus in the New Testament in the light of four texts, Lk 4:18, Acts 4:27 and 10:38, and Heb 1:9. Three of these are Lukan, which is not surprising, given that Luke is at pains to present Jesus as the prophet, indeed as the new Elijah, and that the anointing here spoken of is to be understood in the light of the anointing of the prophet in the Old Testament. In the anointing of Jesus there is no suggestion of a material anointing. He is anointed by God (the Father) with the Holy Spirit in order to preach the Gospel, a prophetic task. This approach is inspired by Is 61:1

We consider first Acts 10:38, which occurs in the course of Peter's address in the house of Cornelius. We begin at v. 36: "(36) You know the word which he sent to Israel, preaching good news of peace by Jesus Christ (he is Lord of all), (37) the word which was proclaimed throughout all Judea, beginning from Galilee after the baptism which John preached: (38) how God anointed Jesus of Nazareth with the Holy Spirit and with power; how he went about doing good and healing all that were oppressed by the devil, for God was with him."

De la Potterie relates this text to Is 61:1, which speaks of the deputation of a human being to the role of prophet. Significantly, in its version of this passage, the Septuagint has the verb *euaggelizo* ("to bring good tidings"), which in New Testament terminology means "to preach the

Gospel." The passage from Acts clearly refers to the baptism of Jesus. The statement, "God was with him," is seen as important, as it reflects the Old Testament formula put in the mouth of God, "I am with you." Thus the presence of God is brought about by the anointing and is directed to the prophetic task of Jesus. This passage is contrasted with Jn 16:32, where "The Father is with me" is seen in reference not to the anointing but to the divine Sonship of Jesus. Mühlen concludes that the presence of the Father to Jesus has two references, one to his divine Sonship, the other to his anointing with the Holy Spirit.

It remains to say that neither Mühlen nor de la Potterie is saying that by the Holy Spirit Luke means the third person of the Trinity as later understood by the Church. But the Lukan doctrine provides a foundation for that belief. This is seen, e.g., in the presence of the definite article in "the Holy Spirit" in Luke's account of the baptism (3:22) in contrast to Mark's account (1:8). This indicates that for Luke the Holy Spirit is not just the power of God as in the Old Testament, but the eschatological gift of the Spirit of God. Thus is provided sufficient justification for developing from Lukan texts theological arguments that presuppose a certain personhood and distinctness on the part of the Holy Spirit.

The next text is Lk 4:18, which is the quotation, by Jesus in the synagogue at Nazareth, of Is 61:1, as fulfilled by his assumption of the prophetic role. We begin with v. 16: "(16) And he came to Nazareth, where he had been brought up; and he went to the synagogue, as his custom was, on the sabbath day. And he stood up to read; (17) and there was given to him the book of the prophet Isaiah. He opened the book and found the place where it was written, (18) 'The Spirit of the Lord is upon me, because he has anointed me to preach good news to the poor. He has sent me to proclaim release to the captives and recovery of sight to the blind, to set at liberty those who are oppressed, (19) to proclaim the acceptable year of the Lord.' (20) And he closed the book, and gave it back to the attendant, and sat down; and the eyes of all in the synagogue were fixed on him. (21) And he began to say to them, 'Today this scripture has been fulfilled in your hearing.'"

This passage must be linked with Lk 4:14, "And Jesus returned in the power of the Spirit into Galilee," because it was in the power of the Spirit in which he returned to Galilee that he spoke in the synagogue. And in turn Lk 4:14 must be linked with Lk 3:21-22, the baptism of Jesus, because the Spirit in whose power he returned to Galilee was the Spirit who descended upon him at his baptism. Again, therefore, the anointing of Jesus with the Holy Spirit is situated at his baptism, and this anointing is to be understood as his deputation to the role of prophet.

The next text, Acts 4:27, is part of the prayer of the community following the release of Peter and John. In vv. 25-26, Ps 2:1-2 is quoted, "Why did the Gentiles rage, and the people imagine vain things? The kings of the earth set themselves in array, and the rulers were gathered together, against the Lord and his Anointed." In v. 27 the fate of Jesus is seen as the fulfillment of the prophecy of the psalm, "for truly in this city there were gathered together against thy holy servant Jesus, whom thou didst anoint, both Herod and Pontius Pilate, with the Gentiles and the people of Israel." Mühlen restricts himself to two comments, first, that the text states that Jesus was anointed, and second that a distinction is drawn between the proper name "Jesus" and the anointing. He could have added that it is by God (the Father) that Jesus is here said to have been anointed. It would be tempting to speculate on the significance of the identification of Jesus in this context with the Servant of God in Deutero-Isaiah, but Mühlen refrains from this, though in fact de la Potterie has an elaborate hypothesis to offer.[17]

The final text Heb 1:09, is evidently regarded by Mühlen as the least important of the four. It is a quotation from Ps 45, and reads, beginning with v. 8, "(8) But of the Son he says, 'Thy throne, O God, is for ever and ever, the righteous scepter is the scepter of thy kingdom. (9) Thou hast loved righteousness and hated lawlessness; therefore God, thy God, has anointed thee with the oil of gladness beyond thy comrades.'" Here it is asserted that Jesus was anointed by God the Father. The only significant comment that Mühlen makes is the same as his comment on the previous text, viz., that a distinction is made between the Son (i.e., the person of Jesus) and the anointing (i.e., his office).

Mühlen then endorses the conclusion of de la Potterie, "One does not find in the New Testament any text which refers to an anointing of Christ at the moment of the Incarnation. ... The true, and in a sense the only, context in which the New Testament speaks of the

---

17   Cf. I. de la Potterie, "L'onction du Christ. Étude de théologie biblique," *Nouvelle Revue Théologique* 80 (1958) 225-52. See English translation, "The Anointing of Christ," *Word and Mystery* (ed. L.O'Donovan) (New York: Newman Press, 1968) 173-79.

anointing of Christ is that of the baptism."[18] De la Potterie is then invoked as support in a criticism of Scheeben for identifying the anointing and the Incarnation. He is further quoted as distinguishing the two themes, "the Christ" and the anointing, saying that in Luke they undergo parallel and unconnected development. (Actually, he understands "Christ" as designating Jesus upon his ascension, as having entered the condition of King-Messiah, while he considers the theme of anointing to belong to the beginning of the public life, the baptism, where Jesus is designated as Prophet.) He points out that while for the Fathers the titles King, Priest and Prophet indicate a manner of being, in the New Testament the anointing is connected with a function of Christ. Mühlen then excludes Lk 1:35 from consideration in relation to the anointing of Jesus, on the ground that it involves an anointing not of Jesus but of Mary.

Notwithstanding de la Potterie's reservations about the title "Christ" as distinct from the theme of anointing, Mühlen, concludes that "Christ," as translation of "Messiah," is connected with the anointing of Jesus with the Holy Spirit (this statement occurs also, it will be recalled, at the beginning of Mühlen's exposition), and not with the Incarnation, while the name "Jesus" is connected with his humanity. Scheeben's understanding of "Christ" as designating "the divine-human compositum" can, he holds, be positively excluded by Scripture.

It is important to note that Mühlen recognizes that what the New Testament presents in temporal sequence must sometimes be understood as being in logical sequence only. Thus the anointing with the Holy Spirit, though presented as taking place at the baptism, must actually have taken place at the first moment of the Incarnation.[19] At the baptism something was revealed which until then had remained hidden. This position is determined by the fact that the Son (together with the Father) is the origin of the Holy Spirit even when incarnate. Since, therefore, the Son is united to the human nature from the first moment of the Incarnation, also from that moment the Holy Spirit, proceeding from him, must anoint the human nature. It is at the baptism that this anointing is manifested. In each instance a divine person is linked with a created reality, the Son with the human nature of Jesus, the Holy Spirit with his created (habitual) grace and consequently (because Christ is head) also with the grace of other humans.

18   "The Anointing of Christ" 181-82.

19   Mühlen 197-214.

Mühlen invokes Aquinas in asserting that in Christ the *gratia unionis* (the grace of union, i.e., that by which the sacred humanity is united to the Godhead) is to be distinguished from habitual grace. The former is the work of the Son, the latter the work of the Holy Spirit.

Clearly, Mühlen bases much of his theology of the anointing on the work of de la Potterie. It will be useful to add at this point some further material on the subject from this source not included by Mühlen. The Old Testament, says de la Potterie, gives only one example of the anointing of a prophet, viz., that of Elisha by Elijah in I Kings 19:16. It is clear that this is not a material anointing. Elisha is anointed with the spirit of prophecy. In 1 Chron 16:22 (which is the same as Ps 105:15) prophets are said, by the device of parallelism, to be "anointed ones." This indicates that the prophets have been given the spirit of prophecy.

Commenting on Acts 10:38, de la Potterie observes that Jesus is said to be anointed with the Holy Spirit and with power. He notes the conjunction of these ideas with that of anointing. We shall bear this comment in mind for later use.

On the baptism passage in Luke (3:21-22), de la Potterie comments that Jesus is there designated as prophet, not as King-Messiah. The argument is that the statement by the voice from heaven refers not to Ps 2, but to the first Servant Song (Is 42:1-9), where the servant is presented as a teacher or prophet. De la Potterie points to the parallel, clearly intended by Luke, between the descent of the Spirit on Jesus at the baptism and the descent of the same Spirit on the disciples at Pentecost (Acts 2:1-11). This is another point that we shall keep in mind.

The descent of the Spirit on Jesus at the baptism, says de la Potterie, cannot be regarded as the inauguration of his Messianic ministry. Indeed the validity of the concept of a Messianic ministry can be disputed. As we have noted already, in the perspective of Luke, Jesus entered upon his Messiahship at his ascension. Luke does not connect the title "Christ" with the anointing at the baptism. The fourth major text given above, Heb 1:9, presents the King-Messiah rather than the prophet, but even there the anointing is not an anointing to Messianic office, but an expression of joy at the enthronement of the King-Messiah in accordance with the custom of throwing perfume on a person being honored.

De la Potterie recognizes that from the point of view of the Fathers, influenced as they were by the Greek concept of being, the anointing of

Jesus as priest, prophet and king must coincide with the Incarnation. These offices are presented differently by the New Testament writers, because, in Semitic fashion, they were concerned with the function of Jesus rather than his being. De la Potterie fears that identifying the anointing of Jesus with the Incarnation leads to a "generalizing" of the sense of the word "anointing" in which the biblical meaning is lost. He regards it as undesirable that the baptismal anointing should come to be seen as nothing more than the revelation of a consecration that already existed in a hidden way.

We begin our critique of the material we have presented here by endorsing Mühlen's rejection of Scheeben's recourse to appropriation as the explanation of the anointing of Jesus through the Holy Spirit. When the sources speak of only one divine person as performing a work, we should be slow to label this as appropriation. Respect for the sources demands that as far as possible, their statements be taken in the proper sense and not metaphorically. Appropriation, therefore, should be adopted only as a last resort, to be abandoned when an acceptable explanation favoring the proper sense emerges. For example, we have seen already that in some cases it was the inadequate philosophical framework of efficient causality that moved theologians to settle for appropriation, so that when formal causality was demonstrated to be a real alternative they were able to accept the proper sense.

We have seen above Scheeben's ways of accounting for the varying statements of the Fathers about the anointing of Jesus, sometimes as an anointing by the Father, sometimes as an anointing by the Son, and sometimes as an anointing through, in, or with, the Holy Spirit. His, however, is not the only possible explanation. Mühlen has a different one, and we a different one again. Scheeben's thought here is determined by his descending Christology, even though, inappropriately, it is expressed in the language of ascending Christology. That is to say, the anointing of Jesus is a theme belonging to ascending Christology, for it is the man Jesus who is the proper object of anointing, by which he is given a unique rank and mission. Ultimately, the verdict as to which theology is correct, Scheeben's, Mühlen's, our own, or some other, will be passed by the sources, in particular by Scripture.

The statements of the Fathers are made sometimes in the context of descending Christology, sometimes in the context of ascending Christology. This variability has to be allowed for. Thus, when Jesus is said to be anointed by the Father, this could mean either that the

Incarnation is the prolongation into the world of the generation of the Son by the Father (descending Christology), or that it is the bestowal by the Father of the Holy Spirit on the sacred humanity (ascending Christology). When the Son is said to anoint himself, this can only be a statement of descending Christology, in which the Incarnation is regarded simply as constituted. When Jesus is said to be anointed "through" the Spirit, this could mean either that it is the Father who anoints him by this means (in the context of either a descending or an ascending Christology as outlined above), or that it is the Son who thus anoints himself (in a descending Christology only). When it is said that Jesus is anointed "in" the Holy Spirit, "in" may mean simply "by" (as it can in patristic Greek), in which case the emphasis falls on the personal activity of the Holy Spirit, whereas "with" emphasizes his instrumental function, passive in relation to the Father or the Son, toward the sacred humanity; or it could concentrate attention on the simple presence of the Holy Spirit to Jesus, prescinding both from the Spirit's relations to the Father and the Son and from his function, whether conceived actively or passively, in regard to the sacred humanity. Scheeben (and Mühlen in following him) oversimplifies in imposing on the Fathers a single, consistent and homogeneous theology of the anointing of Jesus. The fact of the matter is that there are various strands in their theology of the anointing, and the task of the theologian is to select and elaborate from them that which represents the most authentic development from the ways in which the theme occurs in Scripture.

In order to maintain the position of recognizing in the Fathers only the one theology of the anointing of Jesus, Scheeben sometimes has to impose on words meanings that no impartial person could admit. Thus, he says that when "occasionally" the Fathers clearly identify the Incarnation and the anointing of Jesus with the Holy Spirit, by the latter term is meant not the divine person who bears that name, but the Logos as principle of the Holy Spirit. This distortion of the plain meaning of words immediately throws his position into question. We, for our part, hope to have avoided such pitfalls, for we recognize in the Fathers a variety of approaches, among which we attempt to judge with the aid of Scripture and the later organic developments of theology.

We look now at the patristic texts given by Scheeben and Mühlen, in order to see to what extent they support the conclusions drawn from them. We begin with the three texts given by Scheeben in the

Mysterien, and we consider them in the order in which we have given them.

The first was from Gregory of Nazianzus. The Christology here is of the descending type, and the agent of the anointing is the Father. The anointed one is Jesus Christ, specifically in his humanity. It is clear that here the anointing theme is only ancillary to Gregory's effort to express the Incarnation adequately, in terms that foreshadow the later definition of Chalcedon. Hence the ointment is identified only in a general way, as the divinity. While the Christology is in fact inadequate, it is certainly not monophysitic or even Apollinarist. Indeed, Gregory considered himself an opponent of Apollinarius. The text cannot be said to favor strongly any particular theory of the anointing, but it should be noted that at least it does not have the Son as the agent of the anointing.

The second text was from John Damascene. It too belongs to a descending Christology. Here Christ is said to anoint himself, but the statement is immediately weakened by the qualification that it is precisely as God that he anoints and as a human that he is anointed. The fact that this passage comes from the antimonophysitic writings of Damascene shows his real intention. He is less concerned with the anointing as a theological theme than with the distinction of natures, human and divine, in Christ.

The same is true of the third text, also from Damascene. Here the anointing theme is somewhat more developed, in that the Incarnation is seen as a full anointing as distinct from the partial anointing of a prophet. This enables Damascene to say that the anointer becomes a human and the anointed becomes God, not, however, by a fusion of natures, "but by union according to person." It is clear that the anointing theme is here subordinated to the interests of the doctrine of the distinction of natures in Christ. It is interesting to note that only a few lines before this text Damascene writes: "But when there came the fullness of time, an angel of the Lord was sent to her, to announce the conception of the Lord. In this manner she conceived the Son of God, the substantial power of the Father, not of the will of flesh, nor of the will of man, i.e., from intercourse and seed, but of the good will of the Father and the cooperation of the Holy Spirit."[20] Here there is no anointing theology and no preoccupation with the doctrine of the distinction of natures. Under the influence of Lk 1:26-38 roles are as-

---

20   PG 94, 1160.

signed to the three divine persons in the Incarnation. The Father is the initiator, the Holy Spirit the immediate operator, and the incarnate Son of God the outcome of the work. It is clear that Damascene is able to accept the Incarnation of the Son of God as the work of the Father in the power of the Holy Spirit.

We turn now to the *Dogmatik*, and to the two texts from there, in the order in which we gave them earlier. The first was from Gregory of Nazianzus. The observations made about the last text of Gregory's apply again here. Once again, the anointing theme is ancillary to that of distinction and unity in Christ. The anointing theme is not developed, and is used only to convey the idea of impregnation, in this case so great that what is anointed (man) becomes that which anoints (God). The Christology is weak, but it would be anachronistic to accuse Gregory of monophysitism. His use of the anointing theme is too limited to allow the drawing of detailed conclusions for a theology of anointing.

The final text was from Peter Chrysologus. In the context of a descending Christology, he is thinking of the hypostatic union in terms of distinction and unity in Christ. Anointing serves to describe the closeness of this union of God and man, and the point is made that it is a "whole" anointing, comparable to the "presence of the whole of the anointer" in Damascene and the "whole presence of the anointer" in Cyril.[21] However, a different perspective is evident in an earlier sermon of Chrysologus on the Apostles' creed, when he writes: "*Who was born of the Holy Spirit.* In this manner is Christ born for you until a human will change for you the order of birth, so that there will be a new rising in life for you, for whom the old decline remained always in death. *Who was born of the Holy Spirit and the Virgin Mary.* Where the Spirit generates, a virgin brings forth, something wholly divine and not at all human is done, nor is there any room for weakness where power (*virtus*) is linked to virtue (*virtus*)."[22] While it is strange to hear the power of generation, which is proper to the Father, predicated of the Holy Spirit, probably all that Chrysologus meant is that the Father generates by or through the Holy Spirit. In any case, in this text the action of God in bringing about the Incarnation is centered on the operation of the Holy Spirit.

---

21   PG 74, 961. The phrase occurs in a text which we will consider in the next chapter.

22   *Sermo* 57 (PL 52, 359).

Before continuing, we should consider the question raised by the last text, whether our theology of the Incarnation is a form of the Spirit Christology of the second century.[23] In this Christology the Spirit was not the third person of the Trinity, whose existence as a distinct person was not grasped at that time, but rather the second person. It is thought likely that the credal formulation, Who was born of the Holy Spirit and the Virgin Mary, reflects precisely this Christology. However, our Christology has little in common with it. The patristic Christology out of which our own grows is not this primitive one, but the one forged by Athanasius with his homoousion, and therefore the distinct personhood, of the Holy Spirit.

Mühlen's additional text, from Cyril of Alexandria, will be considered in our separate treatment of Cyril. We can now sum up our consideration of the use made by Scheeben and Mühlen of the five patristic texts, two from Gregory of Nazianzus, two from John Damascene and one from Chrysologus. These texts were chosen by Scheeben in the first place because they appeared to support his theology of the anointing, in which the sacred humanity is anointed by the Son in the Incarnation. Our criticism has shown that they do not do even this, since in them the anointing theme is left in a relatively undeveloped state and is subordinated to the theme of distinction and unity in Christ. By the same token, they are equally inadequate as a support for Mühlen's theology, in which the humanity is anointed by the Holy Spirit apart from the Incarnation. In these texts anointing is situated not where it belongs and can be developed, viz., in a context of ascending Christology, but in the descending Christology of the nature-person approach to Christ. Our study of Cyril of Alexandria, which we admit represents only a fraction of the patristic research that needs to be done, will show not only that the question is more complicated than was suspected, but that our theology of the anointing of Jesus is justified as a development of the most authentic strand of patristic thought on this matter.

Mühlen is correct in saying in his critique of Scheeben that in the New Testament "Christ" is basically a title and not a name. This, however, does not make the title "Christ" irrelevant to a discussion of the person of the God-man, as though only a name could be of significance for the understanding of a person, a title being merely a designation of office. This would be so only on the supposition, actually made

---

23   Cf. Kelly 142-45.

by Mühlen, that person and office are to be rigidly separated. But if office (conceived, of course, at a basic, as distinct from a superficial, level) is a dynamic expression of the reality of the person holding it, the title of office is indispensable for the understanding of the person. Hence Scheeben's conclusion that "Christ" expresses the essence of the person of Jesus may not be dismissed, even if the premise on which he bases it is false. We pointed out earlier that de la Potterie has shown that in the New Testament "Christ" and anointing are distinct themes, and that, even though he acknowledges this, Mühlen nevertheless states that in the New Testament the title "Christ" indicates the anointing of Jesus with the Holy Spirit (which happened at the baptism). In fact, "Christ" in the New Testament indicates the appointment of Jesus to eschatological kingship, which happened at his glorification. Even in the Letter to the Hebrews, and more particularly in Heb 1.9, which is the only place in which the Letter speaks explicitly of anointing, there is no suggestion that this appointment took place through an anointing, either real or metaphorical. In the New Testament the etymological meaning of "Christ" is obscured; it has yielded to the meaning that the word has gathered in its history. So far as the New Testament is concerned, then, the Christ theme is not relevant to the discussion of the anointing of Jesus. However, the Fathers combined the two themes, and did so not arbitrarily, but for reasons that can be justified. We shall therefore be entitled to follow and develop this line of patristic theology.

We have established that when the New Testament, specifically Luke, speaks of the anointing of the man Jesus, the occasion of the anointing is the baptism in the Jordan, the agent is the Father, the ointment is the Holy Spirit, and the objective achieved is the constitution of Jesus as the Prophet. As we have seen, Mühlen, who accepts all this, declares that it is, however, necessary to go beyond the statements of Scripture and situate the anointing at the first moment of the Incarnation, so that the anointing at the baptism now comes to be seen as only the revelation of the real anointing, which took place at the Incarnation, without, however, being identical with it. In Mühlen's exclusively descending Christology the Incarnation remains always the work simply of the Son, and the anointing, which is secondary, is the work of the Holy Spirit. We recall that the reason for this position is that the Son is the source of the Holy Spirit, and that therefore, as the Son becomes united to the sacred humanity at the time of the

Incarnation, he must at that same time bestow on the humanity the Holy Spirit proceeding from him. In this theology the effect of the anointing at the Incarnation is the created (habitual) grace of Jesus.

De la Potterie warns, as we have pointed out, against "generalizing" the significance of the anointing at the baptism. Fortunately, Mühlen does not heed him in this. To do so would be to restrict theology to the level of biblical fundamentalism and cast doubt on all development that actually took place in patristic theology in this matter (which de la Potterie does not hesitate to do). "Generalizing" must therefore be done; but unfortunately, Mühlen does not do it correctly, and this we shall now endeavor to show.

One can see easily enough why Mühlen should say that the effect of the real anointing at the Incarnation is the created grace of Jesus. If the radical union of Jesus with God is explained already by the grace of union (the Son), his human sanctification, that which we, the members, have in common with, and derive from, him, the Head, remains still to be explained; and since in us sanctification is the work of the Holy Spirit, clearly (in Mühlen's theology) it will be the anointing with the Holy Spirit at the Incarnation that will explain human sanctification or created grace in Jesus. However, it is not so easy to see how Mühlen can say that the anointing at the baptism is the revelation of that at the Incarnation, for the differences between these two anointings (again, as conceived in Mühlen's theology) are so great as to rule this out.

In the first place, the effect of the anointing at the baptism is the prophethood of Jesus, while that of the anointing at the Incarnation is (for Mühlen) his created grace. For the baptismal anointing to be the revelation of the Incarnation anointing, the prophethood of Jesus would have to be the revelation of his created grace. This cannot be shown in any case, but the problem is compounded in the context of Mühlen's theology, where a total distinction of person (to which corresponds the created grace of Jesus as a state of being or habit) and office (to which corresponds his prophethood) is maintained. Secondly, though Mühlen avoids saying that the Son is the agent of the anointing of the humanity with the Holy Spirit at the Incarnation, this is clearly implied in what he does say, which is that it is as proceeding from the Son that the Holy Spirit anoints the humanity. And yet, according to Scripture the agent of the anointing at the baptism is not the Son, but the Father. Indeed Scripture gives no warrant whatever for the assertion that the Son anoints his own humanity. We conclude, then, that the anointing at the baptism is not, nor can be, the revelation of the anointing at the Incarnation as understood by Mühlen. By no means, however, does this close off the way toward upholding the anointing at the baptism as the revelation of that at the Incarnation when the latter is understood as the anointing by the Father of the sacred humanity with the Holy Spirit, which creates that humanity, sanctifies it and unites it in person to the pre-existent divine Son.

It would be not only an anachronism but also a confusion of cultures to accuse the New Testament of nominalism for its concern with function and events at the expense of being; but modern theologians, with the patristic and Scholastic eras behind them, cannot so easily be acquitted of the charge when they adopt the same attitude, or place the two on the same level. The latter is what Mühlen does when he makes his sharp distinction between person and office in Jesus, and the corresponding distinction of the Incarnation and the anointing as different mysteries. In this approach, function and events are apprehended in purely juridical terms, i.e., as lacking all necessity, and issuing simply from a divine decree that might have been different. However, the question of being must be faced, and part of the answer is that function and events are rooted in being, so that in them being stands revealed. Aquinas showed his appreciation of this when he noted "the practice of Scripture by which a thing is said to happen when it becomes known."[24] Hence person and office in Jesus are not simply distinct, but in the office the person stands revealed; nor are Incarnation and anointing simply distinct mysteries, but in the baptismal anointing the Incarnation stands revealed. But the whole answer is that in this unique instance not simply revelation but the full sacramentality of God's economic action is involved. In the anointing, when referred, as it is through extension (and rightly), by the Fathers, from the baptism to the first moment of Jesus' human existence, the Incarnation is not revealed but formed, and likewise in the bestowal of office (however conceived) the personhood of Jesus is not simply revealed but formed, not in the sense of being brought about absolutely (for the divine Son pre-exists, or exists in eternity), but in the sense of being brought about in humanity. Therefore the only distinction that we admit between Incarnation and anointing (and it is a logical one) is that between two ways of apprehending the one event, in that we

---

24 *Expositio in omnes S. Pauli Epistolas: Epistola ad Romanos* 1, 3.

recognize "Incarnation" as reflecting a descending, and "anointing" as reflecting an ascending, Christology.

Following Aquinas, Mühlen divides the created realities of the Incarnation, viz., the sacred humanity and the habitual grace of Jesus, between the Son and the Holy Spirit respectively. This division reflects the Thomistic theology of the Incarnation, a descending Christology in which the Incarnation is viewed only as constituted, and therefore simply as a union of the Son and the sacred humanity. If in an ascending Christology we can accept the idea of the anointing with the Holy Spirit as forming the divine Sonship of Jesus, we do not need to divide the sanctification of the sacred humanity and its hypostatic union with the Son in this exclusive way, and we can relate them more intimately than is possible in Thomistic theology, where they are related only insofar as the two divine persons are related, since there the former grace is attributed to the Holy Spirit and the latter to the Son.

In the ascending theology proposed here we hold that the sanctification of the sacred humanity precedes the grace of union as its "last disposition," in the sense explained in the last two chapters. This is because we see the action of the Holy Spirit on Jesus as first creating his humanity, then sanctifying it, and then uniting it in person to the preexistent divine Son, in the order not of time but of nature and understanding. Here the sanctification of Jesus' humanity (the resultant sanctity being a created grace) is a necessary stage toward his unity in person with the Son, which is the grace of union. Hence in this theology the created grace of Jesus is more firmly established than in Thomism, and is related more intimately to the grace of union. However, it needs to be emphasized that the created grace intended here is different from what Aquinas, and Mühlen following him, had in mind. For them it was a habitual, i.e., accidental, grace, but for us it is a substantial grace unique to the humanity of the incarnate Son of God. The nature of this grace is well explained by Maurice de la Taille, in the Scholastic language of his day: "Here again we have an actuation by uncreated Act: a created actuation, as before; but this time of a substantial order, not an accidental order, because it brings the human nature into existence, and into an existence that is not of an accidental, but of a substantial order. This substantial actuation is precisely the grace of union; created grace, like sanctifying grace; not, however, like the latter, purely habitual, that is, a simple accidental disposition, but a truly substantial adaptation and conformation to the Word; yet not a substance nor part of a substance; no more so than the substantial existence of creatures forms part of their substance, although it actuates that substance substantially."[25] Clearly, while being the source of habitual grace in us, it dispenses with the need of habitual grace in Jesus himself, rendering it superflous.[26]

Viewed holistically, grace will always consist of an uncreated and a created component together, the former being identical with some aspect of God himself and the latter being both the effect and the last disposition of the former, depending on the perspective chosen, i.e., whether it be descending or ascending. Thus in a descending Christology the grace of union in the Incarnation will consist of the divine Son in his self-giving to the world and the substantial grace of Christ (of which de la Taille speaks), while in an ascending Christology it will consist of the same realities, conceived now as the same divine Son as goal of an upward, Spirit-directed movement from the world and the unique sanctification of the sacred humanity by the same Holy Spirit. Only the latter view enables us to appreciate the true role of the Holy Spirit in the Incarnation. Because a grace is most properly named in terms of its principal component, viz., uncreated grace, and because in the ascending perspective the agent of the divine intervention of the Incarnation is the Holy Spirit, in this perspective and without prejudice to what has already been said about the grace of union, the Holy Spirit himself can be identified as the grace of union, the supreme grace, and thus the source of every other grace.

We noted earlier that Mühlen sees the presence of the Father to Jesus as having two references, one to his divine Sonship, the other to his anointing with the Holy Spirit. Our theology unites these references, in seeing this presence in the anointing of Jesus to divine Sonship by the Father with the Holy Spirit. Admittedly, the New Testament does not itself combine the themes of anointing and Sonship, but we shall soon show that it provides adequate grounds for combining them

---

25   Maurice de la Taille, S.J., "Actuation créée par Acte incréée," *Recherches de science religieuse* 18 (1928) 253–68, trans. Cyril Vollert, S.J. as "Created Actuation by Uncreated Act," in Maurice de la Taille, *The Hypostatic Union and Created Actuation by Uncreated Act* (West Baden Springs, Ind.: West Baden College, 1952) 29–41, at 35.

26   For the author the concept of a substantial created grace in Christ postdated the original publication of this book. It has therefore necessitated an extensive reworking of this section. See Introduction.

in a more comprehensive theology, which was actually initiated by the Fathers.

Mühlen, it will be recalled, excludes Lk 1:35 as relevant to our enquiry, on the grounds that it speaks of an anointing not of Jesus but of Mary. Later we shall try to show in detail the importance of this text, but for the present we shall be satisfied simply with showing its relevance. We have two comments to make. First, the text does not mention an anointing at all, whether of Jesus or of Mary. However, later we shall show that theologically we are entitled to speak of an anointing here, since the elements of an anointing are present. Secondly, that the Holy Spirit is said to overshadow Mary rather than Jesus, far from making the text irrelevant, endows it with the highest significance, for it is this overshadowing or anointing that is so radical as to *bring about* the human existence of Jesus, at the same time sanctifying him and uniting him in person to the divine Son. If it were simply an anointing of the man Jesus already existing, it would lack the radicalness of the anointing that is identical with the Incarnation, and would be on the same level as the anointing of Christians. Hence it is clear that instead of meriting exclusion, Lk 1.35 is an important text for our study.

The remainder of this chapter we devote to showing how both Scheeben and Mühlen are led astray by their exclusive use of the procession model of the Trinity. In the course of this critique we shall show when the return model is appropriate, and draw attention to the enlightenment that it can provide.

Neither Scheeben nor Mühlen contemplates the possibility that the Incarnation might be considered in two stages, formation and constitution. Both regard it exclusively in constitution, from the viewpoint of descending Christology and in the light of the procession model. Since the Incarnation as constituted is a union of the sacred humanity and the divine Son, there is no room in their theology for a function proper to the Holy Spirit in bringing the Incarnation about. According to Scheeben his function is a mere appropriation; according to Mühlen it is a reality, but one that is only consequent upon the Incarnation, an anointing connected with the office of Jesus and with his habitual grace.

This is all the more surprising in that both Scheeben and Mühlen (and Aquinas also) enunciate the principle that a human being is united to God by a process that inverts the order of the three divine persons and thus also the order of the Trinitarian processions, so that he or she is united first to the Holy Spirit, thence to the Son, and thence to the Father. One would expect that, holding the reality and the integrity of the humanity of Jesus as they do, they would apply this principle to Jesus also, but in fact they do not. It is evident from their theology that they regard him as an exception to the principle.

It is now appropriate to look more closely at this principle. We transmit it in Scheeben's own words from the *Mysterien*: "According to the Fathers there *corresponds to the outgoing movement of the three divine persons a return movement*, as the Holy Spirit, by his coming, abiding and working in our soul, raises us up to union with the Son, and through the Son to the Father. Through his mission, the communication of the Holy Spirit, we are made partakers of the divine nature, thereby attaining fellowship with the Son of God, who is born anew in us, and thereupon we enter into relationship with his Father, who then becomes our Father also."[27] A footnote purports to substantiate the claim concerning the Fathers with two references to Cyril of Alexandria, which upon examination reveal only a conviction as to the inverted order of the divine persons in the spiritual life of ordinary people (nothing is said either about Jesus or about the processions). Scheeben expresses the principle again in another passage in the *Mysterien*: "The second procession, which closes the internal processions and communications, is, as it were, the conductor for the external transmission of the first to the creature. The communication of the divine nature from the Father to the Son by generation can find its way to the creature only in the further communication of that nature through love to the Holy Spirit. And so the Holy Spirit appears as the result of the union of Father and Son, therefore as mediator of the union of God with the creature, which is modeled on this relationship."[28] At least these passages reveal Scheeben's conviction that the supernatural order among human beings reflects the inner life of the Trinity.

We agree that in the union of human beings with God the divine persons are encountered in the order Holy Spirit, Son, Father. This is stated in Scripture (Gal 4:6; Eph 2:18). We go further, and hold that this is so also in the case of Jesus. What we disagree with is the assertion that it is so simply because we experience an inversion of the

---

27   Scheeben, *Mysterien* 152.
28   Ibid. 123.

processions of the divine persons. What is being invoked here is the procession model in inverted form.

In the second part of this book we reached the conclusion that the divine Sonship of Jesus was acquired non-sacramentally, bestowed on him by the Father without any offer, but that the divine filiation of ordinary people is acquired sacramentally, bestowed on them by the Father in the sacrament of the offer made (principally) by Christ in his (glorified) humanity. We have also shown that to the offer of divine filiation in the world there corresponds in the Trinity the procession of the Holy Spirit, while to the bestowal of divine filiation on both Jesus and ordinary people there corresponds in the Trinity the bestowal by the Father of the Holy Spirit on the Son. We take it as an accepted position in Catholic theology (to which we will nevertheless give specific attention later) that the divine filiation of humans is the work of the Holy Spirit, Spirit of filiation.

It remains to be shown from the sources that the Holy Spirit is the Spirit of Sonship also for Jesus, in the sense of bringing about the Incarnation itself. For the moment we ask the reader to assume this important point. If, then, for the time being we may take it that it is the bestowal of the Holy Spirit which (in respectively different ways) brings about the divine filiation of both Jesus and ordinary people, this can be linked with the statements given above and lead us to the conclusion that the non-sacramental bestowal of the Holy Spirit by the Father on the sacred humanity brings about the divine Sonship of Jesus, and that the sacramental bestowal of the same Spirit by the Father on ordinary people, principally in the offer made by the glorified Christ, brings about their divine filiation. In relation to the revelation and the operation of the Trinity in Incarnation and grace, we have, then, not one but two, trinitarian models to consider, the procession model and the return model. Scheeben and Mühlen had access to only one of these, the procession model, which they have used both in the usual form and in inversion. This latter use cannot be justified, since there is no ground in the Trinity itself for inverting the procession model. It is therefore unwarranted to think that a merely factual inversion of the order of persons entitles one to invert the model itself. Since in the Incarnation there was no offer of the Holy Spirit to Jesus, but only the bestowal, it is clear that the return model, as well as the procession model, will have a role to play in the consideration of the Incarnation. We shall now show how both models should be invoked in relation to the divine economy. We deal in turn with the revelation and the operation of the Trinity, first relating each vertically to the Trinity in itself, and then relating the application of the two models on each horizontal plane, i.e., the Trinity in itself, its revelation, and finally its operation.

The Trinity stands revealed in Jesus, incarnate Word of the Father, and in the Holy Spirit sent by Christ upon the Church. The Trinity, therefore, is fully revealed in this sending of the Holy Spirit. Just as the single operation of the Trinity is carried forward beyond the generation of the Son to the breathing-forth of the Holy Spirit, so this operation as participated in by the world will have the mission of the Son carried beyond itself to the point where the mission of the Holy Spirit at Pentecost begins. This revelation follows the procession model in that these two missions reflect the processions in the Trinity, and express by succession in time the atemporal order in which the latter occur in the Trinity.

However, the return model also operates here, and indeed in two applications. First, the revelation of the Trinity, which we can say takes place in the resurrection since this is the culmination of Jesus' life, is the revelation in the first instance of the hidden event of the Incarnation, for it is the incarnate Son who in being revealed himself reveals the Father, and acquires the authority to send the Holy Spirit, thus revealing him; and this Incarnation is formed by the bestowal (without any offer) of the Holy Spirit by the Father on the sacred humanity in an act which at the same time creates it, sanctifies it, and unites it in person to the Son. This corresponds to the bestowal of the Holy Spirit by the Father on the Son in the Trinity. Admittedly, the order of the divine persons is the same as the inverse of their order in the processions, but this should not cause us to think that all we have here is an inversion of the procession model. The order, Holy Spirit, Son, Father, which occurs here, is explained by the fact that the Holy Spirit, as Spirit of Sonship (bestowed by the Father), draws the sacred humanity into unity of person with the Son, making Jesus precisely in this humanity Son of the eternal Father. This relates to the bestowal of the Holy Spirit in the Trinity, not to his procession. Hence we have here not an inversion of the procession model but an application, indeed the principal one, of the return model.

Secondly, the return model operates here in that the sending of the Holy Spirit by Christ upon the Church is related to the bestowal by the Father of the same Spirit on this community, which thus becomes one with the Son (sons and daughters in the Son).

We conclude that in the revelation of the Trinity the procession model and the return model are both involved, the former in the sending of the Holy Spirit, the latter in his bestowal, in the Incarnation and at Pentecost.

In the operation of the Trinity both models have a place. The procession model applies, since in the case of ordinary people the offer of the Holy Spirit is made, ultimately by the Father, but immediately in the sacrament of the glorified humanity of Christ. In this offer of grace the revelation of the Trinity in the sending of the Holy Spirit upon the Church is directed to the individual person, and so the model is the procession model, and the order of the divine persons is that of the processions. Then if, and as, the person responds positively to the offer of grace, the offer becomes for him or her the sacrament of the bestowal of grace, i.e., the bestowal by the Father of the Holy Spirit, Spirit of filiation, so that this person is drawn into community with the Son (in the same Spirit) as a child in the Son, and thus is related to the Father. Hence also in the operation of the Trinity both the procession model and the return model are involved, the former in the offer of the Holy Spirit, the latter in his bestowal.

We now relate the applications of the two models to each other on the three horizontal planes. In the Trinity itself the procession and the bestowal of the Holy Spirit are related in that the bestowal is the mode in which the procession is given. In the Trinity as revealed, the revelation takes place, as we said, in the resurrection of Christ, as pointing at the same time back to the hidden bestowal of the Holy Spirit on him at the Incarnation, and forward to the sending of the Holy Spirit by him upon the Church. The sending of the Holy Spirit is therefore the revelation of his bestowal in the Incarnation. At the same time the sending of the Spirit upon the Church by Christ is the sacrament of his bestowal on the Church by the Father.

This leads us to reflect that the revelation of the Trinity that takes place in Christ is more than a mere making-known: it effects the bestowal by the Father of divine filiation on the Church as such. It is, in the fullest sense of the word (from which the other senses are to be derived), sacrament. Christ is the primordial sacrament of God .[29] Although already in his earthly life Jesus was the sacrament of the

---

29   Cf. E. Schillebeeckx, *Christ the Sacrament* (London, 1963).

Father, he entered upon the perfection of his sacramentality in coming fully to himself in humanity, and thus as divine Son acquiring in that humanity universal significance and efficacy. This we understand theologically as happening in the resurrection, though later we will explain why we consider Jesus' death, resurrection, ascension, sending of the Spirit and parousia, simply as different theological aspects of the one reality.

The sending of the Holy Spirit by Christ upon the Church may be compared with the offer of the Holy Spirit through the ministry of Christ to the individual person. Each is a legitimate application of the procession model. However, there is an important difference between them. The offer of the Holy Spirit encounters the free will of the person to whom it is made, and hence will not necessarily involve the bestowal of the Holy Spirit on that person; but the sending of the Spirit by Christ upon the Church is infallibly the sacrament of the bestowal of the Spirit on the Church by the Father. The Church, following Israel of old (Ex 4:22; Hos 11.1), is inescapably "son of God." The free will of individual members plays no part here. The sending of the Holy Spirit by Christ upon the Church is authoritative and permanent. It results in the "marks" of the Church (one, holy, catholic and apostolic), i.e., its indefectibility, whatever be the sins of the individual members. The permanent guiding and enlivening presence of the Spirit, indeed of Christ precisely in and through his Spirit, is promised in the Gospels (Mt 28:20; Jn 14:18; 15:26). We recall here the comment of de la Potterie about the parallel intended by Luke between the descent of the Holy Spirit on Jesus at the baptism and the descent of the same Spirit on the Church at Pentecost. The parallel suggests that though in the latter case the Spirit is sent by Christ, it is, as in the former case, bestowed by the Father. However, we are not hereby suggesting that the bestowal of the Holy Spirit by the Father on the Church was done independently of all human free will, for it was done in conjunction with the free will of Jesus, not just in his glorified humanity but also in his earthly life. Indeed, it is meaningful to speak of the will of the glorified Jesus only if this is understood in terms of his will in his life and at his death. The fact that Jesus merited by his life and death to become the sender of the Holy Spirit, *his* Spirit, upon the Church implies that as head of the future Church and of the whole human race (which he was by virtue of the Incarnation) he freely, as a human being, and in his earthly life, endorsed the Father's radical bestowal of the

Holy Spirit on himself, which in his case alone was done without any offer. That is to say, as mediator of the new covenant he freely made his grace, the Father's Gift of the Holy Spirit to him, the grace of the Church as such. (How this is to be understood we shall explain in the next part.) These theological statements are verified from the earthly life of Jesus from the Gospels, where his obedient acceptance of, and fidelity to, his vocation from the Father to be the bearer of a unique mission to humans are evident.

In speaking of what we call the Trinity as revealed and the Trinity as operative, Scheeben and Mühlen (and Aquinas before them) have used only the procession model, and that not always correctly. This can be seen from what we have said above. Thus, in considering our union with God in the Trinity as operative, they use the procession model in relation to the bestowal of grace, where clearly it has no place, but where the correct model is the return model. The procession model applies to the offer, not to the bestowal, of grace.

In considering the Trinity as revealed, they have used the procession model correctly in relation to the missions of the Son and the Holy Spirit, but they have used it also in relation to what we call the formation of the Incarnation, where it has no place. As we have already pointed out, they show no awareness that the question of the constitution of the Incarnation is preceded by that of its formation. Thus, they say that in the Incarnation it is the Son who is united to the sacred humanity, that the Son is the origin of the Holy Spirit, and that therefore the Son communicates the Holy Spirit to the sacred humanity. This is the way in which they involve the Holy Spirit in the Incarnation.[30]

We now list our objections to the procession model in relation to the Incarnation. We recognize that some of these amount to different ways of saying the same thing, but consider them worth saying even

---

30   Because of its Thomistic and patristic background it is not surprising that this theology should appear also in statements of the magisterium, e.g., Pope Pius XII's encyclical *Mystici Corporis*: "In the first moment of the Incarnation the Son of the Eternal Father had adorned with the fullness of the Holy Spirit the human nature which was substantially united with Himself, that it might be an appropriate instrument of the divinity in the bloody work of the Redemption" (Catholic Truth Society translation, p.20). The teaching conveyed in this and the following statement is that the Holy Spirit plays a decisive role in the economy of the redemption. To this end the procession model is invoked, where clearly the return model is appropriate.

so. We preface them with the observation that some use of this model is clearly justified. Just as the mission of the Holy Spirit is explained by reference to the procession model, so, from the viewpoint of descending Christology and the constitution of the Incarnation, the latter may be understood as we explained in Part Two, in terms of the projection into the world of the generation of the Son by the Father in the Trinity. It is to the thorough-going use of the model, e.g., to the statement that the Son, sent into the world by the Father, in turns sends the Holy Spirit proceeding from him upon his own humanity, that we particularly object.

First, as there was no offer of the Holy Spirit to Jesus, but only the bestowal, it is clear that the bestowal model will be a superior guide, in comparison to the procession model, in understanding the Incarnation and its implications.

Secondly, the procession model considers the Incarnation only from the standpoint of descending Christology. Room therefore must be left for a consideration of it from the complementary standpoint of ascending Christology, and this will require use of the return model.

Thirdly, the return model reveals a far more important role for the Holy Spirit in the Incarnation than the procession model can account for.

Fourthly, it is an over-simplification to say that the Son is the origin of the Holy Spirit. Even in Latin theology the Son is only co-principle of the Holy Spirit along with the Father, not simply principle. Yet if the Father is introduced, even only as co-principle, the point being made by means of the procession model can no longer be sustained, viz., that it is precisely (therefore only) the Son who communicates the Holy Spirit to the sacred humanity. Indeed, the return model shows that this is not so, that it is the *Father* who communicates the Holy Spirit to the sacred humanity.

Fifthly, the statement that the Son, as origin of the Holy Spirit, communicates this Spirit to his humanity, can be challenged on the grounds that there is nothing in the Trinity in itself that can be invoked as warrant for this statement. In the Trinity the Son bestows the Holy Spirit only on the Father, and then in an answering love. We must leave to Part Four a discussion of what precisely it is in the Trinity to which corresponds the fact that Christ in his humanity is the source of the Holy Spirit for other people. But that the Son is the source of the Spirit for his own humanity is unsubstantiated from a consideration of the Trinity, nor is there any text of Scripture that supports it in any way, though, as we noted, some of the Fathers did say it, in what we must call a false development of the procession model. This situation is not affected by the claim that the Son does this purely in his divinity.

This critique is made from the standpoint of notional, constitutive acts. When, however, the situation is regarded *subsequently*, the immediate union between the Son and the sacred humanity does justify a certain, weakened sense of the criticized statement. But then it can be asked, how helpful is it to make this statement? To us it seems that it is not helpful at all, that in fact it is misleading.

The difference between Jesus and ordinary people is not simply that the latter receive the Holy Spirit whereas the former (in his humanity) receives the Son, but that the Holy Spirit, engaging, as Spirit of filiation, both the sacred humanity and ordinary people, draws them into different kinds of union with the divine Son, the former into unity of person with him, and the latter into simple union so that they become sons or daughters in the Son. To regard the sacred humanity as determined in its openness to God simply by the Son, and other people as so determined by the Holy Spirit, as theology has traditionally done, is to acknowledge the uniqueness of Jesus certainly, but at the cost of his supernatural solidarity with others beyond a vague sharing in the divine nature. But if both the sacred humanity and ordinary people are determined by the same divine person, the Holy Spirit, Spirit of filiation, the solidarity of Jesus with ordinary people at both the natural and the supernatural level comes to the fore, but not so as to impair his uniqueness, for the divine Sonship of Jesus does not differ from that of others simply by degree (which is how it differs from one ordinary person to another). The difference between unity in person with the Son and simple community with him in the same Spirit is a difference of kind, not just of degree. The Incarnation is the peak of union between humanity and God, and it lies not just beyond the probability, but beyond the possibility, of achievement by the ordinary person even under the impetus of grace.

The ultimate explanation of this difference of kind is the sovereign will of the Father in his plan for the salvation and deification of human beings (the economy), this will being exercised in its utter freedom and gratuitousness (grace), where nevertheless the necessary consistency of God requires that his free action in the world reflect how he exists and acts in himself, i.e., as Father, Son and Holy Spirit, in procession and bestowal. This requires, as we have shown, an Incarnation of the Son and (with him and through him) a sending of the Holy Spirit. The difference in kind, as we have already explained, is guaranteed by the fact that the humanity of Jesus did not pre-exist the bestowal of the Holy Spirit in his case, while the humanity of others does pre-exist the bestowal in their case. This means that divinity is simply *realized* in humanity in the case of Jesus, whereas in the case of others whatever being they have in the sphere of God is *achieved* through cooperation with grace. In the next chapter we give our own positive presentation of the anointing of the man Jesus by the Father with the Holy Spirit.

8 THE ANOINTING OF JESUS

Having, as it were, laid out the basic materials in the last chapter, we are now in a position to expound positively our own theology of the anointing of Jesus with the Holy Spirit. This was an anointing to divine Sonship, the unique divine sonship in which the man Jesus was made one in person with the eternal Son of God. In this theology there is no element of adoptionism, since the humanity of Jesus is declared not to have existed prior to the anointing. The anointing called his humanity into being, so that from the first moment of its existence it existed as the humanity of the Son of God. This anointing, therefore, brought about the Incarnation of the Son of God. In this theology there are three points, to be considered separately, viz., anointing with the Holy Spirit, the anointing to divine sonship, and the anointing that is identical with the Incarnation.

We deal first with anointing with the Holy Spirit. In our theology the idea of the self-communication of God to humans, presented in the second part of this book, derives from the biblical concept of anointing with the Holy Spirit, which acquired its meaning in reference to the secular Jewish custom, carried over also into religious life, of anointing with oil. When oil is rubbed into the skin, it disappears into the anointed person, penetrating, according to the psalmist, into their very bones (Ps 109:18), and conveying to them health and energy. Anointing with oil was therefore obviously suited to become a sacrament of the communication of the power of God, i.e., of God in his power, or the Spirit of God, to equip the anointed person for a special divine mission. Such a communication, of course, presupposed election for the mission. The ceremony of anointing was connected basically with the appointment of the king (cf. 1Sam 16:12-13); but even in the appointment of a prophet, viz., Elisha (1Kings 19:16), where there was no use of oil, the term was retained in a metaphorical sense to denote the communication of the Spirit in an act of election and mission. However, we do not wish to lay great store by this latter text. In the New Testament the idea of the metaphorical anointing of the prophet arose not from this text but from Is 61:1-2. In the Lukan texts already examined the anointing of Jesus with the Holy Spirit is situated at the beginning of his public life, and signifies his election and deputation to preach the Good News as prophet par excellence.

We now take up our second point, the anointing to divine sonship. This is a concept to which de la Potterie would object as an unwarranted generalization of the biblical concept of the anointing of Jesus, which was an anointing to prophethood. What right have we, with the Fathers but not with Scripture, to say that Jesus was anointed to divine Sonship?

First we must say something about the concept of divine filiation in the New Testament. It is a commonplace of biblical theology to say that in the Old Testament the title "son of God" designated a person or a group elected by God to enjoy his special intimacy and be entrusted by him with a particular function. Thus, e.g., the king was God's son (2 Sam 7:14), as was Israel itself (Ex 4:22). On the evidence of the New Testament it seems that at the time of Jesus "Son of God" was used as a messianic title.[1] This is understandable, since the king was son of God and the Messiah was king par excellence. Quite apart from this, however, one of the most important things that the New Testament has to tell us about the religious consciousness of Jesus is that he called upon God as his Father.[2] Though he did not designate himself Son of God, it was to be expected that he who was known to call upon God as Father (and, in so doing, distinguished himself from other people in his relationship to God) should come to be confessed by his followers as Son of God, no longer purely in a sense corresponding to Old Testament messianic expectations but in a sense corresponding to the actual person of Jesus himself in his unique status before God.[3] Hence as a synonym for "Christ," "Son of God" was achieved early in the history of the Palestinian community, as a result of the resurrection, and is attested in the primitive tradition which is preserved in the New Testament; but as an expression of the unique, mysterious and transcendent reality of Jesus, it is found first in the later and more sophisticated strands of the New Testament, which have been affected by Hellenistic influences.[4]

------

1   Cf. O. Cullmann, *The Christology of the New Testament* (London, 1963) 273-75.

2   Cf. J. Jeremias, New Testament Theology. Part 1: *The Proclamation of Jesus* (London, 1971) 61-68.

3   Cf. W. Pannenberg 53-66.

4   Cf. F. Hahn, *The Titles of Jesus in Christology* (London, 1969) 288-307.

Anointing is Luke's way of presenting the communication to Jesus of the eschatological Spirit of God, which in later theology came to be seen as the third person of the Trinity. Luke sees this communication, situated at the baptism, in functional terms, as equipping Jesus for his unique task. Because of the form that Jesus' ministry actually took and the Old Testament matrix which accordingly Luke has selected in order to give it form, it is presented in terms of prophethood. It would be rash, however, to ascribe an absolute value to the meaning with which Luke, or any other particular evangelist, for the sake of his own theological purpose, endows the communication of the Holy Spirit to Jesus at the baptism. For that matter, even in Luke the prophetic orientation of the baptism is not given with the baptism account itself but only later in the Gospel. The thesis of F. Lentzen-Deis is instructive here.[5] According to him, the events with which the synoptics surround the baptism point to the significance of Jesus in a general way as the Son (Servant) of God designated for his salvific mission. The voice from heaven is declared to echo the first Servant Song from Deutero-Isaiah, Is 42:1-9, but the significance of the fact that the word "servant" has been replaced by "son" cannot be overlooked. It appears that de la Potterie, commenting on Luke's account of the baptism, exaggerates the prophetic theme, first in the Song, and consequently also in the baptism account. Certainly, the Song has the servant as a prophet (v.4), but his kingly role emerges much more strongly, both in the Song as a whole and in v.1, where God's spirit, declared by de la Potterie to be the spirit of prophecy, is more likely to be the spirit of kingship (cf. 1Sam 16:13).[6] Further, if the orientation here is prophetic, it is difficult to explain the substitution of the word "son," which was applied to kings but not to prophets. It is only later, in 4:18, with its reference to Is 61:1-2 and the introduction of the anointing theme in reference to the baptism, that Luke adopts his specifically prophetic interpretation of the baptism. The same point can be made from Matthew, since he too makes his own use of the common material. There Jesus is seen as the fulfillment of the religious destiny of his people, particularly as represented by Moses, so that the baptism is invested with special

---

5   F. Lentzen-Deis, *Die Taufe Jesu nach den Synoptikern: Literarkritische und gattungsgeschichtliche Untersuchungen* (Frankfurt am Main, 1970).

6   Cf. C. Westermann, *Isaiah 40-66* (London, 1969) 93-94.

meaning in the light of the passage through the Red Sea (cf. 1Cor 10:2).[7]

F. Hahn has shown that the Son of God who stands at the centre of the baptism accounts does not merely correspond to the early Palestinian conception of the man adopted by God and endowed with his Spirit. The later Hellenistic element of spiritualization through bestowal of the Holy Spirit as that on which the divine Sonship rests and by which it is attested is more strongly present.[8] We may conclude that the basic Synoptic theology of the baptism is that it is the explanation of the significance of Jesus as the one who is constituted unique ("beloved") Son of God by the bestowal of the Holy Spirit, and directed to his unique saving task in a quite open way, the content of which is supplied by his subsequent life, death and glorification. (We repeat that the adoptionist overtones in the accounts themselves and in the above statement have to be corrected by the theological consideration that the baptism is the revelation of the inner nature of Jesus as possessed by him from the beginning of his life.) Even in the Old Testament the title "son of God," though linked specially with the king (2 Sam 7:14; Ps 2:7), was open to fulfillment in various ways, by angels (Deut 32:8; Ps 29:1; 89:6; Job 1:6), Israel as a whole (Ex 4:22; Hos 11:1; Wis 18:13), and princes and judges (Ps 82:6). While a son of God always had a function, the function is not specified by the title itself. Hence it was a highly suitable title for Jesus. Combining the Semitic elements of election for mission and obedience with the distinctively Hellenistic element of divinization, it was fulfilled by Jesus in both categories in a way corresponding to his transcendent uniqueness. Further, while it indicated function (indeterminately), it came as close as Semitic thought allowed to the expression of status or being.

In Luke the later engrafted theme of anointing (to prophethood), inspired by Is 61:1-2, is important because anointing remains the best biblical and patristic way of expressing the communication of the Holy Spirit, which we now see to be basically connected with divine Sonship. Due account should be taken of the fact that theological development takes place in Luke's gospel itself. The bestowal of the Holy Spirit in the link forged by the baptism account between this bestowal and divine Sonship is transformed by Luke into an anointing (for a task, viz., prophecy). When the question of being is again

7   J.C. Fenton, *Saint Matthew* (Harmondsworth: Pelican, 1963) 58-59.
8   Cf. Hahn 293-94, 337-41.

inevitably asked, only a fundamentalist could forbid the theologian to continue the development of the theological process thus initiated by Luke himself. Though Luke would not, and did not, use the expression "anointing to divine Sonship" or its equivalent, the expression and its underlying theology represent a perfectly valid development of his own theology, a development which was made by the Fathers, and which modern theology is therefore entitled to carry through to its completion.

Next, a word should be said about the bestowal of the Holy Spirit on Jesus and his divine Sonship in the Fourth Gospel. Mühlen noted the motif of the presence of God to Jesus in relation to his anointing with the Holy Spirit in Acts 10:38 and to his divine Sonship in Jn 16:32. In the latter text there is no mention of the Holy Spirit at all, and the theme of divine Sonship is present only in an indirect way, in as much as Jesus speaks of God as the Father, but it is not surprising that a father should be said to be present to his son. It should be noted, however, that John too sees the divine Sonship of Jesus as constituted by the bestowal of the Holy Spirit by the Father. This is done early in the Gospel, in 1:32-34, at the baptism (though the actual baptism of Jesus is not mentioned). In order to avoid adoptionism we must here make the same theological adjustments as with the Synoptics on the same subject. This is the first mention of the Son of God in the Gospel proper (apart from the Prologue), and therefore it is in the light of the bestowal of the Holy Spirit that the divine Sonship of Jesus, a key concept in this gospel, is to be understood.

There is in this gospel a further highly significant text, 3:34-35, where the bestowal of the Holy Spirit and the divine Sonship of Jesus are connected in the context of the Father's love for the Son. Here the uniqueness of Jesus is centered not just on his vocation, which is also affirmed, but in the unique imparting of the Holy Spirit to him, expressed thus: "It is not by measure that he (the Father) gives the Spirit (to Jesus)." All other impartings of the Spirit to humans are limited, but on Jesus the Spirit is bestowed in all fullness. This is the explanation of his unique divine Sonship.

A postscript can now be added to our earlier criticism of Mühlen's distinction of person and office in Jesus. We have seen that in both the Old and the New Testament divine filiation includes both person and office, intimacy and mission, honor and task. To separate these things as Mühlen does, so as eventually to make two distinct mysteries of the Incarnation and the anointing, is to impose on biblical thought a framework that is alien to it. While person and office, honor and task, can, and even should, be distinguished logically, in Scripture there is no person who does not have an office commensurate with their personhood (we prescind from how the office is bestowed); nor is there any such thing as an empty honor; rather in every honor a responsibility or a task is implied. Although Scheeben is wrong in holding that it is the Son who anoints the sacred humanity, he is here closer to the truth than Mühlen, since he recognizes the anointing and the Incarnation to be one and the same divine mystery.

We turn now to our third and most important point, the anointing of Jesus with the Holy Spirit that is identical with the Incarnation. By this anointing the man Jesus was raised from the first moment of his existence to possess, on the two levels of being and experience, a uniquely intimate relationship with God, and this relationship laid upon him a unique responsibility for, and mission to, his fellow humans. Eventually the relationship came to be understood in the Church in terms of unity of person with the pre-existent divine Son, second person of the Trinity (union of the divine and a human nature in the one divine person), and the mission as salvation, worked by Jesus in his life and death and offered to others through his continuing presence in the Church.

At this point a brief examination of the Christology of Pannenberg will be helpful.[9] His ingenious central thesis is that the event which constituted Jesus Son of God was the resurrection. The obvious objection that this is adoptionist is answered with the claim that the resurrection exercised over the earlier, earthly life of Jesus an "inherent retroactive power,"[10] which brought it about that he was Son of God from the first moment of his human existence; however, it was not his conception but the resurrection that was decisive for his Sonship. This explanation certainly keeps the thesis within the bounds of orthodoxy. Also it enables us to understand what is meant by such biblical assertions as that the resurrection made Jesus both Lord and Christ (Acts 2:36); and it is meaningful within the context of what Pannenberg clearly regards as Hebrew "ontology:" "For thought that does not proceed from a concept of essence that transcends time, for which the essence of a thing is not what persists in the succession of change, for

9   Pannenberg, *Jesus - God and Man.*
10   Ibid. 307.

which, rather, the future is open in the sense that it will bring unpredictably new things that nothing can resist as absolutely unchangeable —for such thought only the future decides what something is."[11] For all this, however, the explanation cannot claim our agreement. First, there is the incongruity of making a comparison between a primitive and unreflective biblical supposition and Greek philosophy; and secondly, there is the gratuitousness of the assumption that the supposition is true because it is biblical. In fact, it has no more claim on the modern believer than the most famous of all biblical suppositions, viz., that the sun revolves around the earth. The final objection to it is that it involves what philosophers call backward causation. This renders it ontologically impossible. Hence we must reject the supposition and with it the explanation and the thesis itself. While we are grateful to Pannenberg for his thesis as a persuasive account of one level of biblical thought, we cannot accept it as true in itself, and we are forced to look elsewhere for the explanation of the divine Sonship of Jesus.

However, Pannenberg himself opens the way for us when he says that it was soon felt in the primitive Church that the divine Sonship of Jesus should be located in his earthly life and so should be pushed back from the resurrection into his life.[12] He notes several such attempts in the New Testament, viz., the transfiguration, the baptism, the conception, and lastly the eternity of the pre-existent divine Son.[13] These explanations, however, he regards as less authoritative than the resurrection, because they were later and were the fruit of theological reflection. It seems to us arbitrary that such high importance should be attached to antiquity, and that theology should be held so suspect, particularly as Pannenberg himself holds that in the history of traditions interpretation belongs to the essence of an event, so that for him the concept of brute historical facts is quite unacceptable.[14] One can argue more convincingly the opposite way, that initially the unity of Jesus with God was located at the resurrection because that was the event that summoned the faith of the community into being, but that almost immediately reflection showed that this unity must have existed always, not just from the beginning of his public life, but from the beginning of his human life itself, his conception, and that this

11   Ibid. 136.
12   Cf. ibid. 135.
13   Cf. ibid. 133-58.
14   Cf. G. O'Collins, *Foundations of Theology* (Chicago, 1971) 120.

conception was indeed the incarnation of the pre-existent divine Son. This would at least reinstate the resurrection to its traditional position in doctrine and theology as the event that revealed, not the event that constituted, the divine Sonship of Jesus. However, the full realization of divine Sonship in his humanity was brought about by the death of Jesus as the full achievement of his personal history and hence of his humanity, and this we say without prejudice to the fact that he was already Son of God from the first moment of his human existence; and the resurrection, as we shall have to explain later, is to be understood as (though not *only* as) a theological implication of his death. Hence the resurrection emerges as both the realization and the revelation of the divine Sonship of Jesus. In this view, as can readily be seen, the two opposing schools of "Incarnation Christology" and "resurrection Christology" are reconciled. It cannot be seriously maintained that in this theology, as one step back from that of Pannenberg, the value of the resurrection is diminished. The resurrection is the event in which the divine Sonship of Jesus, bestowed at his conception and realized in his life, stands fully established, revealed and offered sacramentally, particularly in the Eucharist, so that it becomes for humans the decisive saving reality, giving them the opportunity of faith, hope and love.

By reference to Pannenberg we have been able to survey quickly the New Testament theology of the divine Sonship of Jesus, and even before an examination of the texts bearing on his conception appreciate that it was there that his Sonship was bestowed. To revert briefly to our second point before passing on to this examination, it will be useful for us to look at the relation of the bestowal of the Holy Spirit to the divine Sonship of Jesus in those significant parts of the New Testament noted by Pannenberg (apart from the texts dealing with the pre-existence of the divine Son). We have done this already in regard to the baptism, and soon, when we study the relevant texts, we shall do it in regard to the conception. Now we shall briefly consider the resurrection and the transfiguration, bearing in mind that, from our theological viewpoint, in neither place is there question of the actual bestowal of divine Sonship.

In Rom 1:4 Paul, making use of traditional material, sees the resurrection as involving a bestowal of the Holy Spirit (the Spirit of holiness) which results in the divine Sonship of Jesus. Pannenberg, quoting I. Hermann, says that "the connection of the Spirit with the resurrection from the dead, which is present here [Rom 1:4], is inherited from

Jewish eschatology, so that 'the resurrection of the *Kyrios* and his being equipped with the Spirit belong together.'"[15] (The same link is evident also in Rom 8:11.) Of particular interest is that in his deployment of these three themes Paul should see the Sonship of Jesus as constituted by the bestowal of the Holy Spirit. Then, in the transfiguration accounts (Mk 9:2-8 and parallels) there are points of contact with the baptism and the resurrection, both of which have bestowals of the Holy Spirit. The voice of God (the Father) from the cloud and the actual words spoken recall the baptism. The concluding words, "listen to him", echo Deut 18:15, and thus show that the transfiguration belongs to the tradition of the eschatological prophet. While there is no mention here of a bestowal of the Holy Spirit as there was at the baptism, it was by just such a bestowal that this prophet would be constituted (cf. Is 61:1).[16] However, Jesus is again designated Son of God, in what is clearly the developed sense of the title, as is evident from the Hellenistic implications of the technical term "transfigured." The story is linked also with the resurrection, in that Jesus appears in the messianic glory with which that event invested him. We observe, therefore, that the New Testament has a regular tendency to conceive the divine Sonship of Jesus as formed by the bestowal of the Holy Spirit on him by the Father, though for the reasons stated we must always situate this bestowal at the conception of Jesus.

This brings us to the two gospel pericopes, from Matthew and Luke, that speak of the conception of Jesus. Against Pannenberg, we regard these as all the more important in that they reflect the mature consideration of the early community and the evangelists as to the significance of Jesus. Here we find that the question of the unity of Jesus with God is solved not in purely functional terms but in terms of the person of Jesus from the first moment of his human existence. The fact that both pericopes speak also of the future of Jesus, Matthew of his office and Luke of his rank, does not militate against this.

Like Rom 1:3-5, Mt 1:18-25 connects the two themes "Son of God" and "Son of David," but in a different way. The Romans text begins with the Son of David, who is designated Son of God by the resurrection; the Gospel text, on the other hand, begins with the Son of God, who becomes Son of David by adoption. While the expression "Son of God" does not occur in the pericope, that Jesus is Son of God is

---

15   Pannenberg 118.

16   Cf. Hahn 380-82.

conveyed by the assertion that he is "of the Holy Spirit" (vv. 18, 20) and by the denial of paternity to Joseph. It was necessary, then, for Jesus to be adopted by "Joseph, son of David" (v.20) in order to acquire messianic credentials. The divine paternity is implied again in the fact that God exercises the prerogative of a father in naming the child. The fact that Joseph actually announces the name (v.25), far from casting doubt on this, confirms it. The uniqueness of Jesus before God is intimated in several ways, in his virginal conception in fulfillment of prophecy and by the power of God, and in the uniqueness of his mission as Saviour (v. 21), which is implied in his name "Jesus" ("the Lord saves"). When Matthew speaks of the Holy Spirit, he is thinking not of the third person of the Trinity but of God in his creative lifegiving power (cf. Gen 1:2; Jdt 16:14; Ps 104:30). But we have here the germ of the later doctrine, in that the transcendent God is said to make a human being, Jesus, his unique Son and sanctify him for his saving mission by bestowing his Spirit on him in a special act of election and creation. This pericope provides a valid point of departure for our theology of the anointing of Jesus by the Father with the Holy Spirit in an act that creates his humanity, sanctifies it and unites it in person to the divine Son.

More important still is the annunciation pericope of Lk 1:26-38. Here we find the strongest biblical foundation for our theology. As Jesus did not pre-exist the event here narrated, there can be no question of adoptionism. Indeed there is in the text no hint of the theology of the pre-existence of the Son of God, which is clearly a later, but compatible, development.[17] Here Jesus is presented simply as the man who is created as Son of God, and this by the Father (the Lord, God the Most High) in the power of the Holy Spirit. His uniqueness is expressed in terms that include his messiahship referred to as a thing of the future, but it is a messiahship subtly transformed, so that its basic constituent, the divinizing gift of the Spirit in all fullness, is given at the beginning of his life. Hahn expresses the matter thus: "Here the full messianic predicates of Lk 1:32 f. are now applied to the earthly Jesus, and that has spiritualization as its sequel. This new spiritualizing interpretation of traditional Jewish motifs again points to the sphere of Hellenistic Jewish Christianity."[18] The Holy Spirit, as Hahn

---

17   Cf. R. Brown, *The Birth of the Messiah* (London, 1977) 291, 314 (note 48), 316 (note 56).

18   Hahn 298.

remarks, quoting Dibelius, is conceived as "creative vital energy," [19] but the creative act at the same time sanctifies Jesus (v.32) and makes him unique Son of God (vv.32, 35). "On the basis of this begetting by the Spirit," writes Hahn, "divine sonship is now predicated of Jesus. Here, then, otherwise than in the story of the baptism, the divine sonship is not established by the indwelling Spirit, by virtue of whom Jesus is installed in his earthly messianic office, but by a special act which precedes the whole of his work on earth." [20] He sums up his treatment by saying, "The divine sonship was provided with another basis in the theologumenon of the virgin birth in the narrative of the annunciation to Mary. There it is a matter of the lifegiving power of the Spirit, who effects the conception without the participation of any man. The divine sonship rests upon the creative act of election and separation in the mother's womb." [21]

While the theme of anointing does not belong to this context so far as strictly biblical thought is concerned, the propriety of calling this communication of the Holy Spirit an anointing from a theological point of view is beyond question. De la Potterie had observed, as we noted, the conjunction, in Acts 10:38, of the themes of the Holy Spirit and of power with that of anointing. While anointing is not mentioned here, the Holy Spirit is said to be bestowed, and power to rule as Messiah is said to be basically endowed. The theologian, therefore, takes only one logical step when he identifies this action of God as an anointing.

An important point made by Hahn should be noted now. He remarks that election from the mother's womb was not unknown to Scripture, and gives Judg 13:05, Is 49:07, Jer 1:05 and Gal 1:15 as examples.[22] Being graced from the beginning of one's existence, therefore, does not necessarily imply that one is thereby made unique Son of God. However, it is question of whether logically the priority has an existing person graced to become a child of God (adoptive), or an act of grace that founds the existence of a man as Son of God in the unique sense. Hahn answers the objection himself in a comparison that he makes of Jesus and John the Baptist: "It may be pointed out that endowment with the Spirit in the mother's womb is not spoken

19   Ibid. 296.
20   Ibid. 296-97.
21   Ibid. 299.
22   Ibid. 326, note 116.

of here as in Lk 1:15 in the case of John the Baptist. The story of the virgin birth is so far no rectilineal extension of the statements about Jesus as the bearer of the Spirit. Rather the Spirit is understood here not as a gift but as the creative power, and otherwise than in the story about the Baptist it is just in this that the divine Sonship of Jesus rests. It is of interest that in the narrative of the birth of Jesus in Lk 1 and 2 statements about His possession of the Spirit are avoided." [23] When Hahn says that the Spirit is not understood as a gift, it is clear that he means a gift to an already existing man. He is not considering the possibility, affirmed by ourselves as a fact, that the exercise of creative power is at the same time also a gift, though in a somewhat different, indeed a uniquely radical, sense, viz., of founding even the basic human existence of the man. Jesus, then, receives the Gift of the Holy Spirit par excellence.

The point has already been made that one of the differences between Jesus and ordinary people is that with Jesus the bestowal of the Holy Spirit was non-sacramental, while with others it is necessarily sacramental. Now in the New Testament the bestowal of the Holy Spirit on Jesus is expressed in terms of his anointing; and the anointing is presented there as sacramental, as happening to an already existing human. This, however, does not constitute a real difficulty. Once it is realized that, theologically speaking, the baptismal anointing is the proclamation of the original anointing, which took place at the Incarnation, the problem disappears. This anointing was non-sacramental, since it was a bestowal without an offer, the bestowal being so radical that it brought the humanity of Jesus into existence.

We are now in a position to conclude that the central thesis of our theology of grace, viz., that the Father anointed the man Jesus with the Holy Spirit in an act which at the same time created him, sanctified him and united him in person to the divine Son, is found in seminal form in Scripture.

It is not difficult to see why the theology of the anointing of Jesus with the Holy Spirit was generalized by the Fathers into a theology of the Incarnation. In Scripture the anointing was the election of Jesus and the communication of divine power to him for a specific function. The concept was well suited to convey the idea of the more radical election and the communication of divinity that constitute the being of Jesus, i.e., the Incarnation, even though the New Testament itself

---

23   Ibid. 326-27, note 117.

did not use it in that way. The Fathers took their cue not only from the baptism of Jesus, but from the fact that he was called Christ, and from the application of certain Old Testament passages to him in the New Testament. The most important of these applications is the citation of Ps 45:6-7 in Heb 1:8-9, which provided the Fathers with an explicit link between the anointing and divine Sonship, though no such link was positively intended by the author of Hebrews, who invoked the psalm for quite a different purpose, viz., to show the superiority of the Son over the angels. Since, as we have seen, it is supported by other and weightier considerations from the New Testament, we are entitled to take up and develop this patristic theology, which opens out into a theology of the self-communication of God.

It is not possible in the scope of this book to undertake a comprehensive study of the teaching of the Fathers on the anointing of the humanity of Jesus. We have said something already on this subject in our critique of Scheeben and Mühlen. We shall complement this now with a brief chronological study of the teaching of a single Father, St. Cyril of Alexandria, who is one of the most important witnesses from antiquity on this matter. It should be noted, however, that a comparable exercise has been performed by J. Verhees in regard to the theology of St. Augustine.[24] Here the conclusion is reached that the unity of person of the man Jesus with the divine Word is the work of the Holy Spirit. The addition of the testimony of the great Father of the West to that of Cyril in the East provides formidable support from the ancient Church for the theology which we here propose. Apart from some final observations, our treatment of Cyril will bring our present chapter and part to their conclusion.

We begin with his commentary on Is 61:1-3, "The Spirit of the Lord is upon me, therefore he anointed me , . . ," which O. Bardenhewer dates before the outbreak of the Nestorian controversy in 429.[25] Cyril places the text on the lips of Christ, as though the Incarnation has already taken place. He writes, "And yet, existing by nature as God, the Only-begotten is the Saint of saints, and himself sanctifies every creature, since he is born of the holy Father, and sends as his own the

---

24   J. Verhees, "Heiliger Geist und Inkarnation in der Theologie des Augustinus von Hippo. Unlöslicher Zusammenhang zwischen Theo-logie und Ökonomie", *Revue des Études Augustiniennes* 22 (1976) 234-53.

25   O. Bardenhewer, *Geschichte der altkirchlichen Literatur* 4 (Freiburg im Br., 1924) 38.

Spirit proceeding from him, both to the powers above and to those who acknowledge his appearance. How, therefore, did he come to be sanctified? For existing as both divine and human, he gives the Spirit to the creature in the divine way, and receives it from God the Father according to the human way. This we say to be the anointing. Thus he clearly establishes the cause of the Incarnation. For saying that it was from the Father, he was obliged to add, 'Therefore he anointed me, he sent me to announce good news to the poor, . . .'"[26] The idea that the Son as God bestows the Holy Spirit on himself as man is found also in another work of Cyril's, his commentary on St. John's Gospel, which Bardenhewer dates at about the same time as the commentary on Isaiah.[27]

Cyril begins in the quoted passage by considering the Only-begotten apart from the Incarnation. He declares that, thus considered, the Son is holy in himself, and does not need to have the Holy Spirit bestowed on him in order to be holy. It is only as a human that he is anointed with the Holy Spirit. As we shall see from its prominence in the passages here assembled, this was an important consideration for Cyril. It was dictated here, as elsewhere, by the equality of the three divine persons. When, therefore, he asks, "How, therefore, did he come to be sanctified?" he is thinking of the Only-begotten in the state of Incarnation. He approached the matter from two sides, the divine and the human. From God's side, which we would call the viewpoint of descending Christology, he has the Son bestow the Holy Spirit on his own humanity. He does not distinguish between the constitution and the formation of the Incarnation, and he is dominated by the idea from descending Christology that the hypostatic union is a union of precisely the Son with human nature. He is therefore unable to invoke the fact that for Jesus the Holy Spirit is the Spirit of Sonship. Nor is he in a position to apply the distinction of the procession and the bestowal of the Holy Spirit within the Trinity.

The imperfect state of Cyril's theology on this point makes all the more significant his statements on the human side, where he is guided by the ascending Christology of Scripture. For Cyril the Father was certainly the "he" who sent Jesus to announce good news to the poor. As it is the same "he" who is said to have anointed Jesus, it was the *Father* who anointed Jesus as a human, and indeed with the Holy Spirit. It is

26   PG 70, 1349-52.

27   PG 74, 549. Cf. Bardenhewer 41.

precisely this anointing that Cyril identifies with the Incarnation, even though this does not square with what he has said on the side of God. The descending and the ascending elements of his Christology are left unreconciled.

From the viewpoint of descending Christology—and if one is determined to make use of the theme of anointing—one would have to say that the Incarnation is an anointing by the Son, in that it is a communication of precisely the Son to the sacred humanity. From the viewpoint of ascending Christology, the Incarnation (the term itself, we recall, belongs properly to descending Christology) is an anointing by the Father, and with (and "by" only in this sense) the Holy Spirit. The two viewpoints are reconciled by the insight that for Jesus the Holy Spirit is the Spirit of Sonship, i.e., the Spirit who unites the sacred humanity to the person of the divine Son. It is this key element, which we have shown to be based on Scripture, that is missing from the theology of Cyril here.

It is appropriate to introduce at this point the single text, from Cyril, that Mühlen adds to those collected by Scheeben. Mühlen uses this text as additional evidence that the teaching of the Fathers was that the anointing of the humanity of Christ which they identified with the Incarnation was an anointing by the Son. If this interpretation of the Fathers is correct, in the opinion of Mühlen the anointing by the Holy Spirit would have to be secondary and consequent in relation to that by the Son, in as much as the Holy Spirit proceeds from the Son, and it would therefore have a different significance. For Mühlen, as we have seen, the Son is responsible for the Incarnation, and the anointing by the Holy Spirit is connected with the (created) grace possessed by Jesus.

The text given by Mühlen is from Cyril's commentary on the Letter to the Hebrews, and reads as follows: "But the Son is anointed when he came into the world, that is, when he became incarnate. For then he entered into communion with creation, uniting the creature to himself, and anointing the humanity with the divinity, so as to make the two of them one."[28] There is no doubt that in this text the anointing is identified with the Incarnation, and that it is an anointing by the Son.

There is, however, in the text a discordant note, which Mühlen ignores, viz., the statement that the Son *is anointed* (i.e., the passive voice). Our comment on this is that it is the only element from ascending

---

28   PG 74, 961.

Christology in a text that otherwise reflects a descending Christology. Apart from this exception, Cyril here treats the theme of anointing within a descending Christology. Also, in the last passage that we examined Cyril treated the anointing within a descending Christology. This, as we saw, did not prevent him from treating it in the same passage within an ascending Christology also, even though the result was an unresolved situation. If the anointing is going to be situated in a descending Christology, then it has to be an anointing by the Son. We note that in the last text some degree of reconciliation was sought by Cyril in that in both his descending and his ascending Christology the anointing was considered to be done *with* the Holy Spirit. There the non-resolution lay in the fact that in the descending Christology the anointer was the Son, while in the ascending Christology it was the Father. Here, however, where Cyril has the Son as the anointer, by his silence on the matter he conveys the impression that the Son anoints his humanity not with the Holy Spirit but with himself.

There is, however, a serious objection against Mühlen's use of this text. He has cited only the latter part of a short, self-contained paragraph that is announced at its head as a commentary on the words, "Therefore God anointed you", from Heb 1:9. The earlier part of the paragraph reads, "You see that God is anointed by God. For when he became man, remaining what he was, then also, from the human point of view (literally: according to us humanly), he is anointed for the apostleship. For his humanity is anointed by the divine Spirit, but he (the Spirit) did not work as on simple humans, like prophets and patriarchs. But the anointing was, as it were, the whole presence of the anointer."[29] The text then continues as given by Mühlen.

With the addition of the first part of the text, the balance of ascending and descending Christology that we find elsewhere in Cyril is redressed. While the second sentence of the first part begins with descending Christology, it becomes ascending from the words "from the human point of view." As we would expect under these circumstances, the anointing is said to be by the Holy Spirit. In being distinguished from lesser anointings, and in having its uniqueness stressed (it alone conveys the whole presence of the anointer), the anointing is identified with the Incarnation. Interestingly, the anointing is conceived functionally, in that Jesus is declared to be anointed for the apostleship, probably in reference to the anointing and sending of Is 61:1

---

29   Ibid.

(a text much loved by Cyril), "Therefore he anointed me, he *sent* me to announce good news to the poor" (in LXX). The uniqueness of the anointing precludes the possibility of understanding "apostleship" in any sense in which an ordinary person could be an apostle. The apostleship to which Jesus is anointed is his unique prophetic ("to announce good news") mission from the Father, commensurate with his dignity as Son of God. It is the Incarnation itself, conceived in functional terms.

In its entirety, this text approximates to the last one that we examined. In its ascending Christology, each has as the anointed reality what we would call the human nature of Christ, the last text saying "the creature," and this one "his humanity." Perhaps the reason for this precision is that each considers the anointing also within a descending Christology, in which the Son is the anointer, and indeed anoints himself, which calls for an explanation, viz., that as God he anoints himself as a human, i.e., the divinity anoints the humanity. Where the anointing is considered only within an ascending Christology, in which the anointer is the Father, as in other texts that we shall examine, such precision is not demanded, as one can be satisfied with the statement that the Father anoints the Son, though, as we shall see, on these occasions Cyril is careful to point out (for another reason) that it is only as incarnate that the Son is anointed. In its ascending Christology this text does not state, as does the last, that the Father is the anointer (with the Holy Spirit), though this is implied in the statement that Jesus is anointed as apostle, since it was the Father who sent him on his mission. The text itself witnesses to Cyril's difficulty, as in the first part the Son is said to be anointed with the Holy Spirit, while in the second the Son is said to be the anointer. (As we have remarked, the problem is solved by seeing that for Jesus the Holy Spirit is the Spirit of Sonship, uniting the humanity to the person of the pre-existent divine Son). We detect, therefore, in this passage, the same non-resolution of ascending and descending Christology that we discovered in the last passage.

From these observations it will be clear that the text quoted by Mühlen may not be used simply as he has done. While we have pointed up the unresolved condition of Cyril's theology of the anointing of Jesus, we hope to have shown that it represents a stage toward the position that we have adopted, a position that we base ultimately on the New Testament and that we claim to be free of the precise shortcomings that we have discovered in both Scheeben and Mühlen's theology of the anointing. The next passage from Cyril is taken from his first letter, which because of its anti-Nestorian contents must be dated after 429, and hence is later than the passages that we have looked at so far. "The Word, who was existing in the form and equality of God the Father, humbled himself, therefore, when, being made flesh (to use the language of John), he was born of a woman, and having his birth from God the Father, submitted for our sake to undergo a birth like ours. If there be any who teach differently, let them explain how among us the Word from God the Father would be considered and called Christ. For if Christ is named from being anointed, who was it that the Father anointed with the oil of gladness, that is, with the Holy Spirit?"[30]

The first sentence of this text is based on Phil 2:5-11, from which "form", "humbled", "equality" and "a birth like ours" are borrowed, the former two directly, and the latter two indirectly. Like the Philippians text, this text speaks of the Incarnation. Cyril is concerned to convey, against Nestorius, that the person of Jesus is identical with that of the Word, that in the Incarnation the Word humbled himself in relation to the Father, and that apart from the Incarnation he did not humble himself. The anointing is identified with the humbling, and so with the Incarnation. Cyril continues at some length with the idea that it is impossible that the Word be, and be called, Christ apart from the Incarnation.

In this text, the first sentence represents descending Christology, the last ascending Christology, and the middle sentence is a link between the two. In the middle sentence the divine being, "the Word from God the Father" (descending Christology), is identified with the human be-ing "called Christ" (ascending Christology). It is the person of the Word who is said to have been anointed, but only as incarnate. Further (and this, of course, comes from the last sentence), he is anointed by the Father, and with the Holy Spirit. The advance in relation to the two passages examined so far, however, may be only apparent rather than real, for in all three the anointed one is the person of the Word incar-nate (though in saying "the creature", the first, is more precise), in their ascending Christology all have him (at least equivalently) anointed by the Father with the Holy Spirit, and in their descending Christology the first and the second have the Son as the anointer, while the third is

---

30   PG 77, 25.

simply silent on the matter. If pressed, Cyril might have answered that here too the Son was the anointer, in which case the same unresolved situation would obtain in this passage as in the last.

Continuing, Cyril alerts his readers to the danger of saying that the Word was anointed apart from the Incarnation. He warns against understanding the anointing of ordinary people with the Holy Spirit in grace as a multiplication of the Incarnation. First, for the sake of argument, he puts the offending contention: "And the divinely inspired John will testify, saying, 'And you have an anointing from the Holy One.' Therefore, we ourselves would perhaps be equal to God."[31] This idea Cyril rejects in language so strong that his Latin translator feels constrained to tone it down: "But as for us, even if we are anointed with the Holy Spirit, and possess abundantly the grace of sonship, and are called gods, at least we shall not be unmindful of the measure of our nature. For we are of the earth, and are counted among servants; but he is not one of us (literally: "he is not among whom we;" Latin: he is not contained by the laws of our nature), but he is by nature truly Son, and Lord of all, and from heaven."[32] If Cyril feels that he must here stress the difference between Jesus and ordinary people, it is only because he has just been stressing their similarity, in that both he and they are recipients of anointing with the Holy Spirit, and is concerned lest the two anointings be placed on the same level. Even though each is an anointing by the Father with the Holy Spirit, the uniqueness of the anointing of Jesus must be upheld.

We turn now to a text from the *Liber de recta fide, ad reginas.* "And to the angels he says, 'Who makes his angels spirits and his ministers a flame of fire,' but to the Son he says, 'Your throne, O God, is forever,' and 'The rod of your righteousness is the rod of your kingdom. You loved justice and hated iniquity, therefore God, your God, anointed you with the oil of gladness above your companions.' If he is the maker of angels, having a throne forever, having loved justice and hated iniquity, and therefore is said to be anointed with the oil of gladness by God the Father, what, then, have we to say, coming to such knowledge about him? For if he makes his angels spirits and has a throne of divinity, how is he anointed with the oil of gladness? Indeed it is as God that he makes the angels, but it is as man that he is anointed. The anointing takes place not in regard to the divine nature, but in regard to the

---

31   PG 77, 28.

32   Ibid.

wise execution of the divine plan. The Christ, then, is God and man: the same person is God according to nature, but (became) man like us according to the divine plan, when he was born of a woman according to flesh."[33]

This text presents the mixture of descending and ascending Christology that by now we have come to expect of Cyril. However, the anointing is discussed only in the context of ascending Christology. Hence it is no surprise to read that the Father is the anointer, though the fact that he anoints with the Holy Spirit is not mentioned in this text. The familiar idea that it is only as man that the Son is anointed is stated. On its own, this is not enough to establish identity between the anointing and the Incarnation, but the identification is actually made in the last sentence, where the anointing is situated at the Son's birth from a woman, i.e., at the beginning of his human life.

The next passage from Cyril is the first chapter, titled "What is Christ?", from his *Scholia de Incarnatione unigeniti*, dated by Bardenhewer after 431.[34] There are four paragraphs. In the first, the literal meaning of the word "Christ" (anointed) is explained, and it is immediately added that in Scripture the prophets too are called "Christs," although they were anointed by the Holy Spirit "mentally," i.e., spiritually. The second paragraph states that Christ the Saviour also was anointed, but that his anointing was not done with oil, nor was it (simply) a prophetic anointing, or a deputation for a task, such as happened in the case of Cyrus, who also is called a "christ" in Scripture. Cyril here says nothing positive about the anointing of Jesus, but the uniqueness that he attributes to it by his negative statements suggests that for him it is identical with the Incarnation.

The third paragraph continues, "But it (the anointing of Jesus) was something more. For since because of the sin of Adam sin reigned over all, the Holy Spirit departed, and it (human nature) fell into evil of every kind. Therefore, it was necessary that mounting once again by the mercy of God to its original state, it be deemed worthy of the Spirit. Therefore, the only-begotten Word of God became man. To those on earth he appeared with an earthly body, and was made free of sin, so that in him, and him alone, human nature, crowned with the praises of

---

33   PG 76, 1252.
34   PG 75, 1369-72. Cf. Bardenhewer 52.

innocence, might be enriched with the Holy Spirit, and thus reformed for God through holiness."[35]

With sure theological instinct, Cyril here situates Jesus with those whom he has come to save, and considers his anointing-Incarnation not just in itself, as an honor for him, but in the light of its purpose for humankind, viz., salvation. (The previous paragraph began with the words, "On Christ, the Saviour of us all, we say that an anointing was done . . .") This approach becomes even more explicit in the remainder of the chapter.

There is no reason to suppose that here Cyril conceives the anointing as done by any other than the Holy Spirit. To suggest, e.g., that the sacred humanity is anointed by the Son primarily, and by the Holy Spirit only in that he proceeds from the Son, is not only to go beyond the text, but to introduce an element quite foreign to it. It is to ignore the fact that already in this passage Cyril has spoken of spiritual anointing (as distinct from that done with oil) as done by the Holy Spirit. Further, from the fact that Cyril here compares the anointing of Jesus with that of other people, it is evident that, in the skilful mixture of descending and ascending Christology in the text, it is within an ascending Christology that he here approaches the question of the anointing of the sacred humanity. We have seen elsewhere that where Cyril does this, he conceives the anointing as done by the Holy Spirit. We conclude, therefore, that in this passage Cyril regards the Incarnation as a special, indeed unique, case of anointing by the Holy Spirit. However, as in other places where this is said or implied, no explanation is offered as to how this theology is squared with the descending theology of the Incarnation of the divine Son.

As we have pointed out, in the third paragraph Cyril begins to consider the anointing of Jesus in the light of its purpose, the salvation of humans. Human beings needing salvation are conceived ideally, as "human nature," from which the Holy Spirit is said to have "departed," leaving it in the condition where it needs to regain the Holy Spirit. The regaining of the Holy Spirit for human nature is said to have happened in the anointing of Jesus, which needs to be participated in by others if the divine plan that human nature as such is to regain the Holy Spirit is to be fulfilled. The acquisition of the Holy Spirit by Jesus is equated, without explanation, with the Incarnation, and its

---

35   Ibid.

uniqueness stressed by the statement that it is in Jesus alone that human nature is enriched with the Holy Spirit.

The third paragraph continues, "The grace that takes Christ, the first-born among us, as its beginning, thus passes into us, and therefore the blessed David, teaching us, sings to the Son, 'You loved justice and hated iniquity, therefore God, your God, anointed you with the oil of gladness.'"[36] Paragraph four follows, "Therefore, as we said above, the Son was anointed with the praises of innocence as a man like us (literally: according to us humanly), human nature being illumined in him, and indeed made worthy to be allotted a share in the Holy Spirit, who will not depart as he did in the beginning, but rather will be pleased to dwell in it. Therefore it was written, 'The Spirit came down upon Christ and remained on him.' Therefore the Word of God is called Christ, the Word who is a man for us and like us, and who came in the form of a slave. He was anointed humanly according to the flesh, but he anoints divinely with his own Spirit those who believe in him."[37]

In these words Cyril presents Jesus as the one who, having received the Holy Spirit, becomes in turn the source of this Spirit for others. As the last sentence expresses it, the anointed one becomes the anointer. However, as anointer, he is presented as one who anoints others, not as one who anoints himself or his own humanity. We defer to later a discussion of the question, in what sense, if at all, Jesus may be called an anointer of others. We note Cyril's concern not to place those who receive the Holy Spirit from Jesus on the same level as Jesus himself. His uniqueness has to be preserved, and this Cyril does by saying that he is the "first-born," and that grace had its "beginning" in him.

Very interesting is the contrast of the two verbs "depart" and "remain." Here we find a patristic base for our theology presented earlier, that with Jesus faith flowed from his divine Sonship, while with ordinary believers divine filiation results from faith. The Holy Spirit "remains" with Jesus (cf. Jn 1:33) because in his case the bestowal of the Spirit uniquely precedes his human free will (creating his human nature, and at the same time sanctifying it and uniting it in person to the preexistent divine Son). It was not possible, therefore, for Jesus to reject the Holy Spirit by sin. However, the Holy Spirit can depart from ordinary believers, for in their case his bestowal remains on them

---

36   PG 75, 1372.
37   Ibid.

only in the sacrament of an on-going offer that can at any time be refused in a sinful act of the free will in which he is rejected. However, even though the Holy Spirit may depart from individual believers because of their sin, thanks to the Incarnation he is guaranteed to remain forever with human nature as such. It can never happen again that the Holy Spirit will simply depart from human nature.

The final passage is taken from the dialogue *Quod unus sit Christus*, which according to Bardenhewer is one of the last anti-Nestorian writings of Cyril.[38] We begin with the end of a speech by B, one of the dialogists. "Since it is quite inappropriate to attribute it (the name "Christ," "Anointed") to the Father or the Holy Spirit, nor, in all likelihood, will it pertain to the Only-begotten himself, rather it is rightly given to the one born of the seed of David, of whom it would not be totally improper to think and to say that he was anointed by the Spirit."[39] Here, in strained and guarded language, we are told that of the three divine persons only the Son is anointed, not, however, in himself, but only in relation to his Incarnation. The anointing is set in the context of an ascending Christology. In linking the anointing with the birth of Jesus rather than some later event in his life, Cyril shows that for him the anointing is the Incarnation. Further, the anointing is done by the Holy Spirit.

The dialogue is then taken up by A, who asserts that the equality of the three divine persons requires that the Only-begotten be anointed only in his humanity. He continues, "However, dear friends, I should say that the name 'Christ' and the thing itself, that is, the anointing, came to the Only-begotten with the ways of the emptying, bringing clearly the explanation of the Incarnation to those who listen. For it would be well worth-while to observe that it was according as he appeared as man that he was anointed."[40] A clearer identification of the anointing and the Incarnation could scarcely be desired. A little later in the speech the same point is repeated in somewhat different language: "Since the divine and most holy Scripture says that he became flesh, it would be fitting, then, that the anointing happen to him in relation to the enfleshment that is his."[41] Both texts set the anointing within a descending Christology, as is evident also from the nature of

38   PG 75, 1276-77. Cf. Bardenhewer 54.

39   PG 75, 1276.

40   PG 75, 1276-77.

41   PG 75, 1277.

the biblical texts referred to, viz., Phil 2:7 and Jn 1:14, respectively. Perhaps this is the explanation of the precision of the second text in saying that it was the humanity, rather than the person of the Word incarnate, that was anointed.

Later still in the same speech A says, "He was sanctified with us when he became one of us. That it was truly the Son who was the anointed one, according as he became flesh, that is to say, perfect man, the divinely inspired David will affirm, saying to him, 'Your throne, O God, is forever, . . . Therefore God, your God, anointed you with the oil of gladness above your companions.' Observe, therefore, how, calling him God and assigning him a throne forever, he says that he was anointed by God, it is clear that it was by the Father, with a certain excellent anointing above his companions, that is, us."[42] In the last sentence of this text the Christology is ascending, and it is therefore no surprise to find Cyril stating that in the anointing that is identical with the Incarnation the Father is the one who anoints the Son in his humanity. Again, against Nestorius, the identity of person of Jesus and the Son is stressed.

Further, it is clear that Cyril understands both the Incarnation and grace as anointings with the Holy Spirit, and in the last sentence of the text he makes a comparison between them. It is not a very thorough comparison, nor could it have been, since the important element from ascending Christology that the anointing of Jesus was an anointing to the unique divine Sonship is lacking in his theology. However, he is concerned to bring out the uniqueness of the Incarnation in relation to grace, and this he does when he says that the anointing of Jesus was more excellent than that of ordinary people.

By a variety of expressions Cyril shows that he grasps the difference between what modern theology calls descending and ascending Christology. He uses the two terms "Incarnation" and "anointing." Since it is God who becomes man, and man who is anointed, it is clear that the term "Incarnation" belongs to descending Christology, and "anointing" to ascending Christology. Though Cyril uses the theme of anointing in its proper context of ascending Christology, we find that he uses it also within descending Christology. In his ascending Christology he develops the theme very well. He is clear that the anointer is the Father, and that he anoints with the Holy Spirit. The one who is anointed is the divine Son, not, however, in himself, but

---

42   Ibid.

only as incarnate. At times he is pushed, apparently by his simultaneous use of the theme of anointing in a descending Christology, to make the precision that it is the humanity of the Son that is anointed. For Cyril this anointing is identical with the Incarnation.

Cyril is less assured when he treats the theme of anointing in his descending Christology. This is not surprising, since, properly speaking, this theme has no place there. Used there, it can only signify the communication of divinity to humanity, by analogy with the communication of oil, with its properties of power and health, to the human body. Here, then, the anointing is the communication of the divine Son to the human nature in the Incarnation. This makes the Son the anointer. He can be considered either as anointing by himself, in that the hypostatic union is a union of himself with the humanity, or as anointing with the Holy Spirit who proceeds from him. In this last conception the primary anointing is by the Son, and the anointing by the Holy Spirit is secondary. This conception we may set aside, since, as we have seen, it is unsupported by Scripture, and contradicted by the Trinity in itself, to which conforms the activity of the divine persons in the revelation and the operation of the Trinity in the world. However, no one can reasonably object to Cyril's use of the idea of anointing to denote the immediate communication of the Son to the sacred humanity in the Incarnation. It only remains to comment that this conception applies to the Incarnation as constituted, and does not seek to discover how it was formed, or came about.

Cyril was unable to resolve the tension between his descending and his ascending Christology in relation to the anointing. This was not just because one element of his descending Christology is shown to be incorrect in the light of a more developed theology of the Trinity, for this element does not always appear in his theology, and the problem is still there when it does not. Basically, he was unable to reconcile the various elements of his Christology because he did not see, and therefore use, a factor that can be distilled from Scripture, viz., that the Holy Spirit, bestowed by the Father on the humanity of Jesus, anointed it in the most radical possible way, by at the same time creating it, sanctifying it, and uniting in person to the pre-existent divine Son. In a way that makes Jesus the paradigm for all others, the Holy Spirit was the Spirit of Sonship for him. Having used this element from ascending Christology to understand the formation of the Incarnation, when we change our viewpoint to that of descending Christology and consider the Incarnation as constituted, we can then understand how the Incarnation, at the same time as it is an anointing by the Father with the Holy Spirit, can be, and is, an anointing by the Son.

It remains only to note, with approval, that in his ascending Christology Cyril took account of the fact that both the Incarnation and grace were anointings with the Holy Spirit, and was at pains to uphold the uniqueness of the anointing of Jesus in the Incarnation.

It is clear that much more work needs to be done on the theology of the anointing in Cyril and in the other Eastern Fathers. However, we consider that the brief study essayed here authenticates our theology of grace as genuinely based. This theology states that grace is the extension to humans of the Holy Spirit, the Father's love for the Son in the Trinity. This grace appeared fully in the world in the person of Jesus Christ, the Incarnation, in which the Father bestowed the Holy Spirit as Spirit of Sonship on the human nature of Jesus in the most radical way, creating it, sanctifying it, and uniting it in person to the pre-existent divine Son, making him divine Son in humanity. In his resurrection, i.e., in the Church, Jesus becomes the sender of this same Spirit, in that he is authorized to offer him to all people, to be received in faith. The accepted offer is the sacrament of the bestowal of the Holy Spirit *as* Spirit of sonship by the Father, changing them from sinners to sons and daughters, "sons in the Son," in that the same Spirit who made Jesus unique Son of God in humanity is now possessed also by them.

It should be noted that there is no conflict between what is said here and the theology of divine formal causality presented in the second part of this book. The perspective adopted there was that of descending Christology, and it was stated that it is the Son who exercises divine formal causality in regard to the sacred humanity. Here, on the other hand, the perspective is that of ascending Christology. The humanity of Jesus is seen to be so exalted by the Holy Spirit as to be rendered one in person with the Son, but this does not allow the Holy Spirit to be characterized as either substantial or accidental form in regard to the Son incarnate. The substantial form of Jesus is the Son: he *is* the Son. And though Jesus, uniquely , *possesses* the Holy Spirit, he does not possess him as accidental form, for there is no created accident in him corresponding to this possession. *His* holiness is simply that of God, in which he was created.[43] In the Incarnation the Son and the Holy Spirit remain distinct divine persons, each acting in his own property, the Son as the revelation of God, the Holy Spirit as his power and love. Further, this remark applies to the hypostatic union not just in its formation but afterwards as well. Just as creation can be regarded as both an act and an ongoing process, so the hypostatic union can be regarded as both an event and a continuing process, and therefore as a perpetual work of the Son and the Holy Spirit respectively. By contrast, the grace of other humans, because of the accidental character of sanctifying grace, can be referred as a work of divine formal causality to the Holy Spirit alone. These observations are necessary to fill out the theology of divine formal causality outlined in Part Two.

In Part One we reached the conclusion that the most basic statement that can be made about the Holy Spirit is that he is the love with which the Father loves the Son. This brings home to us the fact that as the Father's love the Holy Spirit rests properly on the Son and on no other. When, therefore, the Father freely directs his love beyond the Trinity to personal being created for the purpose of receiving this love, it will necessarily draw that being into union of some kind with its proper object, the Son in the Trinity. There, "in the order not of time but of nature and understanding", the Father bestows the Holy Spirit as his love on the Son already constituted. Outside the Trinity, however, the Father's bestowal of the Holy Spirit will *bring about* divine filiation in the recipient, whom, in our case, it encounters in a state of alienation from him. Hence it is clear that it is by no extrinsic title that for personal being outside the Trinity the Holy Spirit is the Spirit of sonship (filiation). The union with the Son thus brought about will be, according to the will of the Father, either, in the case of the Incarnation, unity of person with the Son by the most radical possible bestowal of the Spirit, or, in the case of grace, union of persons, human persons with the Son as sons and daughters in the Son by a less radical bestowal. The basic difference between these two bestowals, as we have observed several times, is guaranteed by the fact that the former

---

43   See p. 140 (Chapter 7) where this statement is amplified in the light of a later development in my theology based on the thought of de la Taille. The holiness of Jesus is there explained also in terms of a unique substantial created grace (which is not, however, a substantial form) identical with the divine Sonship as received by the sacred humanity. Simply put, it *is* the sacred humanity.

creates the humanity of Jesus in unity of person with the Son, while the latter encounters already existing human persons.

The space that we have devoted to the anointing of Jesus is only in keeping with its importance in the theology of grace, for if our conclusion is correct (as we believe it to be), the principal barrier to a synthesis in Catholic theology of grace is overcome. As long as the great grace of Jesus, the grace of union, is referred simply to the Son, a full synthesis remains impossible; but once it is realized that this grace is precisely the fullness of that given to ordinary people, viz., the Holy Spirit, Spirit of divine filiation, the way to the desired synthesis is opened. We move on now in Part Four to consider the anointing of ordinary people with the Holy Spirit. Here we find further justification for considering the theology of grace under the rubric of anointing, for Jesus Christ, the paradigm of grace, and all others who receive grace are thereby embraced within the one approach.

PART IV

THEOLOGY OF THE INCARNATION AND GRACE IN THE LIGHT OF THE RETURN MODEL

2. THE SENDING OF THE HOLY SPIRIT TO HUMAN BEINGS

9 THE SENDING OF THE HOLY SPIRIT AND THE RETURN MODEL

In this part of the book we pursue our investigation of the theology of the Incarnation and grace in the light of the return model of the Trinity. In the last part we concentrated on the Incarnation in the light of this model, and so now in this part we must address ourselves to the question of grace in the light of the same model. Here we find that because of the necessary sacramentality of grace the bestowal of the Holy Spirit by the Father will take place principally in the sacrament as which Jesus is constituted by his death and resurrection. This means that as well as considering the invisible bestowal by the Father, we shall have to consider the visible sending of the Holy Spirit by Christ, and the range of sacraments, culminating in the Eucharist, by which this sending encounters individual humans. Before we do this, however, the very first question we must face (and it will be the task of the present chapter) is that of the relation of the sending of the Holy Spirit to the Trinity in itself. The answer which emerges will justify our linking of the sending of the Holy Spirit by Christ with the return model rather than the procession model, which at first sight might appear more appropriate.

Since the Trinity as revealed and operative corresponds to the Trinity in itself, we now put the question, what is it in the Trinity in itself to which corresponds the sending of the Holy Spirit by Christ upon the Church and the continued sending of the same Spirit through its ministry? Theologians who address themselves to this question usually answer it by saying that the sending of the Spirit by Christ is a projection or continuation of the procession of the Spirit through or with the Son in the Trinity, i.e., they answer it in terms of the procession model.[1] This, however, is not fully satisfactory. The principal disadvantage

---

1   An interesting exception is Hans Urs von Balthasar (cf. his *Love Alone: The Way of Revelation* [London, 1968] 93; *Engagement with God* [London, 1975] 36-37; *Elucidations* [London, 1975] 41), who catches up the saving activity of Christ into the dialogue between the incarnate Son and the Father. While this approach cannot be characterized as an appeal to the return model of the Trinity, it nevertheless approximates somewhat to it.

of this "out-going" model is that it neither states nor implies the purpose of the breathing-forth of the Holy Spirit in the Trinity, and so inevitably, even if unintentionally, conveys the impression that this final stage of the divine operation is without purpose. On the other hand, the sending of the Holy Spirit by Christ, conceived along these lines, clearly has a purpose, viz., the gracing of humans. This, however, gives rise to the danger of conceiving the purpose of the breathing-forth of the Holy Spirit in the Trinity as ultimately and necessarily the gracing of humans. If this were conceded, however, the freedom of the Father in sending the Son and the Holy Spirit into the world, and therewith the transcendence of God, would be compromised.

The solution to the problem lies in conceiving the procession of the Holy Spirit according to the "circular," or return, model. With it the transcendence and freedom of God are guaranteed, and it is readily seen that the Trinity is self-enclosed and self-sufficient, and that the breathing-forth of the Spirit in the Trinity has a purpose, viz., he is breathed forth as the mutual love of the Father and the Son. Yet, mysteriously, the three divine persons freely will not to be the sole participants of their life but to share it with created beings, and here is given the reason for both the creation of humans and their world and the missions of the Son and the Holy Spirit. Far from the Trinity being dependent on humans, then, the converse is true. If they are to receive grace, it will be only because they are assimilated to the inner life of God. While it is true that this implies a (logically) previous reaching-out to humans on the part of God, positing them in being and challenging them spiritually in the sacraments of grace, these actions are to be seen only as moments of their assimilation to God. This we have explained already in Scholastic terms in our exposition of the relation of efficient and formal causality.

As we have explained, this assimilation takes place through the gracious bestowal, by the Father, of the Holy Spirit, whom in the Trinity he "by nature" bestows on the Son, on the only created beings capable of receiving him, viz., humans precisely in their spirituality, thus drawing them into union with the primordially rightful object of this bestowal, viz., the Son, so that for humans the Spirit becomes the Spirit of filiation. This the Father does in the first place by a non-sacramental bestowal that is so radical and total that it creates an individual human nature, viz., that of Jesus, sanctifies it and unites it in person to the Son. Having realized in his life and death the unique Sonship given him as grace at his conception, Jesus alone of all human beings acquires the authority to send the same Spirit to others. This he does in his continuing ministry, and those responding in faith to his offer receive the Spirit bestowed now sacramentally, but still, of course, as Spirit of filiation, by the Father. Necessarily, their filiation is less radical than that of Jesus, and they become sons and daughters *in the Son.* Thus in the divine economy is the assimilation of humans to the life of the Trinity complete.

However, the question remains, to what in the Trinity in itself does the sending of the Holy Spirit by Christ correspond? In a word, the answer to this question is that it corresponds to the bestowal of the Holy Spirit by the Son on the Father. We have now to justify this answer, but before we do, we point out that here we have for the first time the second moment of the procession of the Holy Spirit coming into play in the economy. In the last part we saw the relevance of the first moment of this procession to the Incarnation, viz., the bestowal of the Holy Spirit by the Father on the Son, and in the process we gained some insight into its application to the regeneration of humans as sons and daughters of the Father in grace as well. Now in this part we take up the second of these matters in some detail, and in so doing we shall see the relevance of the second moment of the procession of the Holy Spirit, the bestowal of the Holy Spirit as answering love by the Son on the Father. We shall see that it applies to the sending of the Holy Spirit by Christ to humans and to the faith and love of those thus graced.

We now present our argument in brief form, and we shall then go on to develop its various parts in detail. The key to understanding the relation of the sending of the Holy Spirit by Christ to the Trinity in itself is the profound unity of the double commandment of Jesus, to love God and to love the neighbor. The sending of the Holy Spirit by Christ is the supreme and all-inclusive primary act of his love of God, i.e., the Father. Flowing as its total act and expression from his humanity endowed in the most radical possible way with the Father's Gift of the Holy Spirit, Spirit of Sonship, Christ's love of the Father is nothing other than the Holy Spirit himself. It corresponds to the bestowal of the Holy Spirit as love by the Son on the Father in the Trinity in itself. Thus the relation of the sending of the Holy Spirit by Christ to humans to the bestowal of the Holy Spirit by the Son on the Father in the Trinity is evident.

With ordinary people, faith in God is the act which at the same time brings about and flows from their divine filiation. In either construction it is their response to the Holy Spirit sent from the Father as Spirit of filiation and as his love for his sons and daughters (in the Son) in the sacrament of the sending of the Spirit by Christ. "To show that you are sons, God has sent the Spirit of his Son into our hearts, crying, 'Abba! Father!'" (Gal 4:6). In the order of the operation of the Trinity this love of sons and daughters for the Father also corresponds to the bestowal of the Holy Spirit as love by the Son on the Father in the Trinity in itself. And according to the unity of the double commandment of love, the love of humans for the Father has as its primary act their love of the neighbor. They cannot, like Christ, send the Holy Spirit to their neighbor, but their love, expressed in many ways, some of them quite humble, finds its highest expression in their intercession on the neighbor's behalf. The profound communion of graced people with Christ can hence be appreciated, and indeed is visible in its highest expression, the Eucharist. They commune with him in the same Spirit, given to him in unsurpassable fullness and sent by him to them; they commune with him in love of the Father, in that their love is caught up in his because enabled by the same Spirit (the same is true of prayer, cf. Rom 8:26); and they commune with him in love of the neighbor, since in the medium of the same Spirit they are sons and daughters in him and hence brothers and sisters of him and of each other.

The first matter calling for comment is the unity of the double commandment of Jesus, love of God and love of neighbour (Mk 12:28-31 and parallels). Rahner has shown that these two commandments are linked not simply extrinsically, by the will of Jesus, but intrinsically, so that they constitute a single commandment.[2] Here we shall content ourselves merely with stating his conclusions. The two loves are related in that "the categorised explicit love of neighbor is the primary act of the love of God."[3] Further, "the love of God unreflectedly but really and always intends God in supernatural transcendentality in the love of neighbor as such, and even the explicit love of God is still borne by that opening in trusting love to the whole of reality which takes place

---

2   Cf. K. Rahner, "Reflections on the Unity of the Love of Neighbor and the Love of God," *Theological Investigations* 6, 231-49.

3   Ibid. 247.

in the love of neighbor."[4] The other matter calling for comment is that the sending of the Holy Spirit by Christ is the supreme act of his love for humans. This point we develop with the aid of the theology of death which we have invoked already and the above-mentioned theology of the unity of the double commandment of love. What emerges from this will be an alternative to the theory of vicarious satisfaction as the explanation of the meaning and value of the death of Jesus in relation to both the Father and human beings.

In recent theology death is seen as more than simply the event that stands at the end of the row of all the events of a person's life. It is the event that crowns their personal history, and subsumes it in a single act which expresses and affirms the whole meaning and value of their life. In death the changeable and earthly character of a person's life ceases, and that life assumes its definitive and transcendental form. For better or worse the gradual free formation of the person within the endowed nature is then complete. Since faith, at least in the transcendental sense, is the most basic determinant of personhood and its quality, no one can escape the demand to affirm this faith in the act of death. If, under grace, it is affirmed, the affirmation is option for the self-fulfillment that takes place in God and is traditionally called heaven; if it is denied, the denial is option for self-assertion apart from God, a sinful option doomed to the frustration that is traditionally called hell. This theology, which is called that of final option, should be seen not as a simple alternative to that of fundamental option, but rather as its complement. This latter theology, of which we shall have more to say in the next part, states that in reaching moral maturity a human assumes over against God a stance of either transcendental faith or transcendental unbelief. This option, which is a state rather than an act, is strengthened, weakened, or even reversed, according as a person lives in accordance with it or not. Rooted in their history, it makes a person what they are by the time that they arrive at their death, and hence greatly influences their final option.

We now link the theology of death and the theology of the radical unity of the double commandment of love in the statement that the death of a just person, in as much as it is their supreme act of love of God, is also their supreme act of love of neighbor, even if it is experienced as the act of their life in which they are most isolated from the neighbor. If Rahner's thesis of the unity of the double commandment

---

4   Ibid.

is true (as it surely is) both in general and in regard to the humblest specific acts of love, it must be supremely true in regard to that act which subsumes and reaffirms the whole love-value of a person's life, viz., the death of a just person. The truth of our contention can be seen also from a consideration of the doctrine of the communion of saints. This implies that a person's loving service of the neighbor, which is the expression of their divine filiation in as much as it implies spiritual brotherhood or sisterhood to the neighbor, reaches its highest point (which does not abolish the need or value of humbler forms of service, but rather unifies and directs them and is built up in them) in their intercession with God on the neighbor's behalf. It further implies that when a person dies their intercession, far from ceasing, attains a new and definitive status, in that in death a just person acquires the "state of perfection" or eschatological divine filiation (cf. Rom 8:23) and brotherhood or sisterhood to the neighbor. This is evident from the Church's practice (to which great importance is attached) of invoking the intercession of the saints, particularly of Mary, the greatest of them. The status accruing to the intercession of a just person on their death is proof of the fact that their death is their supreme act of love of neighbor as well as of God, for the bestowal of this status by God signifies that in accepting their death as orientated toward himself God accepts also its orientation to the neighbor and makes this latter orientation effective. If this were not so, we would be forced to say that this status comes as something quite extrinsic to the person's being and life and to the act that sums up and expresses them.

We now apply these general considerations to the specific case of Jesus. The nature with which he was endowed at his conception was a human nature. The person, endowed at the same time, who had to come to expression in that nature was a divine person, the Son. This is not to suggest that the Son had to change or develop in himself. Being divine, he was unchangeable. That which was founded in being, changed, and developed, was the human nature. Here we must contrast ordinary people with Jesus, for with them the (human) person comes into existence only with the nature, and gradually grows in being as the nature expands, whereas with Jesus the (divine) person preexisted the human nature, and, as God, always possessed the fullness of being, so that this person could only come to *realization* or *expression* in the nature, as it increasingly, in the course of the human history of Jesus, endowed that nature with being, which it did in cooperation with Jesus' exercise of virtue in that nature. Of all created being only human nature has the capacity for a divine person to come to expression in it, since only human nature has spirituality or openness to God, so that the infinite can be realized in it. As we explained in our outline of the theology of death, it requires the death of a person to bring their personhood fully into being. In the case of Jesus, therefore, it required his death to bring the divine person fully into realization in his humanity. We conclude that, even though the divine Sonship was bestowed on Jesus at the beginning of his life, it needed his history and his death for him to realize fully in his humanity the reality of the Son of God, and therefore for him to be fully constituted as mediator between God and humans.

It is apposite at this point to offer an observation about the resurrection of Jesus. The actual faith-content of this doctrine is the full coming into being in the world, and therefore the full saving presence, of the Son of God, which took place precisely in the humanity, and therefore through the death, of Jesus of Nazareth. We should not allow ourselves to be deflected from this appreciation by theological discussion regarding the nature of the ontological reality of the resurrection. This discussion, intriguing as it is in itself, is concerned with weighing the concrete ways in which the New Testament, determined by the anthropologies of its day, reports this event. Nor should we be over-impressed by efforts to replace the Incarnation with the resurrection as the centre of the mystery of Christ.[5] The most basic fact about Christ is the Incarnation, and on it the resurrection and the other mysteries depend. This is not to make them superfluous or to downgrade them, or to devalue Jesus' human history. The way in which we have described the resurrection above witnesses to its vital importance as the historical realization of the saving mystery, but it must be borne in mind that it could not have this significance but for the Incarnation.

We remarked above that the love of a just person for their neighbor assumes its highest form in his intercession on the neighbor's behalf, and that in their death this intercession attains a new and definitive status. What an intercessor prays for in lived reality, even if they may not know it consciously, is that God (the Father) through Christ (the Son) will bestow grace (the Holy Spirit) on the neighbor. As a son or daughter (in the Son) they can thus approach the Father, but they

---

5   For example, and particularly, Pannenberg, *Jesus - God and Man* (London, 1968), but also G. O'Collins, *The Easter Jesus* (London, 1973).

themselves lack the authority to send the Holy Spirit to the neighbor. It is the possession of this authority, which derives from Christ's unique divine Sonship, that makes his intercession unique and paradigmatic. Over and above (but including, and taking its point of departure from) the sense in which all humans are brothers and sisters by nature, Christ, as unique Son of God, is (at least potentially) the brother of all humans by grace also in a unique sense, i.e., a sense in relation to which that in which ordinary people are brothers and sisters by grace (i.e., in the same Spirit) is only analogous and derived. The uniqueness of Christ as brother is seen in the fact that of all humans he alone can and does create the community of the brotherhood and sisterhood of humans by grace, viz., the Church, in that by virtue of his authority he alone can and does send from the Father to humans the Spirit of divine filiation which he himself received from him in all fullness. Jesus exercised this authority even during his earthly life, but because his divine Sonship was then not fully realized in his humanity and his authority, therefore, was not fully established, any sending of the Spirit by him then was necessarily limited. Because he was human, death connoted for him too a transition to a new and definitive status as intercessor; but because he was unique Son of God in humanity it was in relation to his unique form of intercession that this was so. Through his death his divine Sonship was fully realised in his humanity, and hence his authority to send in his humanity the Holy Spirit upon the Church became fully established. His love of the neighbor, which flowed as act from his unique divine Sonship in humanity precisely in its orientation to the neighbor as spiritual brotherhood, was also thus brought to completion. This Sonship, authority and love (which simply constitute the one personal reality in its being, dignity and act) were made effective by the Father in the sending of the Holy Spirit by Christ from him at Pentecost and thereafter in the Church. This sending is contrasted with that which took place during Jesus' earthly life in that it was full and universal, the Messianic outpouring of the Spirit foretold by the prophets.

Hence we link theologically not only the resurrection but also Pentecost with the death of the man who was unique Son of God. It was therefore not just the result of a divine decree but was required by the Incarnation in its full historical realization that the Spirit was not given (fully) before Jesus was glorified (cf. Jn 7:39). Along with the resurrection and the sending of the Holy Spirit at Pentecost, also the ascension of Jesus can be understood in relation to his death, in that his surrender to the Father in faith, which was accomplished only in his death, constituted his attainment precisely in his humanity to the Father, and hence can be portrayed as an elevation to the Father's side. The order, presented in the New Testament chronologically, of resurrection, ascension and sending of the Spirit, is explained by seeing the resurrection as the full coming to himself in humanity of the Son of God (through death), the ascension as his consequent attainment to God (the Father), and Pentecost as his consequent effectiveness for the neighbor (in sending the Holy Spirit to them).

With Jesus, as with ordinary people, the primary act of his love of God (the Father) was his love of the neighbor, and the supreme act of his love of God, his death, was thereby also his supreme act of love of neighbor, which we have shown to be, in his unique case, the sending of the Holy Spirit at Pentecost. The double orientation of the death of Jesus, as love of God and love of neighbor, is so clearly and abundantly attested by the New Testament that we shall be content to review its evidence quite summarily. The Letter to the Hebrews calls his death a "sacrifice for sins" (10:12). As a sacrifice, it was an act of love orientated to God. It was the supreme self-offering of Jesus to the Father in love and obedience to his will. And as a sacrifice precisely for sins, the death of Jesus was an act of love orientated to the neighbor, for whose sins alone it was a sacrifice.[6] The conception of the death of Jesus as a sacrifice for sins formed the biblical foundation for the theology of vicarious satisfaction developed by Anselm. The basis for both these models in the life and consciousness of Jesus as attested by the Gospels is the responsibility that he assumed for his fellow-humans before God, a responsibility that was vindicated and confirmed by

---

6   Regrettably, the death of Jesus conceived as a sacrifice has been misconstrued by many as an act of appeasement exacted by a vengeful and sadistic, and therefore anthropomorphic and literally incredible, God. What is intended by this theological model, which, after all, is only one way among several in which the New Testament interprets the death of Jesus, is that his death was acceptable to God because it signified his unqualified adherence, unchecked by concupiscence, to his vocation and mission in the face of all obstacles, particularly death, the last and greatest of all, and so constituted the adequate expression of his whole life of faith. God cannot be held accountable for the sins of humans which provided the trial that served to evoke the fullness of Jesus' faith, which was the enabling factor in the full realization of his divine Sonship.

the Father in raising him from the dead. The Fourth Gospel, in addition to interpreting the death of Jesus in terms of his love of God (14:31), interprets it also as his love of the neighbor, since it has him say, "Greater love has no one than this, that he lay down his life for his friends" (15:13). And it has been suggested that the significance of the statement, "He bowed his head and gave up the spirit" (19:30), is that Jesus sent the Holy Spirit to humankind in the same act (which we stress was his supreme act of love) in which he gave up his human spirit to the Father in death.[7] The same double orientation is evident in the words of institution of the Eucharist (Mk 14:22-25 and parallels) and in the theology of covenant presented both there and in the Letter to the Hebrews, in which Jesus, as the mediator of the covenant established precisely in his death, relates on the one side to God and on the other to humans, to both, however, in love. We do not suggest that the New Testament teaches the precise profound relation of love of God and love of neighbor in the death of Jesus which later reflection has laid bare, but the fact that it so clearly sees the death of Jesus as orientated to both God and the neighbor in love provides us with convincing evidence that Rahner's thesis of the radical unity of the double commandment of love is supremely true in the case of the love of Jesus as it came to full expression in the act of his death as his self-giving to the Father and his sending of the Holy Spirit from the Father to humans.

Our efforts in the preceding pages have enabled us to see that the sending of the Holy Spirit by Christ at Pentecost and thereafter in the Church, as the primary act of Christ's love of the Father, corresponds to the bestowal of the Holy Spirit as love by the Son on the Father in the Trinity in itself. The purpose of the sending of the Spirit by Christ is that humans may be drawn through the response of faith into divine filiation with and through him, so that they too, with him, will love the Father with the love of sons and daughters, corresponding to the same Trinitarian love spoken of above. By analogy with Christ, their love of the Father also will have as its primary act their love for each other in the medium of the same Spirit. The double bond of love forged by the Holy Spirit creates the community that we know as the Church. Thus we are enabled to see the Trinity as the centre of all being, and the created world as achieving its purpose in becoming assimilated through

---

7   Cf. R. Brown, *The Gospel according to John* (XIII-XXI) (The Anchor Bible) (New York, 1970) 931.

humans to its life. We now proceed in the next chapter to examine more closely the sending of the Holy Spirit by Christ to his fellow human beings.

IO THE SENDING OF THE HOLY SPIRIT

This chapter is devoted to an important question in the theology of grace, the sending of the Holy Spirit to humans. In it we shall undertake four tasks. The first is to distinguish the different roles, divine and human, involved in the sending of the Spirit. This is necessary because, in contrast to the bestowal of the Spirit on Jesus, his bestowal on ordinary humans must be sacramental; and this immediately introduces two elements, the categorial action of an agent in the world, and the transcendental action of God, with the former serving as the sacrament of the latter. Our second task will be to investigate the sources, Scripture and the Fathers, on the question of the anointing of humans with the Holy Spirit. This follows logically upon the previous section, since here we have a categorial anointing by Christ, the equivalent of his sending of the Spirit, and a transcendental anointing by the Father. This section is important because it connects the grace of humans with the grace of Jesus as studied in Part Three. Our third task will be to present a summary of our theology of grace to that point. It will be the appropriate place for such a summary, since on conclusion of our second task our theology will be essentially complete, as it will only remain, in the following two chapters, to examine the concrete forms of the sacramentality of grace, which has already been established in principle, and then, in Part Five, to integrate a number of questions from the theology of grace, till then not treated in this book, into our synthesis. Finally, our fourth task will be to complete the exercise, begun in Part Two, of situating our theology of grace in relation to the biblical theology of covenant. The acquisition of a theology of the sending of the Spirit will enable us to do this.

We begin, then, with our first task, of distinguishing the various roles, divine and human, involved in the sending of the Spirit. Clearly the role of the Father in the sending of the Spirit is divine. Just as the Holy Spirit proceeds ultimately from the Father in the Trinity, so he is sent ultimately by the Father into the world (Jn 14:26; 15:26). The role of Christ in the sending of the Spirit is also divine, but it is distinguished from that of the Father in containing also a human element. In transcendental theology the divine being of Christ is explained as, in part, a determination of his human being, and similarly his divine operation may be explained as a determination of his human operation. This would mean that the action of Christ in sending the Spirit is to be characterized as "theandric," i.e., literally, divine-human, or better (for our purposes), human-divine. That Christ is in fact the sender of the Spirit is attested by Scripture (Jn15:26; 16:7; 20:22; Acts 2:33; Rom 8:9; 2 Cor 3:17; Eph 4:7). He is the historical and visible sender, while the Father remains the transcendent and invisible sender (Col 1:15; 1 Tim 1:17; 6:16).

Through the resurrection Christ becomes co-sender of the Spirit with the Father. He becomes "co-sender" (the economic term) because he becomes, in his humanity, as fully one in being as it is possible for a human to be with the "co-principle" (the trinitarian term). Through the resurrection, which is the completion of Jesus in nature and in grace, he becomes the full realization of divinity in humanity, i.e., the realization of the Son, who with the Father is co-principle of the Holy Spirit. The Father had bestowed the Holy Spirit, Spirit of Sonship, in all fullness on him precisely so that, realizing this grace in his life and death, he might in turn become the source of the same Spirit for all humans. However, the divinity of Christ, as divinity realized in humanity, cannot simply be equated in every respect with that of the Father, which is divinity given. Hence the sending of the Spirit by Christ must be related to, rather than simply identified with, the sending of the Spirit by the Father.

The authority by which Christ sends the Holy Spirit is that which he acquires as Son of God realized in humanity. Here we must show between Jesus and other humans a contrast which applies both to earthly life and to life after death. An ordinary person can only intercede with God (the Father) to send the Holy Spirit upon his neighbor, but Christ has the authority actually to send the Holy Spirit. Jesus is affirmed in Heb 7:25 to be a constant intercessor in heaven with the Father on behalf of humans, but the same text asserts that he is an intercessor in a unique sense, viz., in that he can save humans. The authority of Jesus was a datum of his consciousness even in his earthly life, though its basis was not objectified by him in the precise way that it later was in the Church. This consciousness is evident in his earthly life in, e.g., the fact that he forgave sin (Mk 2:5 and parallels; Lk 7:48). (This forgiveness, as we shall soon see, involved a limited sending, or giving, of the Holy Spirit.)

From what has been said, the importance of differentiating accurately between divine and human roles in the sending of the Holy Spirit will be clear. As to the roles specifically of the Father and Christ in this action, the difference is expressed in the statement that the role of the Father is purely divine while that of Christ is theandric; but when it comes to describing these roles with the aid of particular terms, we find it necessary to divide these into three categories. The first is that comprising terms that apply to both the Father and Christ, but analogously, the analogy residing in the fact that while each is divine, in the case of the Father the divinity is given and in the case of Christ it is realized in humanity. Thus, e.g., it is said of the Father and Christ that each "sends" the Holy Spirit, but here the Father acts as the simply divine principle while Christ acts as Son of God in humanity. The second category is that comprising terms that apply to the Father alone, and therefore not at all to Christ. This is possible because these terms pertain only to the aspect in which the Father differs from Christ, mentioned above. Thus, e.g., in the sending of the Holy Spirit only the Father "regenerates" humans as sons and daughters (Tit 3:4-6). Finally, the third category is that comprising terms which for the sake of clarity we restrict by definition to the Father in his given divinity. Thus, e.g., when we say that Christ sends the Holy Spirit but that only the Father bestows him, we restrict "bestow" to indicate only the appropriate action of the Father in his pure divinity, whereas of itself the word could just as easily be used as a synonym for "send" in the sense in which Christ is said to send the Spirit. However, this is not arbitrariness or nominalism. There is a basis in fact for thus restricting and differentiating, viz., that ultimately God (the Holy Spirit) is given (bestowed) by him who is purely and simply God (the Father).

Such words as "communicate," "give" and "anoint" belong to the first category. Each assumes that Christ himself possesses the Holy Spirit and asserts that he imparts him in his own way to humans. Let us take each word in turn. While "communicate" clearly belongs to this category, we should bear in mind that "self-communication" belongs to the second category, because "self" stands for the Father, who communicates himself to humans in the two modalities of Incarnation and grace. With regard to "give," in the Letter to the Ephesians there is a passage (4:7-13) in which "give" is used presumably of Christ in the context of grace. We note that Scripture, speaking of the Holy Spirit (and not, therefore, of the precise biblical concept "grace," i.e., favor) in relation to "give," "gift," etc., always has him given by the Father (cf. Lk 11:13; Jn 3:34; 4:10; 14.16; Acts 8:18-20; 11:15-17; 15:8; Rom 5:5; 1 Cor 12:8; 2 Cor 1:22; 5:5; 1 Jn 3:24), never by Christ. Surely, this is no accident. For this reason, and also because it is so close in meaning to "bestow," "give" is best assigned to the third category.[1] A scrutiny of the Ephesians passage reveals that it is by no means certain that the giver of grace in v.7 is not the Father, and that in any case the "gift" of vv.7 and 11, where the giver is clearly Christ, is identified in v.11 as simply the allotment of different vocations in the Church. With regard to "anoint," we shall see soon from the sources that there is ample justification for regarding Christ as anointer of humans with the Holy Spirit.

Grace, understood theologically as the Holy Spirit coming to humans in the economy of salvation, may be considered as the grace of God (the Father) (over 50 times in Scripture) in as much as the Father bestows the Spirit on humans in grace; as the grace of Christ (about 20 times in Scripture) in as much Christ sends the Spirit to humans; and (though the expression does not occur in Scripture, the closest to it being "the Spirit of grace" [Heb 10:29]) as the grace of the Holy Spirit in as much as the Holy Spirit in his economic involvement is grace. There is something to be said for each designation, and none can claim exclusivity. To call grace the grace of Christ emphasizes an aspect of Christianity that is basic to it, viz., that it is primarily not a system but a cult centring on a historical person, Jesus of Nazareth, who was confessed as the Christ. But to call grace the grace of God, where "God" stands for "Father,"[2] places this Christocentricity in perspective. Christ belongs at the centre of the religion that bears his title

---

1   Hence we cannot agree with the ICEL translation of the words *a te, Pater, misit Spiritum Sanctum, primitias credentibus* in the Fourth Eucharistic Prayer as "he (Christ) sent the Holy Spirit from you, Father, as his first gift to those who believe." The fact that in reference to Jn 15:26 Christ is said here to send the Holy Spirit from the Father makes the Holy Spirit the gift of the Father rather than of Christ. Further, if the biblical image of gift is to be used at all, the biblical usage of always having the Father as the giver should be respected. In any case, the biblical image of first fruits in the Latin, reflecting Rom 8:23 (where the first fruits of the Spirit are given not by Christ but by the Father [cf. v.14]), is exchanged arbitrarily in the translation for the image of gift.

2   Cf. K. Rahner, "Theos in the New Testament," *Theological Investigations* 1 (London, 1961) 79-148.

(or name) only in the sense that he is "the way," that no-one comes to the *Father* except by him (Jn 14:6). True, grace is merited and mediated by Christ, and conforms humans to him, but primordially it is the grace of the Father, and ultimately its purpose is to make humans *his* sons and daughters. Finally, to call grace the grace of the Holy Spirit is to focus attention on the "forgotten" person of the Trinity, *in* whom the Father conforms humans to his Son.

The differentiation of the roles of the Father and Christ in the sending of the Holy Spirit should not lead us to conceive this sending as two categorial actions, laid, as it were, side by side. This can be seen immediately from their nature, i.e., the fact that one is transcendental, i.e., emanating from God in his pure divinity, and the other theandric. The precise relationship of Christ and the Father in regard to the sending of the Holy Spirit is expressed in the statement that the sending of the Spirit by Christ, both upon the Church at Pentecost and to individuals thereafter, is the *sacrament* of his bestowal by the Father. That is to say, the sending of the Spirit by Christ is the perceptible, experienced act, flowing from the humanity of Christ (theandric), in which the invisible (transcendental) sending by the Father is signified and accomplished; and the mode in which this sending by the Father is given is the bestowal in which the Church is constituted as such and individuals are regenerated as children of God.

In relation to the sending of the Holy Spirit in grace it is necessary to speak also of the offer of grace. Like "send", the term "offer" in this context belongs to the first of the three categories that we have distinguished above. The sending of the Holy Spirit by the Father is both visible and invisible, visible in that it is made through the sending by Christ (per Filium), invisible in that, remaining so, it is accomplished in the sacrament of the sending by Christ (Filioque), thus exemplifying in the economic order the statement of Aquinas about the Trinity in itself, that the Holy Spirit proceeds from the Father both mediately and immediately. The offer of grace by the Father, however, can only be perceptible, not imperceptible, since an offer must be experienced as such. However, the transcendence of the Father is not jeopardized here, since the perceptibility of his offer comes from the fact that it is made in that of Christ.

"Offer" and "send" are also to be contrasted, in that the offer of grace presupposes a free human will to which the offer is made in such a way that it can be either accepted or rejected, whereas the sending of the Holy Spirit presupposes acceptance. However, even when conceived categorially, i.e., as done by Christ, offering and sending are not to be distinguished as though they were two distinct and successive actions. To do this would be to succumb to Semi-Pelagianism, which sees the effectiveness of God's grace as dependent on its acceptance by humans. Offering and sending are the numerically one action of Christ, but the distinction recognizes the existence of two elements, the sovereignty of God and the freedom of humans, that are present in every interaction of God and humans in grace. To speak of the offer of grace implies the freedom of humans; to speak of sending the Holy Spirit implies the sovereignty of God. We do not suggest that this terminology helps toward the solution of a problem that not only remains unsolved but, as we shall later show, is insoluble in principle. It is precisely because the two elements cannot be included in a single synthesis that it is necessary here to distinguish between sending and offering, not in themselves but in their outcome, i.e., according as the offer is in fact accepted or not. Thus we may say simply that the offer of grace by Christ is the sacrament of its bestowal by the Father, or, more comprehensively, that the offer of grace by Christ, if accepted, is the sending of the Holy Spirit by him, and this in turn is the sacrament of the bestowal of the Holy Spirit by the Father.

In the revelation of the Trinity there was no offer, but simply the bestowal, of grace. This we see firstly in the Incarnation, where there was no human will in existence to receive the offer of grace, but where the will itself was created by the Father's bestowal of the Holy Spirit, which in its utter radicalness created and sanctified the humanity of Jesus and joined it in person to the divine Son. However, we do not rule out all cooperation of human free will in the acceptance of the grace of the Incarnation. Though there was no offer of this grace to Jesus, the offer was made to humankind to accept it as the grace of its salvation. This was the offer made to Mary and accepted by her (cf. Lk 1:38) on behalf of humankind and particularly of the future Church, which she then began to represent. The uniqueness of Mary among the saints is attributed not just to the fact that she was the physical mother of Jesus but to the fact that in faith she accepted on behalf of believers God's offer of salvation to humans (cf. Mk 3:35) and lived her whole life in the light of this faith.

Secondly, in the formation of the Church at Pentecost there was no offer of grace to the community as such but simply its bestowal. Of course, the grace by which the community was formed was offered to individuals, since ultimately all grace, even that destined for the community, must be borne by individuals. This grace could have been refused by those to whom it was offered, but divine providence ensured, as it still ensures, that without violation of individual freedom sufficient people accepted it for the community to come into being and to continue. But here too there was an individual human will which cooperated in the bestowal of grace on the community, viz., that of Jesus. In the exercise of his human will in his life and death, Jesus ratified by his obedience to the Father (cf. Heb 5:8) the grace he had been given at the Incarnation. This obedience involved the assumption by him of responsibility before God for the salvation of humans. The acceptance by the Father of the obedience of Jesus gave effect to this assumption of responsibility, and so made the grace of Jesus the grace of the Church. This idea is contained seminally in the traditional teaching that Jesus merited his own glorification and the grace given to humans. It is clear from this that in the formation of the Church as an act calling for the interaction of God and humans, the human cooperation came not from the community as such but from Jesus in his obedience.

Thus is established a parallel between the sacred humanity and the Church. However, it should be remembered that while both were created by the bestowal of the Holy Spirit, they were not created in exactly the same way. The sacred humanity was created absolutely, from nothing, but the Church was created only relatively, i.e., from an existing group of humans. Hence, while the bestowal of the Holy Spirit in the former case had to be non-sacramental, in the latter it could have been, and in fact was, sacramental, i.e., accomplished in signs, despite the absence of an offer. In this case it was simply the *sending* of the Holy Spirit (by Christ) that was the sacrament of his bestowal by the Father.

The grace in which the Church was created at Pentecost, while including the grace of individuals, was the grace of the Church as such, the grace that assured its continuance and advancement. Foremost in this connection, because of its link with the Eucharist, is the special priesthood of bishops and priests. This is a particular participation in Christ's grace of headship, i.e., the grace by which he is the source of the Holy Spirit for others, viz., the Gift of the Holy Spirit made in all fullness to him by the Father at the Incarnation, realized in his human history, and consequently sent by him as his own Spirit to others at

Pentecost. The recipients of the above-mentioned participation in the grace of headship do not become simple multiples of Christ, for the grace is not given to them as it was to him. They merely participate, though in a stable way, in the grace that remains that of Christ himself. The participatory quality of this grace and their stability in it are guaranteed by the traditional teaching of the sacramental character received in ordination. Concretely, they receive with the Spirit of Christ a participation in his authority to send the Spirit to others, so that their sending of the Spirit is a participation in, and continuation of, his sending of the Spirit at Pentecost. It must be noted, however, that this apostolate and priesthood are fully effective only in conjunction with the lay apostolate and the priesthood to which it belongs, viz., the common priesthood, entered upon by baptism.[3]

Next after the special priesthood must be mentioned Christian marriage, the sacrament through which "the domestic Church"[4] is constituted by the same Spirit who constitutes the universal Church. The unity and indissolubility of marriage are guaranteed by the traditional teaching of the marriage bond. In addition to these "institutional" forms of grace, and serving the same end, are those specifications of the Gift of the Holy Spirit which technically are called charisms (cf. 1 Cor 12:28, 4-11; Eph 4: 11-13). A charism may be defined as "a gift or aptitude which is liberated and empowered by the Spirit of God and is taken into the ministry of building up the body of Christ which is the Church."[5] Because they have to do with the guidance of the Church, charisms too are participations in the headship of Christ, though in a different way from the special priesthood. While for the sake of clarity we have here contrasted community grace and personal grace, strictly speaking there is no such thing as purely personal grace. For example, the gift of tongues is presented in 1 Cor 14:4 as a personal grace, but that it has also a community dimension is evident from vv. 12-13 and 27-28. Even when given to a private individual, the Gift of the Holy Spirit has an orientation toward the community, which finds expression both in worship (particularly the Eucharist) and in the apostolate.

---

3   Cf. A. Grillmeier, *Commentary on the Documents of Vatican II* (ed. H. Vorgrimler) 1 (London, 1967) 156-9.

4   *Lumen Gentium* 11.

5   *Theological and Pastoral Orientations on the Catholic Charismatic Renewal* (Malines) (Notre Dame, Indiana, 1974) 5.

This brings us to our second task, an investigation, from the sources, of the theme of the anointing of humans with the Holy Spirit. This material has been covered by Mühlen in a different perspective.[6] To him we are indebted for most of the patristic references. We begin with the statements of Scripture on this subject.

The first biblical text is 2 Cor 1:21. We begin at v.19 and continue to v.22. "(19) For the Son of God, Jesus Christ, whom we preached among you, Silvanus and Timothy and I, was not Yes and No; but in him it is always Yes. (20) For all the promises of God find their Yes in him. That is why we utter the Amen through him, to the glory of God. (21) But it is God who strengthens us with you in Christ, and has anointed us; (22) and he has put his seal upon us and given us his Spirit in our hearts as a guarantee."

Mühlen makes the following comments on the text, in dependence on de la Potterie.[7] It is commonly agreed that v.21 is set in the context of baptism. The Greek text has the juxtaposition of two pairs of participles joined by "and": "strengthening" and "having anointed," and "having sealed" and "having given," the second pair pertaining to baptism, the first to the acquisition of the faith that leads to baptism. Anointing, therefore, pertains to the action of God that brings about the faith necessary for baptism. It is therefore a spiritual anointing, which is manifest in the response of faith. We may conclude that this anointing is a participation in that of Jesus (although his was not brought about in the same way), since for the only time in his writings Paul has used the verb "to anoint," and this immediately after saying "Christ," which means "Anointed." Though the title is not used in this meaning here, it is apparently its use that has on this occasion moved Paul to speak of the anointing of Christians. The fact that "anoint" is in the aorist tense and "strengthen" in the present is significant. As the meanings of the words themselves also suggest, the anointing is a single completed action, the strengthening an ongoing process. The anointing, therefore, has to do with the first acquisition of faith, and the strengthening with the action of God in keeping it alive from that point on. The single action is identified in v.19 as the preaching of Jesus Christ, the Son of God. This is not just words about Christ, it is the Corinthians' faith-evoking encounter with him that took place in preaching. The result of this encounter is union with Christ (cf. I Cor 12:12-13; Heb 3:14;

---

6   Cf. H. Mühlen, *Una Mystica Persona* (Paderborn, 1968) 224-42.

7   I. de la Potterie, "L'onction du chrétien par la foi", *Biblica* 40 (1959) 12-69.

6:4), which is brought about by the bestowal of the Spirit. Though the text links this union and the gift of the Spirit, it does not present their connection as intrinsic, as I Cor 12:12 does with the aid of the image of body-spirit unity, perhaps because here the Spirit is conceived simply as that of the Father. Here the anointing of Christians is not specifically a sharing in the prophethood of Christ, whose own anointing is so presented elsewhere in the New Testament (Luke), but rather is linked with their personal salvation.

To these observations it should be added that the anointer is God (the Father), and that while the ointment is not identified, there is ground for taking it to be the Holy Spirit, since it is he who is said to be given as a guarantee. Also, the solidarity with Christ initiated by the anointing is presented as solidarity precisely with the Son of God, so that, while this is not stated in the text, the anointing is directed to a participation in Christ's divine Sonship. Finally, while no active role is ascribed to Christ in the text, it may be concluded that he too, in his own way, is the anointer, since the anointing takes place in his personal contribution to the encounter that happens when he is preached.

We turn now to the second, and last, biblical text, 1 Jn 2:20, 27, and we shall begin from v.18. "(18) Children, it is the last hour; and as you have heard that antichrist is coming, so now many antichrists have come; therefore we know that it is the last hour. (19) They went out from us, but they were not of us; for if they had been of us, they would have continued with us; but they went out, that it might be plain that they all are not of us. (20) But you have an anointing from the Holy One, and you all know. (21) I write to you, not because you do not know the truth, but because you know it, and know that no lie is of the truth. (22) Who is the liar but he who denies that Jesus is the Christ? This is the antichrist, he who denies the Father and the Son. (23) No one who denies the Son has the Father. He who confesses the Son has the Father also. (24) Let what you heard from the beginning abide in you. If what you heard from the beginning abides in you, then you will abide in the Son and in the Father. (25) And this is what he has promised us, eternal life. (26) I write this to you about those who would deceive you; (27) but the chrism which you received from him abides in you, and you have no need that anyone should teach you; as his chrism teaches you about everything, and is true, and is no lie, just as it has taught you, abide in him."

The word we have translated "anointing" in v.20 is actually the word for chrism, but in the context of the verse it clearly stands for the act of anointing, whereas in v.27 it stands for chrism since it is said to abide. From v.20 it is not clear whether the anointer, called the Holy One, is the Father or Christ. However, in v.27 the chrism is probably to be said to come from Christ, since the person from whom it is declared to be received is most likely the same as the one who in v.25 promises eternal life, and this is clearly Christ. On this interpretation the Holy One would be Christ. The majority of commentators holds that the chrism is to be identified as the Holy Spirit. Mühlen, depending on de la Potterie, discusses this question, which is put as a choice between the alternatives of the Holy Spirit and the genuine preached word of Christ. The majority opinion is based on the fact that the chrism bestows knowledge of all things, which is the function Jesus attributes to the Paraclete in Jn 14:17,26; 15:26; 16:13. On the other hand, the chrism is said to be true and no lie, which would indicate that it is the truth of Christ, presented in the word of preaching. A further indication is that what is said in v.24 to "abide" is what was heard from the beginning, i.e., the word, and that in v.27 it is the chrism that is said to abide. De la Potterie offers the middle position: "The oil of anointing is indeed the word of God, not, however, in so far as it is preached exteriorly in the community, but in so far as it is received by faith in the heart and remains active there, thanks to the action of the Spirit."[8] The text of 1 John does not contain a complete theology of anointing, but the elements are there. De la Potterie has synthesized them, not, however, completely. We suggest that they can be synthesized into a theology that goes beyond the coinciding actions postulated by de la Potterie. The preached word, filled with the presence of Christ through the power of the resurrection, is the *sacrament* in which he, through his minister, offers the Holy Spirit to humans, and in which the Father bestows the same Spirit on those who respond to the offer in faith. The Spirit is the Father's gift, a gift which in its giving enables the free act, faith, by which it is received, so that faith too is his gift, and indeed before it is the work of humans.

The process is aptly called anointing, for just as anointing with oil conveys health and energy, so does the word of preaching convey the Holy Spirit and the gift of faith. John has chosen the theme of anointing probably because he wants to make the distinction of those

---

8   Ibid. 44.

in whom faith has really taken root and those in whom it has not. Anointing, we recall, penetrates to the very bones of a person (Ps 109:18). This faith is that which dawns before baptism and leads to it, and so the anointing, as in the previous text, is a spiritual anointing before baptism. The presence of this faith is normally, but not infallibly, signified by baptism. The false teachers too had been baptised, but unlike the Christians who remained, had not been anointed, a fact that stood revealed in their departure. The idea of anointing is reinforced by that of "abiding," in which personal appropriation and interiority are conveyed. As in the previous text, the Christian's encounter is not just with words, but with Christ himself, so that through the anointing the believer abides in Christ. This is the Johannine way, redolent of the branches abiding in the vine of Christ (Jn 15:1-11), of speaking of solidarity with Christ, brought about through the anointing. The trinitarian dimension of grace emerges clearly from the text. If Christ conveys the Spirit, the Spirit in turn establishes union with Christ the Son, and the person who has the Son also has the Father.

If we leave aside for the moment the particular theme of anointing with the Holy Spirit, we may state that the more general theme of the role and works of the Holy Spirit according to the New Testament has been investigated quite fully, and therefore it will be sufficient for us to make only passing reference to it here. The Holy Spirit is sent by the Father, but also by Christ in so far as the Father's saving work is accomplished in him. Speaking of the following as works of the Holy Spirit, R. Koch asks, "What effects do the Pauline new creation or the Johannine rebirth entail?" to which he replies, "Above all, sonship of God, the victorious act of faith, burning love for the brethren and the bearing of inspired witness."[9] To this familiar list we would add one further effect, viz., the forgiveness of sins, and as it has not received a great deal of attention, we shall now offer some comment on it.

According to Is 43:25 God alone can forgive sins. The hearers of Jesus had this in mind when they said, "Why does this person speak thus? It is blasphemy! Who can forgive sins but God alone?" (Mk 2:7 and parallels). The forgiveness of sins is an act of divine power, and therefore an act of the Spirit of God, in which the messianic, and hence eschatological, renewal was to be accomplished (cf. Ezek 36:26). Hence we are not surprised to find in the New Testament that it is

---

9 "Spirit," *Encyclopedia of Biblical Theology* (ed. J.B. Bauer) 3 (London, 1970) 885.

through the Holy Spirit, borne and sent in all fullness by Jesus the Messiah, that the forgiveness of sins takes place. If this theme is less than prominent in the New Testament, it is perhaps because greater stress is laid there on the more positive works of the Holy Spirit. Even so, the following case can be made from the New Testament.

Bearing in mind that in the Pauline theology Christ and the Church are mediated to each other by the Spirit, we see that when Paul has the Father reconciling humans to himself through Christ (Rom 5:10-11) in the Church's ministry of preaching (2 Cor 5:18-19) received by humans in faith (Rom 3:25), the forgiveness of sins contained in this reconciliation must be accomplished in the Holy Spirit. Further, if in the Pauline theology faith is brought about by the action of the Holy Spirit (which is not just a conclusion of the last argument but can be shown independently), the forgiveness of sins which takes place in justification by faith must also be the work of the Spirit. Hence this theology leads to the conclusion that the forgiveness of sins is a work of the Holy Spirit sent by Christ from the Father.

In the Johannine theology we find an explicit linking of the sending of the Holy Spirit and the forgiveness of sins, in Jn 20:22-23: "And when he had said this, he breathed on them, and said to them, 'Receive the Holy Spirit. If you forgive the sins of any, they are forgiven; if you retain the sins of any, they are retained'" (cf. Acts 2.38). Commenting on another Johannine text, Jn 1:29, S. Lyonnet observes that for the Fourth Gospel Christ has come to take away the sin of the world "in the sense that he communicates to man the Holy Spirit—we shall understand later that he does this by the Cross—and thus gives him the strength to sin no more."[10]

The fact that Jesus forgave sins in his lifetime implies a certain sending of the Spirit by him even then, as the two are inseparably linked by Scripture, as we have just seen. However, according to the Fourth Gospel, Jesus showed awareness that the full eschatological gift of the Spirit through him lay in the future and was dependent on the outcome of his life (cf. Jn 7:39). This can only mean that while the divine Sonship remained only imperfectly realized in him, i.e., while he yet lived, any sending of the Spirit by him was necessarily limited, merely a foretaste of the eschatological gift.

---

10   S. Lyonnet, "Péché. IV. Dans le Nouveau Testament," *Supplément au Dictionnaire de la Bible*, Fascicle 38 (Paris, 1963) 492.

In the theology that we draw from the New Testament we see the forgiveness of sins and divine filiation as the principle results, negative and positive respectively, of the sending of the Holy Spirit by Christ. Under these can be subsumed the other effects mentioned by Koch. Faith and neighbor-love we have already related to each other as the one basic religious attitude now in its direct reference to God, now in its encompassment of the neighbor as well. Testimony is the expression of faith for the edification of the neighbor, and therefore a work of neighbor-love. Faith and divine filiation we have already related as respectively the act and the being of the one reality. The great social operation of the Holy Spirit, the creation and the sustenance of the Church, is by no means overlooked in this synthesis, for when faith becomes neighbor-love there is set in motion a dynamism that comes to rest only in the full communion of humans with each other in Christ, which is the Church; and divine filiation, it should always be remembered, is a social as well as a personal reality, i.e., fiiliation in the Son. The forgiveness of sins is an important work of the Holy Spirit, for human beings are found by God not friendly or even neutral, but hostile and averted, so that their movement of faith toward God under the impulse of the Holy Spirit must have conversion as its first moment, which implies the forgiveness of sins on the part of God as the first moment of his gift of filiation in the Spirit. Since in the New Testament the anointing of humans with the Holy Spirit is directed to the creation of faith, we are justified, in developing a theology of this anointing, to see it as resulting in the two-sided gift of which we have been speaking, the forgiveness of sins and divine filiation.

Turning now to the Fathers, we take our first text from St. Ignatius of Antioch to the Ephesians, 17,1: "The Lord received ointment on his head in order to breathe incorruption on the Church. Be not anointed with the stench of the teaching of the prince of this world; may he not lead you away captive from the life set before you. Why do we not all become wise, having received the knowledge of God, that is Jesus Christ? Why do we perish in foolishness, not recognizing the gift which the Lord has truly sent?"[11]

The words about the Lord receiving ointment on his head are a reference to the Gospel story of the anointing of Jesus by a woman, who remains unnamed in Matthew (26:6-13) and Mark (14:3-9) and is identified as Mary, sister of Lazarus and Martha, in John (12:1-8).

---

11   PG 5, 657.

In Mark and Matthew it is the head of Jesus that is anointed, while in John it is the feet. Ignatius has followed the former version in this respect probably because he wants to bring out the continuity of the anointing of Christ by God and the anointing of the Church by Christ. This he does by having the anointed head of Jesus itself breathe incorruption on the Church. In Mark and John the ointment is specified as nard, which is aromatic and used for embalming. Hence Ignatius's statements about incorruption for the Church and the stench of false doctrine. The intended contrast is between fragrance and incorruption on the one hand (qualities connected with nard) and stench and corruption on the other. As we have intimated, the anointing to which Ignatius refers is a symbol of the invisible and spiritual anointing which Jesus received from God.

The first sentence, in saying that Jesus breathed incorruption on the Church, refers to Jn 20:22, where Jesus is said to have breathed on the disciples and said, "Receive the Holy Spirit." The inference is that the anointing that Jesus himself received in order to be able to do this was itself an anointing with the Holy Spirit, and that the breathing of incorruption on the Church by Jesus was an anointing by him with the Holy Spirit. Here as well as in the New Testament we find the connection of this anointing with the acquisition of faith and the connection of faith with life, presumably the "eternal life" of the Fourth Gospel, in contrast to the death brought by false doctrine. We note that this life-giving knowledge of God surpasses the level of mere knowledge and is identified with the actual person of Jesus Christ. This can be understood only in the light of the Pauline doctrine that the Spirit is the mode of presence and operation of the risen Lord. The Holy Spirit is again referred to obliquely at the end, where Ignatius speaks of the gift truly sent by Christ. The use of the very personal verb "send" strongly suggests that this is the Holy Spirit, as would also the noun "gift" were it not for the fact that in the New Testament this particular word (*charisma*) is restricted to created gifts while another word (*dōrea*) is used for the Holy Spirit; but even so, it remains reasonably clear that the gift meant here is the Holy Spirit. The gift is recognized in the word of true doctrine by which it is conveyed.

We move now to St. Clement of Alexandria, beginning with his *Cohortatio ad gentes*. The first text is as follows: "I shall anoint you with the oil of faith, by which you put off corruption; I shall show you the bare pattern of righteousness by which you mount to God."[12] The speaker is identified previously as Jesus, so therefore it is clear that he is the anointer. We note again the link between this anointing and the acquisition of faith, though the word of preaching by which faith is roused is not mentioned. As with Ignatius, anointing is understood with the aid of the idea of embalming. The anointing, it is said, bestows incorruption. Thus material anointing and its result, incorruption, are made the symbols of the spiritual realities of faith and its result, eternal life. With the anointing is linked assimilation to Jesus, "the bare pattern of righteousness," which in turn raises humans up to union with God. While this is the work of the Holy Spirit, in fact he is not mentioned in the text.

The context of the passage provides useful additional material. Thus, incorruption is described as "grace;" further, Jesus is made to say that he will give graciously "the Word, knowledge of God, my whole self." Again we see the effort to go beyond mere knowledge. The knowledge of God that Jesus imparts conveys his whole self to the believer. This is intelligible only if the word of Christian teaching, in its authority and its direct relation to the sacred humanity, conveys the Holy Spirit as mode of presence and operation of the risen Lord. Jesus is spoken of as "Christ," which in this precise context suggests that the anointing he gives is a participation in his own. The idea of assimilation to him is expressed in words different from those of the text: "I want to renew you according to the archetype so that you become like me."

The next text, also from Clement, is from *Paedagogus*, 11, 8, and is a comment on the gospel incident of the anointing of Jesus by the woman in the Lukan (Lk 7:36-50) and Johannine versions, in which it is the feet of Jesus, and not the head, that are anointed. The text is as follows: "And not to press the matter too far, the anointed feet of the Lord are the Apostles receiving a share in the Holy Spirit according to the prophetic word about the fragrance of the ointment."[13] The prophetic word appears to be Jn 12:3b: "... and the house was filled with the fragrance of the ointment." This is prophetic in the sense that just as the fragrance filled the whole house (*oikia*), so did the teaching of the Apostles fill the whole world (*oikumene*) (a reference to Rom 10:18 and Ps 19:4 to which allusion is made several times in the context of the passage), and this because the anointing which Jesus him-

12   PG 8, 241.
13   PG 8, 465.

self received from God filled his whole body from head to foot, which is to say, on the spiritual level, that the anointing received by Jesus, head of the body (the Church), spread down to the Apostles, the feet of the body.

The anointing of the Apostles, for which the anointing of the feet of the Lord is symbolic, involves, we are told, a "share" in the Holy Spirit. This suggests that the anointing of Jesus himself was with the *fullness* of the Spirit. There is, in any case, a spreading of anointing from Jesus to the Apostles, and then a spreading of the word and of faith from them to believers throughout the world. But it is clear from elsewhere in Clement's writings that he regarded preaching as an anointing: "'… but the word of the Lord remains,' having anointed the soul and united it to the spirit."[14] The anointing of Jesus with the Holy Spirit, then, spread as a partial anointing to the Apostles and from them, through their preaching, to believers throughout the world.

The next text is from Origen, the *Contra Celsum*, VI: "Thus, knowing that Christ has come, we see that through him many christs have been made in the world, who, like him, loved righteousness and hated iniquity, and therefore God, the God of Christ, anointed them with the oil of gladness. But he, having loved righteousness and hated iniquity more than did his companions, received the first fruits of this anointing, and as it were, the whole anointing of the oil of gladness. But his companions, each according to his capacity, shared in his anointing. Wherefore, since Christ is the head of the Church, so that Christ and the Church make one body, the oil has gone down from the head to the beard—the symbol of the perfect man—of Aaron, and this oil, going down, reached to the collar of his robe."[15]

In this text Origen has applied the familiar Ps 45:7 to Christ in comparison with his followers. He wants to affirm at the same time the uniqueness of Christ's anointing and the solidarity of Christians with him in this anointing. The uniqueness is brought out by the statement that Jesus receives the first fruits of the anointing destined for humans. One is reminded of I Cor 15:20,23, where Paul has Christ as the first fruits among his companions. The first fruits of a harvest are a special part which can serve to represent the whole. The image therefore suits Origen's purpose well. However, it can also convey the incorrect impression that the anointing of Christ, for all its excellence,

14   PG 8, 1208.
15   PG 11, 1417.

is still only part of the anointing intended for humans. Origen therefore adds that Christ receives the whole of this anointing. Therefore the anointing of his companions can be understood only as a share in his anointing. To illustrate this difficult concept, Origen borrows from Ps 133:2 the image of the anointing of Aaron as high priest. He makes the head of Aaron stand for Christ, and his beard for Christians, or the Church. He legitimizes his choice of image by observing that a beard is the symbol of the perfect, i.e., the mature, man. This makes it suitable for illustrating something which is at the same time a profound and perfect unity in itself, viz., of Christ and Christians in the Church (this being intimated in the allusion to Col 1:18), and a unity with the perfect human, Christ, head of the Church. With the aid of this image one can easily grasp how Christ the head receives the whole of the anointing and how at the same time Christians can share in it according to their capacity. The one anointing, of the head, spreads to, and anoints also, the beard, and this thoroughly, so that the oil permeates right to the collar of the robe.

The context of the passage shows that the anointing is with the Holy Spirit, for the christs are declared to be "bodies filled with the divine Spirit." In the text it is God (the Father) who is the anointer and the one who unites Christians with Christ in the single anointing. In the image Christ himself is passive, and so it is not stated how the anointing spreads from him to Christians. However, the context shows that Origen's thought is by no means constricted to the limits set by the image, and indeed an active role for Christ does emerge. In allusion to Mal 4:2 he is said to be the sun of righteousness which sends out its rays to those who wish to receive it. Hence, though the image selected by Origen does not of itself allow one to conclude that Christ (as well as the Father) is the anointer of Christians, the wider context of the passage does permit this conclusion to be drawn.

We consider now a text from St. Irenaeus, *Adversus haereses*, III. Commenting on the baptism of Jesus in Matthew, he writes: "For Christ did not then descend on Jesus, nor indeed is Christ one person and Jesus another. But the Word of God, who is Savior of all and Ruler of heaven and earth, who is Jesus—as we have shown above— who both assumed flesh and was anointed by the Father with the Spirit, was made Jesus Christ." Having cited Is 11:1-4 and 61:1-2, he continues: "For according as the Word of God was a human from the root of Jesse and a son of Abraham, the Spirit of God rested on him and he was anointed to preach the Gospel to the poor." He concludes: "Therefore the Spirit of God descended on him, the Spirit of him who through the prophets had promised that he would anoint him, so that receiving of the abundance of his anointing, we might be saved."[16] In this text the Father is the anointer, the divine Word as human is the anointed one, and the Holy Spirit is the ointment. There is an unresolved clash of descending and ascending Christology ("the Word of God ... who both assumed flesh and was anointed by the Father with the Spirit"), and the question of whether the anointing is the same as the Incarnation is avoided by expressing the former in its functional orientation: "he was anointed to preach the Gospel." It is this very same anointing, in its abundance, which Christians receive when they respond in faith to this preaching, but for them (as distinct from Jesus) the anointing is orientated to salvation. While the Father remains the ultimate anointer, we may conclude that Christ too is the anointer of Christians, since it is the preaching of his word that conveys the anointing to them.

To conclude our treatment of the Greek Fathers on this question, we refer to our study of Cyril of Alexandria on the anointing of Jesus. In the fourth paragraph of the text quoted from his scholia *De incarnatione unigeniti* we saw Jesus as the one anointed by the Father with the Holy Spirit, who in turn anoints with the same Spirit those who respond to him in faith: "Therefore it was written, 'The Spirit came down upon Christ and remained on him.' Therefore the Word of God is called Christ, the Word who is a human for us and like us, and who came in the form of a slave. He was anointed humanly according to the flesh, but he anoints divinely with his own Spirit those who believe in him."[17]

Finally, we look briefly at two Latin Fathers on this question, Tertullian and St. Augustine. In his treatise *Ad martyras* Tertullian speaks of "your master, Jesus Christ, who has anointed you with the Spirit."[18] Jesus himself, as Tertullian says in his *De baptismo*, "was anointed with the Spirit by God the Father."[19] As Tertullian believed

---

16 *Sancti Irenaei Libros quinque adversus Haereses* (ed. W. Harvey) 2 (Cambridge, 1857) 32-33 (PG 7, 871-72).

17 PG 75,1372.

18 " ... epistates uester Christus Iesus, qui uos Spiritu unxit, ..." CCSL 1, 5 (PL 1, 624).

19 " ... spiritu unctus est a deo patre ..." CCSL 1, 282 (PL 1, 1207).

that Jesus bore the Spirit in all fullness,[20] the anointing of Christians by Christ must have been a participation in his own anointing by the Father.

The last text is taken from St. Augustine's Exposition of Psalm 26. "In two persons (the king and the priest) was prefigured the single future king and priest, one Christ with the office of each, called Christ from the chrism. But not only was our head anointed, but his body also, i.e., ourselves. He is king because he rules and leads us, and priest because he intercedes for us. And indeed he was the only priest who was also the sacrifice. The sacrifice he offered to God was none other than himself. For he would not find apart from himself a most pure spiritual victim, he who like an immaculate lamb redeems us by the shedding of his blood, incorporates us into himself, and makes us his members, so that in him we too might be Christ. Therefore anointing belongs to all Christians; ... This anointing will perfect us spiritually in that life which is promised us. ... For we are anointed now in sign, and by the sign itself is prefigured something of what we shall be. And we must desire some ineffable future thing, and groan in the sign, so that we may rejoice in that thing which is prefigured by the sign."[21]

While mentioning chrism, the text gives no hint as to who or what it is. Nor does it say whether the anointing of Jesus took place at his conception or glorification, though the priesthood to which he is said to be anointed is clearly linked with his death. However, it is valuable for its testimony to the anointing of Christians. While this is not detailed, it does at least affirm that they are anointed through their union with Christ the anointed one, the union being presented in terms of the mystical body. Further, Christ is said to incorporate them into himself, though how this is done is not stated, beyond that it is through the power of his death. Christ draws those destined to belong to him to share in the anointing he himself received from God. One is entitled to conclude from this that Christ, as well as the Father, is the anointer of Christians. Lastly, the sacramental and saving nature and the eschatological orientation of the anointing of Christians are affirmed in the text, as well as the transcendental character of the response of faith made categorially to the sign by which the anointing is done.

---

20   Cf. W. Bender, *Die Lehre über den Heiligen Geist bei Tertullian* (Munich, 1961) 103-07.

21   CCSL 38, 154-55 (PL 36, 199-200).

We are brought thus to our third task, a summary of our theology of grace to this point. In presenting this, we distil some conclusions from our study of the New Testament and the Fathers just completed, and combine them with the major conclusions of the earlier parts of our work.

From our study it is clear that "anoint" is a first category word, i.e., it applies in analogous senses to the action of both God the Father and Christ. The Father anoints with the Holy Spirit both Jesus and ordinary humans. When he anoints Jesus, it is by a radical act which creates (and is therefore non-sacramental) and sanctifies the sacred humanity and unites it in person to the pre-existent divine Son. When he anoints ordinary humans, he does so less radically. His act finds them already existing as (sinful) persons, and therefore it must be sacramental. The supreme sacrament in which he does this, subsuming all others, is Christ. In this act Christ himself acts, as the human who is Son of God. He anoints in that he authoritatively sends the Holy Spirit to humans, first by constituting the Church through the power of his death (Pentecost), and thereafter by his continuing ministry in this Church, where his offer of the Holy Spirit becomes a sending of him for those who respond in faith. The anointing by Christ is the sacrament of the anointing by the Father. There is no question here of two categorial acts. There is the one transcendental act, the communication of the Spirit of God to the spirit of humans, and the categorial mode, the sending by Christ, in which it is accomplished. The basis of this unity is the oneness of Jesus with God, given already as grace, the economic homoousion, in the Incarnation, and realized historically by Jesus in the obedience of his life and death. When the Father anoints humans, he forgives them their sins and re-creates them as his sons and daughters (in the Son) by the bestowal of the Spirit of filiation through the medium of their faith. Since Jesus received this Spirit in all fullness, the Father's action toward humans is not, nor can be, a new act of anointing, distinct from that by which he anointed Jesus, but is rather the embracing of them in that same act according as they respond in faith to the offer made by Christ. The Father's single act is directed in all its creative radicalness to Jesus, and from him to other humans in accordance with their response of faith to his offer. And as for Jesus the Father's act resulted in both an honor and a task, viz., unique divine Sonship and the work of salvation, so for humans it results also in honor and task, viz., participated divine filiation and a share in the apostolate.

The anointing of humans by the Father is a purely divine or transcendental act, since it is the communication by the Father of his Spirit to the spirit of the human being. Since no creature could be the medium of this act without reducing it, this communication must be direct. This, however, is no obstacle to its sacramentality. The role of Christ in this act is theandric, i.e., human-divine, which requires it to be human at base, and therefore categorial. When someone accepts the offer of Christ, it becomes for him a sending of the Holy Spirit by Christ. This, however, is the limit of Christ's function. We can say this in all confidence, for we know that the Holy Spirit as sent by him makes humans not his children, but those of the Father. This shows that the sending by Christ is no substitute for the sending, or bestowal, by the Father; nor is it a medium through which the Father's act is filtered. Sacrament of the Father's act, it draws this act into history, without destroying its transcendentality.

The offer and sending of the Holy Spirit by Christ in the Church is the authentic re-creation and presentation of the sign of Christ there, ultimately in ministry. In the texts we have studied this sign was, for reasons we have noted, the preaching of Christ in the ministry of word. This is clearly a presentation of Christ in his glorified humanity, since it is a development and specification of the Gospel, which is Christ's very word, and at the same time is filled with the power of the Spirit. However, what we say about preaching applies even more strongly to the ministry of sacrament. Like preaching, the seven sacraments are presentations of Christ in his glorified humanity. The relation of the ministry of word to that of sacrament in this special technical sense is, as we shall show in the next chapter, the ordering of a beginning precisely to its completion. The seven sacraments belong to the highest plane of ministry, which itself is an inclined plane, with the Eucharist at the highest point, since it presents Christ not under some particular aspect as do the other individual sacraments, but in all saving fullness. For this reason we shall consider it on its own in the chapter after next. Precisely as sign, sacrament as well as word should be taken into account in relation to the anointing of humans by Christ. He is the anointer, the sign is the ointment, and the Holy Spirit and faith, corresponding to health and energy in the original image, are what is conveyed. Christ anoints in word and sacrament in that these constitute a sign which in its meaning and challenge to faith is truly communicated to humans. The actual conveying of the Holy Spirit and faith in this anointing is explained by its sacramental character, for it is the sacrament of the action in which the anointer is now the Father and the ointment the Holy Spirit. Christ, therefore, anoints with the Holy Spirit only in the two following restricted senses: he authoritatively sends the Spirit; and this action is the sacrament in which the strict communication of the Spirit by the Father is accomplished. In the action of Christ we see, added to the transcendental character of grace, its free, historical and contingent character.

The sacramentality of grace is required by the composite nature of the human its recipient, i.e., as a composite of matter and spirit. While the body of a human cannot be a medium through which the Holy Spirit is filtered, it plays a necessary mediating role in the bestowal of the Spirit, in that the sign that serves as sacrament must be received in the bodily senses. Not only is grace acquired in this bodily way, but once acquired its presence is also expressed in bodily ways, in acts of virtue and especially of fraternal love. These actions of spiritual exchange, accomplished in the mediation of bodies, lead to the creation of community and even leave their mark on the lower world of material reality, the extension of the human body (cf. Acts 4:32). Not only is the community dimension of grace expressed at its fullest in the Eucharist, but this sacrament is the means by which the community, as Church, is summoned into full existence, celebrated as it is by virtue of a community grace, viz., priestly ordination. Thus we see Eucharist and Church, in their mutual relationship, as grace in its most intense visibility. In these acts the very nature of God stands revealed as he offers himself to humans.

It must be remembered, however, that it is the Son of God and indeed precisely in the man Jesus, and not the Holy Spirit or the Father, who is made visible. In itself grace, the Gift of the Holy Spirit, is invisible. It becomes visible only in its effects, viz., of drawing creatures into unity of being (the Incarnation), or union (grace), with the divine Son, the revelation of God, or into the condition of being a reflection of him (the world as affected by the grace of humans).

The theology of anointing is readily translated into a contemporary setting, for it corresponds closely to the theology of the self-communication of God. Thus, the anointing by the Father is the self-communication of the Father in his Spirit, in Incarnation and grace. It is explained in Scholastic categories by the theology of divine formal causality, as exercised by the Son (in the perspective of descending Christology), or by the Holy Spirit (in the perspective of ascending Christology).

It remains to relate what has been said to the Trinity. The anointing of Christians by Christ is seen first in its relation to the procession model of the Trinity, since the sending of the Spirit by Christ from the Father corresponds to the procession of the Spirit both Filioque and per Filium in the Trinity. As a person responds in faith, the Father bestows the Spirit on them, thus making them a child of God in participation of Christ. We are thus brought into the domain of the return model of the Trinity, whereby the Holy Spirit is conceived as bestowed by the Father and the Son on each other as their mutual love. Of course, as a human person, a human is unable to bestow the Holy Spirit; but what they do bestow on the Father is their love, which is human love raised to a new level through the Father's bestowal of the Holy Spirit on them. It is a love in the Holy Spirit, who thus becomes the bond between the new child of God and the Father. It is a created participation in the love of Christ for the Father, which in fact is the Holy Spirit. Because of the unity of love of God and love of neighbor, this love of Christ found expression in the sending of the Holy Spirit by him to humans. If humans are one in spiritual being with Christ through the one anointing by the Father, they are one with him also in act. His act was his unsurpassable love of God and neighbor which effected the reconciliation of God and humans. Their act is their indispensable personal conversion to God, which includes also love of neighbor, the whole in the medium of the Holy Spirit. It is at the same time included in Christ's act and inalienably their own. Its principal realization, subsuming all others, is the Eucharist.

This chapter can now be rounded off by the execution of our fourth and last task, the situation of the theology of grace just summarized in the framework of the fundamental biblical theology of covenant. Here we take up and complete our treatment of this theme in Part Two.

Jesus was the mediator of the new covenant (Heb 9:15; 12:24), the covenant in the Spirit (2 Cor 3:6). This was the eschatological covenant foretold by the prophets, in which the Spirit of God would be poured out on all humans (Joel 2:28-29). The early confession of Jesus as both suffering servant and Messiah facilitated this identification. A mediator had to be chosen and endowed with authority, and election for covenant resulted in a relationship of filiation to God (Deut 14:1-2; Ex 4:22; Hos 11:1), on the basis not of merits but of God's love (Deut 4:37-38; 7.6-7; 9:4-5). The attitude of the covenant partners, *hesed* and *hēn*, from which the idea of grace derives, we identify as the Holy Spirit himself, since it was he who, as the Father's love, was poured out in all fullness on Jesus in the Father's creative act of election, laying down the basis of his future merits, and he whom Jesus directed with authority to humans, calling for penance and answering love. The covenantal grace is therefore rightly identified as the Gift of the Holy Spirit. And because this Spirit is Spirit of filiation, the children of God by the covenant are such because made so by this Spirit. This is true both of Christ the unique Son, and others, who are sons and daughters in the Son. That the new covenant is enacted precisely in the death of Jesus is both stated in Scripture (Mt 26:28; Mk 14:24; Heb 9:15) and explained by the theology of death which we have invoked, whereby a human reaches full stature and effectiveness, in both nature and grace, precisely in death. The Eucharist, memorial of the death of Jesus, is the supreme form of the covenantal encounter between God and his new people in the Holy Spirit. We hope with this brief account to have shown that our theology of grace has the biblical theology of covenant as its matrix. And now, having discussed the sending of the Holy Spirit by Christ, we move on in the next two chapters to investigate the ways in which he sends the Spirit to humans today.

11 THE RANGE OF SACRAMENTS OF GRACE

In this chapter we consider briefly the range of sacraments of grace, i.e., the range of occasions when the offer of grace is made as the sacrament of its bestowal for those who accept. We begin with the humblest of these, viz., what we have called secular sacraments, and work through on an ascending scale, considering in turn the world religions, Judaism, and finally Christianity. The supreme sacrament of the Christian religion, the Eucharist, we reserve for special treatment in the next chapter.

We begin, therefore, with the fully secularized person, who has no religious allegiance and is not affected by religion in any way. There will also be, of course, those who, while uncommitted to religion, are motivated unconsciously by some residual form of it, but in considering the extreme case, which certainly occurs (particularly in places where religion has been suppressed and atheism propagated), we include the less extreme also. In the divine plan the means of grace for these secular people are secular sacraments, i.e., encounters undergone precisely in the world, in which the offer and the bestowal of grace take place.

According to Rahner,[1] in the events of life a person will often be challenged to perform an action or make a decision calling for real self-transcendence. When this happens, the real object of the act is God as he is in himself, and the act takes place under the influence of grace and is an act of faith fulfilling the requirements of Heb 11:6. This, of course is not apprehended "categorially" by the person in question, who will objectify the experience in quite different terms, perhaps

---

1   K. Rahner, "Anonymous Christians," *Theological Investigations* 6, 390-98; "Atheism and Implicit Christianity," *Theological Investigations* 9, 145-64; "On the Theology of Ecumenical Discussion," *Theological Investigations* 11, 24-67; "Anonymous Christianity and the Missionary Task of the Church," *Theological Investigations* 12, 161-78; "Observations on the Problem of the 'Anonymous Christian,'" *Theological Investigations* 14, 280-94; "Faith. I. Way to Faith," SM 2, 310a - 313b; "Missions. II. Salvation of the Non-Evangelized," SM 4, 79b – 81a.

even those of atheism. "Transcendentally," however, it is God who has been affirmed, and in saving faith. In addition to being both transcendental and categorial, i.e., real and complete, both theism and atheism can be either simply transcendental or simply categorial. It is the latter alternatives that are intended here with the terminology "transcendental" and "categorial." Rahner sees transcendental theism as present when, e.g., "a person undertakes and lives the duty of each day in the quiet sincerity of patience, in devotion to his material duties and the demands made upon him by the persons under his care,"[2] or affirms "indescribable joy, unconditional personal love, unconditional obedience to conscience, the experience of loving union with the universe, the experience of the irretrievable vulnerability of one's own human existence beyond one's own control, and so on."[3]

In Rahner's theology, however, more than simple theism is involved in acts of this kind: Christianity itself is involved, albeit in an anonymous form. Since "the Incarnation of God is the uniquely supreme case of the actualization of man's nature in general,"[4] when under the influence of grace a person affirms their own transcendence, they in fact affirm Christ in faith, even if on the conceptual level they do not know him, or, if they do, reject him. Such a person, then, is an "anonymous Christian." In this way Rahner integrates two biblical articles of faith, the necessity of faith in Christ for salvation and the universality of God's saving will, and he finds support for his theory in certain statements of the Second Vatican Council.[5]

Late in his career Rahner discovered a more satisfactory way of grasping and expressing this insight. It assumes not only that every person is permanently and constantly under the influence of grace, but that the uncreated dimension of this grace is the Holy Spirit as the Spirit of Christ, this latter expression being understood in a special sense to be explained. Rahner wrote, "Since the universal efficacy of the Spirit is directed from the beginning to the zenith of its historical mediation, which is the Christ event (or in other words the final cause of the mediation of the Spirit to the world), it can truly be said that this Spirit is everywhere and from the beginning the Spirit of Jesus Christ,

---

2   Rahner, "Anonymous Christians" 394.

3   Rahner, "Faith" 312.

4   Rahner, "Anonymous Christians" 393.

5   *Lumen gentium* 16; *Ad gentes* 7.

the incarnate divine Logos."[5] He expressed the special sense of "Spirit of Christ" by means of the Aristotelian term "entelechy," though in a sense different from that intended by Aristotle. For Rahner the word had the meaning it had acquired in the theology of his own day, which was "an intrinsic tendency" within something "by virtue of which it is orientated toward some goal."[7] Thus he could say, "From the beginning this Spirit is always and everywhere the entelechy of the history of revelation and salvation."[8] In other words, by the will of the Father the Holy Spirit is intrinsically directed to Christ, and inasmuch as he is bestowed on other humans, will lead them to Christ and incorporate them in different degrees into his Mystical Body. Even if not all thus influenced will arrive at this end with full intellectual appropriation, to the extent that they accept the divine prompting they will still achieve the end, though in an "anonymous" way only.[9]

In general, this theology of Rahner commends itself as consonant with the sources of revelation and with modern knowledge of the human person, and as reasonable in itself. We now offer two comments on it.

First, Rahner makes only the briefest reference to a factor which is of the highest importance, viz., that in the response of faith a person not only achieves fulfillment but averts loss: "A refusal of this offer would therefore not leave man in a state of pure unimpaired nature, but would bring him into contradiction with himself even in the sphere of his own being."[10] It must be remembered that much is at stake when for the first time a person is fully engaged by God in a sacrament of grace. If they accept the offer of grace, they become a child of God. However, the process is not a passage from a state of neutrality: it is rescue, salvation, from a state of aversion and sin in which they

---

6   Rahner, "Jesus Christ in the Non-Christian Religions," *Theological Investigations* 17, 46.

7   John Russell, "Entelechy," SM 2, 232b.

8   Rahner, "Jesus Christ in the Non-Christian Religions," *Theological Investigations* 17, 46.

9   This paragraph did not occur in the first edition of my book. It represents a later development in my thinking, for which see my articles, "The Spirit of Christ as Entelechy," *Philosophy & Theology* 13 (2001) 363-98, and "A Trinitarian Response to Issues Raised by Peter Phan," *Theological Studies* 69 (2008) 852-74.

10   Rahner, "Anonymous Christians" 393-94.

are imprisoned and which therefore (through concupiscence) impels them constantly to sinful self-affirmation, i.e., an affirmation of self that is at the same time a rejection of God in grace. The experience of grace, therefore, is one of liberation. On the other hand, if they refuse the offer, the refusal is the sinful self-affirmation just mentioned, and their condition of sinner is only deepened further.

Secondly, Rahner's theology raises the question of the sense (or senses) in which the grace given in secular sacraments (and hence also all grace except that given to Jesus himself) may be called grace of Christ. All grace is grace of the Father, in that he is the ultimate source of grace (cf. Jn 1:17). And all grace is grace of the Holy Spirit, in that it is he primarily who is given in grace, all created gifts given under this name being secondary or consequential upon his presence. Moreover all grace is grace of the divine Word or Son, in that he is present and operative in whatever sacrament is the vehicle of grace. This is so because every sacrament of grace presents a revelation, however partial or imperfect, of God, and it is the divine Word who is the revelation of God, just as in the Trinity he is the self-expression of God. In addition to all this, however, all grace is the grace of Christ. The key to understanding this statement is that the Holy Spirit, the one who primarily is given as grace, is always the Spirit of Christ as entelechy. Even if, for Christians, he is the one given them at Pentecost, he does not thereby cease to be Spirit of Christ as entelechy. As I wrote in an essay on the work of Peter Phan, "The change from the Spirit of Christ as entelechy to outpoured Spirit of Christ is wrought deep in the person of Jesus as the nub of his historical existence, and marks the completion and perfection of the Holy Spirit as Spirit of Christ. In other words, the two meanings of 'Spirit of Christ' are related: in the person of Jesus the Spirit of Christ as entelechy is completed and perfected as outpoured Spirit."[11] This more enlightened view enables us to answer an objection sometimes brought against Rahner's earlier theology, viz., that it embraces an idealized projection of the imagination, the "perfect human," rather than the actual person of Christ. For grace as here conceived directs us, by the will of the Father, not to a projection but to the historical personage of Jesus.

We conclude, therefore, that the person who meets God in a secular sacrament is engaged in an encounter in which the Son offers them the

---

11   David Coffey, "A Trinitarian Response to Issues Raised by Peter Phan" 864.

Holy Spirit in grace, and that if they respond positively they are linked both historically and eschatologically to Christ, so that the grace they receive is truly the grace of Christ.

In the more perfect sacraments of grace, to which we now turn, we find a growing aptness to evoke from the human person an affirmation of their transcendence, in that the sacrament approximates more and more in itself to the person who is thus affirmed, viz., Christ. This increasing approximation takes place in regard to both being and revelation, to the point where in the Incarnation there is real union of being between the Word and the sacrament, i.e., a hypostatic union of the Son and the sacred humanity, and the unsurpassable revelation of God is achieved.

The non-Judaic religions, e.g. Hinduism, Buddhism and Islam (which contains some elements of both Judaism and Christianity), constitute the next level of sacraments of grace. While they exceed purely secular sacraments in that they present explicitly religious truth, they possess less of such truth than does Judaism, and what truth they do possess is to some extent marred by error. Nor are they ordered as directly to Christianity as Judaism is, i.e., through a positive divine covenant destined to give way to a more perfect one. Nevertheless, they are ordered to Christianity, in that the partial religious truth that they contain is ordered to the total truth given at least potentially in the Incarnation. The truth possessed by these religions is the result of the sincere striving of humans after God, which striving is itself a response to his grace encountered sacramentally in their lives, grace that is surely given, since God wills the salvation of all. Their truth does not consist merely in the personal insights of individuals, but is formed within homogeneous traditions in which gifted and saintly people interact with each other and their communities over long periods to build up tested and reliable bodies of truth, which are thus fitted to be the principal sacraments of grace for those who belong to these religions.

On this matter the Second Vatican Council has said, "The Catholic Church rejects nothing that is true and holy in these religions. She looks with sincere respect upon those ways of conduct and of life, those rules and teachings which, though differing in many particulars from what she holds and sets forth, nevertheless often reflect a ray of that Truth which enlightens all men and women."[12] Thus these

---

12   *Nostra aetate* 2.

religions present, in the ways mentioned, signs of God, which, as we have explained in reference to secular sacraments, contain (more than these latter do) the presence of the divine Word, not, to be sure, as incarnate, but nevertheless as truly revelatory of God and in a saving way. They contain him in that they signify him (as God revealed), and thus present sacraments in which he acts as sent by the Father and as himself sending the Holy Spirit in grace. In these sacraments, therefore, the Son of God makes the offer of grace to humans, and when accepted it is the sacrament of the bestowal of the Holy Spirit in grace by the Father.

The body of Christian doctrine will have all the advantages that the teachings of the other religions have, as outlined above, but it has the all-important additional advantage that it rests ultimately on the beliefs and teachings of a man, Jesus of Nazareth, who was the Word of God incarnate. His religious convictions, which he imparted to his followers, pertained to his response, as a man situated historically in his community, to the grace given him by God, except that his grace was unique, viz., that of the Incarnation. This ensured that from him as "the unique, *supreme*, case of the total actualization of human reality,"[13] the fullness of religious truth would derive throughout the history of the Church under the guidance of the Holy Spirit. The other religions, including Judaism, lack this potential universality. They will always present the religious experience of individuals who, however gifted and graced, are less than God incarnate, and this limitation will also affect the quality of the contribution of their communities. Hence these religions are in principle unable to transcend the particular cultures of which they are to some extent the product and which they have helped to form, and their history has consistently shown that they have failed in their attempts to do this. Christianity, on the other hand, though constantly tempted to settle for identification with particular cultures, has shown on a number of important occasions that it has the innate power to break through the barriers of these cultures and establish itself as the truly universal, or catholic, religion. It has this power as a direct result of the Incarnation. To the extent, however, that Christianity is divided in itself, this power is weakened, for division fosters a detrimental kind of cultural identification.

---

13 K. Rahner, "On the Theology of the Incarnation," *Theological Investigations* 4 , 110.

Among the non-Christian religions Judaism occupies a special place, for the Jewish people were chosen by God to live in covenant with him and be prepared by his grace to produce Jesus Christ, mediator of the new and eternal covenant (cf. Heb 9:15; 13:20). As part of this preparation there was a continuing revelation, which reached its completion in Christ. In the revelation to Israel there was no union of being between God and the medium of revelation. The medium simply comprised distinct symbols that were expressive of God. Except on an understanding of revelation as purely verbal (which cannot be sustained), such union between the medium and God must first be given before distinction of persons in the Godhead can be apprehended. Speaking concretely, with the prophets there was never any question of such union between themselves and God, and so the question of distinction in God simply did not arise; but in the context of the accepted unity of Jesus with God, it was necessary for Jesus to distinguish himself from the Father, and thus (and only thus) could the distinction of Father and Son be made accessible. In the Trinity in itself, of course, this distinction is based on the necessary fact that the Son proceeds from the Father, but this is something known only as a result of the Incarnation. Hence the Incarnation is the ground given in the world for penetrating to the distinction of the Father and the Son in the Trinity. Likewise the sending of the Holy Spirit by Christ upon the termination of his earthly life is the ground given in the world for attaining to the knowledge of the Holy Spirit as a distinct divine person.[14] With hindsight the Christian may superimpose the distinction of Father and Son on the Old Testament, as the distinction of God and his Word, or of God revealing and God revealed, but they should

---

14   Recognizing that our entire grounds for distinguishing the persons of the Trinity are given in the world, we can all too easily conclude to a purely economic Trinitarianism, such as that of P. Schoonenberg (cf. *The Christ*, 83-86, especially note 16). This compromises the divine transcendence, and was already found inadequate when it occurred in the ancient Church in the theology of Marcellus, 4th c. bishop of Ancyra. It would likewise be a mistake to think that the truth of the Trinity in itself is fully expressed when we have said of it what can be said on the basis of its grounds given in the world. While the Trinity as revealed tells us true and important facts about the Trinity in itself, it by no means presents, or can present, the whole truth of the Trinity, which surpasses human intelligence and categories of thought.

remember that the ground for making this as a real distinction is given with Christianity, not with Judaism.

From the standpoint of Christianity, then, we may say that in the revelation to Israel the divine Word was present, as the (partial) revelation of the Father in the world, just as he is the self-utterance of the Father in the Trinity. He was present only in that the medium of revelation signified him (as God revealed), which admittedly it did relatively adequately (in comparison with other religions) because it resulted from his positive, free and gracious intervention into history. This kind of presence allowed for (without determining) a future complete presence, where he would be not only signified by the medium but also united in being with it, and this actually happened in the Incarnation, where the medium was the sacred humanity. Thus the Incarnation was, and is, the total possible revelation of God in the world. The revelation made to Israel was the means by which the Father, with and through the Son, sent the Holy Spirit in grace to the members of the Jewish faith. In its writings, teaching, religious services, etc., the Son made them the offer of grace, and, when accepted, this offer was for them the sacrament of its bestowal by the Father.

Not only was this so in the past, it is so also in the present, for the Old Law was abrogated (cf. Eph 2:15; Heb 10:9) only in the sense that in the divine economy it was surpassed and fulfilled by Christ (cf. Mt 5:17; 2 Cor 3:9-10). This does not imply that it has ceased to be the means of grace for those who in good faith still adhere to it. Though Judaism does not have sacraments in the special technical sense, it presents highly developed sacramental forms in which grace is offered and bestowed.

We are thus brought to consider the place of the Christian religion in the sacraments of grace. By the divine economy the supreme sacrament in which the offer of grace is made by the Father is the glorified Christ, who from Pentecost on acts most fully through the special (or ministerial) priesthood, particularly in its highest exercise, the Eucharist, in which the full saving reality of Christ is contained. In the exercise of this ministry the offer of grace is made by Christ, for by ordination and appointment the priest is authorized to act in his person. In this exercise the sign of Christ is presented by the priest, either by word alone or by a combination of word and act, with sometimes material elements (bread, wine, water, oil) also involved. This presentation of the sign of Christ is guaranteed to be effective (provided the conditions required of the recipient are also fulfilled) by the authority of Christ vested in the priest. When the recipient, then, accepts the offer of grace thus made, the ministerial act becomes an authoritative sending of the Holy Spirit in the name of Christ. Just as in the Trinity in itself the Father generates the Son, and through and with him breathes forth the Holy Spirit; and as in the revelation of the Trinity the Father sends Jesus Christ, and then through and with him sends the Holy Spirit at Pentecost; so in the operation of the Trinity the Father sends the priest, in that the latter is invested at ordination with the person of Christ, who lives always as sent by the Father; and then through and with the priest the Father sends the Holy Spirit, in that the priest, participating in Christ precisely as sending the Holy Spirit, himself sends the Spirit. Like the single operation of God in the Trinity in itself and in the revelation of the Trinity, the single ministerial act has two respectively corresponding moments (distinguished by order not by time), the first being that in which the sign of Christ, established at ordination, is activated, and the second being that in which the Holy Spirit is sent. The word-element of the sign of Christ comes from the teaching and preaching of the Church, which reflects the mind of the glorified Christ, which is in continuity with the words of the earthly Jesus, recorded as Gospel in the New Testament.

The priestly ministry is given in two forms, the ministry of word and the ministry of sacrament. In each of these the sign of Christ is presented and the Holy Spirit bestowed in grace. Each has something of both word and sacrament. The difference between them we may describe as one of objective emphasis. By the will of Christ there is in the seven sacraments a particular dignity which guarantees that, provided the requisite conditions on the part of both the minister and the recipient are fulfilled, the action of God will take place (cf. the technical expression *ex opere operato*). In the ministry of word this precise dignity is lacking, though the sign of Christ is still present and the minister still acts authoritatively. While here too the recipient must be disposed for the ministry to be fruitful, more responsibility is laid on the minister to exercise his ministry in a personal way calculated to be effective. However, because in the ministry of word the emphasis lies on the first moment of the ministry (sign of Christ) and in the ministry of sacrament on the second moment (bestowal of the Holy Spirit), there exists between the two forms of the ministry an order, viz., of the ministry of word to that of sacrament. Clearly, this order corresponds to that which exists between the generation of the Son and the breathing-forth of the Holy Spirit in the Trinity, though the correspondence is not exact. The order within the ministry is evident in the actual rites of the sacraments, notably in the Mass itself, where the Liturgy of the Word precedes and is ordered to the Liturgy of the Eucharist.

As we have intimated above, it is not only through the priestly ministry that the offer of grace takes place, though there it is made most poignantly, since there alone Christ, unsurpassable sacrament of God, is present as fully as the structure of human nature can allow and sends the Holy Spirit in continuation of Pentecost in the authoritative ministerial act. The offer of grace is made also through the lay apostolate, as exercised in the ministries of lector and acolyte, but also in any way that the layperson witnesses to Christ by word or act, whether consciously or unconsciously, and so realizes in their own life and hence manifests to others the spiritual and invisible Christian character that they received in baptism. Married people exercise this apostolate in a special way, in relation to each other, their family, and any who meet the love of Christ in their home. The same is true of religious, who witness to Christ by their commitment to the evangelical counsels. In all these ways the sign of Christ is presented, but less solemnly than in the exercise of the ministerial priesthood. Further, it is clear that the layperson lacks the authority to send the Holy Spirit. They may intercede with God (the Father) to send the Holy Spirit (through Christ) to the other person, either explicitly, or implicitly in the deliberate apostolic word or act; or they may unknowingly be a means of grace in that they witness unconsciously to their Christian commitment. Whatever be the level of consciousness and will in the exercise of the lay apostolate, the other person, when they respond affirmatively to the sign of Christ thus presented, responds to Christ himself, and it is Christ thus encountered who in continuation of Pentecost sends the Holy Spirit to them. Thus it happens, according to the divine economy, that this person is led by the exercise of the apostolate of the common priesthood to that of the special priesthood and so ultimately to the Eucharist. The ministerial priest, of course, will exercise the special priesthood only on specific occasions. At other times he will exercise the common priesthood, which he does not lose at priestly ordination.

The words of Augustine are apposite here: "I am a bishop for you, and a Christian with you."[15]

In the separated Christian Churches and Ecclesial Communities likewise the sign of Christ is presented and operates as the sacrament of grace. Speaking globally, we may say that this sign is diminished in them to the extent that through their separation from Rome they have lost the unity of faith and therefore something of its total content. Doctrine, it should be realized, is no mere abstract matter, but has to do with the intellectual content of the sign of Christ, though here a remark of the Second Vatican Council should be heeded, viz., that "when comparing doctrines, they (Catholic theologians) should remember that in Catholic teaching there exists an order or 'hierarchy' of truths, since they vary in their relationship to the foundation of the Christian faith."[16] On particular occasions, however, e.g., sermons, where truth is proclaimed but totality not even attempted, the sign of Christ can be presented in the separated communities just, as truly as, or even more truly than, in the Roman Church under comparable circumstances. We cannot enter here into the vexed question of the existence of the priestly ministry outside the Roman Church. In some instances, notably in the Eastern Orthodox Church, it is acknowledged to exist, but in others the issue is by no means so clear. Suffice it to say that where this ministry does exist our remarks made earlier about the priestly ministry apply, and where it does not (presuming that this is sometimes the case) our remarks about the lay ministry apply. However, it will be clear from what has been said above that ministry, whether clerical or lay, in the separated communities can only suffer from their lack of full communion with Rome. Likewise, ministry in the Roman communion would be greatly enriched by the reunion of Christians, when the best aspects of the various traditions would be united in a new and pregnant synthesis.

Christians move, perhaps sometimes even unconsciously, backwards and forwards along the whole, or almost the whole, range of the sacraments of grace, from secular sacraments to the Eucharist. Indeed, for the greater part of their lives they are exposed to secular sacraments, and they will encounter specifically religious or Christian ones only comparatively rarely, and then as high points of their spiritual life. This is not to say, however, that their spiritual life will lack unity. They

---

15   *Sermo* 340 (PL 38, 1483).

16   *Unitatis redintegratio* 11.

will bring to the Eucharist a spiritual momentum that has been built up in ways that, though humble, are indispensable, and in turn their experience of the Eucharist will send them back to the world with a strength and an outlook that will transform their experience there and enable them to respond more authentically to it. Having now placed the Eucharist in perspective, we are in a position to give it, in the next chapter, the special consideration which it requires.

12 THE EUCHARIST:
PRINCIPAL SACRAMENT OF GRACE

The Eucharist is the principal realization of Christ, who is the great sacrament of grace, subsuming all others. It is therefore the very embodiment and visible presence of grace in the world, the offer of grace, and if its implications are faced sincerely, the divine challenge that evokes from humans the most authentic Christian faith and love.

Because historically Catholic approaches to the Eucharist have been greatly influenced by it, we begin our study with a consideration of the theology of transubstantiation. We say the "theology" of transubstantiation, and henceforth in this chapter, more briefly, "transubstantiation," to indicate simply the *explanation* of the doctrine of the Eucharistic change. This is to be distinguished clearly from the dogma of transubstantiation. The distinction is important, because while the dogma is clothed in the concepts of the theology, it is the doctrine that is binding on the faith of the Church, and not the theology. It is not the object of our criticism here. The conviction that in the Eucharist it is precisely by transubstantiation that bread and wine are changed into the body and blood of Christ arose in the medieval schools, first appeared in official teaching in the Fourth Lateran Council (DS 802), and received definitive form in the Council of Trent (DS 1642, 1652). The truth that is binding for faith, however, is that by the power of God bread and wine are truly changed, so as to become the body and blood of Christ, i.e., Christ in his full saving effectiveness, with the result that he becomes present in the Eucharist in his total being, though under signs rather than in the historical form in which he had once walked Palestine. This presence, called technically the "real" presence, was therefore more than a purely "symbolic" or simply spiritual presence, in which the reenactment of the last supper would serve to recall him to mind and make him present through the faith of the participants. Already, then, we see that Trent had to concern itself with two matters, the real presence (against Zwingli), and, more fundamentally, the Eucharistic change (against Luther). Because the immediately preceding discussion had been conducted in the framework of the

Aristotelian philosophy of nature (a theology of transubstantiation, be it noted, existed also prior to the introduction of Aristotelianism), the conciliar doctrine too was bound to be formed in the same mold of thought, and so it was there declared that the substances of bread and wine are changed, respectively, into those of Christ's body and blood, only the forms of bread and wine remaining, and it was denied that Christ is present along with the bread and wine (consubstantiation or companation). The fact that transubstantiation was a technical and non-biblical term was no objection to it, since a precedent existed in the choice of "homoousios" at Nicaea as a new term by which the faith of the Church at that time could be articulated and saved.

While then, the Eucharistic change was conceived and expressed at Trent in the framework of Aristotelianism, it is simply the reality of the change, and in no way the supportive philosophy, that pertains to the faith there defined. It appears that the Tridentine Fathers themselves, though it was not possible for them to conceive the change in any but Aristotelian categories, showed at least some awareness of this.[1] All the more, then, for us, separated as we are from them by a gulf of time and culture, and with the advantage of the considerable progress made in the meantime in both philosophy and theology, the distinction of content and form in regard to this doctrine is both possible and obligatory. If we do not accept the challenge, we are in danger of falling prey to a conciliar fundamentalism no less damaging to the cause of faith than the biblical variety.

It will not be necessary here to go into the problems about the theology of transubstantiation in detail. Suffice it to say that believers today seek a theology of the Eucharist that will grasp this central sacrament against the background of their total Christian faith rather than that of an impersonal and a-religious philosophy whose validity is called into question as a result of modern philosophical and scientific criticism. Since they are aware of the problem, modern defenders of the theology of transubstantiation do not claim that its underlying philosophy is strict Aristotelianism. They realize that this would demand a relation of accidents to substance that transubstantiation could not allow, and further, would require all four termini, bread, wine, body and blood, to be substances in the strict sense, which clearly none of them is. Transubstantiation is therefore upheld by them only as utilizing a

---

1 Cf. E. Schillebeeckx, *The Eucharist* (London, 1968) 54-58; J. Powers, *Eucharistic Theology* (New York, 1967) 39-40.

popular form of Aristotelianism and saying only that the *realities* of bread and wine are changed respectively into those of the body and blood of Christ, which does require them, of course, to cease to be bread and wine.

However, at least the two following difficulties remain. First, if it is no longer possible to defend a purely physical interpretation of the resurrection of Jesus, we must reckon with the problem presented by the physicality of the body and blood into which the bread and wine are thought to be thus changed. Biblical scholarship assists us here, by pointing out that body and blood are the language of sacrifice, so that the body and blood of Christ are Christ sacrificed,[2] i.e., Christ as he now exists in heaven as a result of his sacrificial death, in the eternal state of self-offering to, and acceptance by, the Father for the salvation of humans, and therefore Christ given again, as it were, for people of all ages, which the New Testament sees as accomplished in the Holy Spirit sent by him from the Father upon the Church. The Eucharist is identified with the sacrifice of Calvary in that the death and res-urrection of Jesus were the gateway through which he entered upon this transcendental state. (We note in passing that a later session of Trent was to declare the identity of the Eucharist with the sacrifice of Calvary [DS 1743].) We are not suggesting that the bread and wine become the Holy Spirit. The New Testament, while recognizing the Spirit as the mode of activity of the risen Christ, does not confuse the two, and neither should we. We shall return to this theme, but already enough has been said to show that the simple change required by a theology of transubstantiation of the bread and wine into the separate realities of Jesus' physical body and blood will not do. It is no objection against this to point out that it was over the bread that Jesus said, "This is my body," and over the wine, "This is my blood." It was the meal in its *unity* that he mysteriously identified with his self-sacrifice. Using, as he did, the sacrificial language of body and blood, it was only to be expected that he would identify the solid that was broken, the bread, with his body, and the red liquid that he poured out, the wine, with his blood.[3]

The second difficulty is that because transubstantiation is conceived as a change taking place wholly within the world, it requires the bread and wine to cease to exist as such in order to be able to become the

---

2   Cf. J. Jeremias, *The Eucharistic Words of Jesus* (London, 1966) 220-25.
3   Cf. ibid. 223.

body and blood of Christ. If bread and wine remain, they cannot have been changed into the body and blood of Christ. This is why Trent condemned companation. Yet there is nothing in the institution narratives that requires this conclusion. If a satisfactory explanation could be proposed by which the bread and wine could be understood to be changed into the sacrificed Christ without ceasing to be what they were originally, the doctrine of the Eucharistic change would be seen not to demand that the bread and wine cease to exist, and a serious difficulty in the way of the faith of many people in the Eucharist would be overcome. This demand would then be seen to stem purely from the theology of transubstantiation.

Of course, the defenders of this theology do not concede that it is a change wholly within the world. Rather, they conceive it as a change from the sphere of the world to the sphere of God, in that the bread and wine are changed into the body and blood of the glorified Christ as he lives now in heaven. In any event they realize that to accept it as a change taking place wholly within the world would be to turn Holy Communion into cannibalism. Hence they are prepared to recognize that the formula that in Holy Communion we eat the body of Christ and drink his blood (to which we shall return later) must contain a metaphorical element as well as a real one. However, despite their laudable intentions, the very concept of the change of one material reality into another, however much the second may be said now to belong to the sphere of God (through glorification), locks this theology inescapably and wholly within the world. The tell-tale signs of this are, as we have indicated, the dependence of transubstantiation on an overly physical understanding of the resurrection of Jesus, and its insistence that the bread and wine cease to exist.

If the Eucharistic change is unique, as Trent says it is, it cannot be explained by any theology or philosophy. To attempt to explain it would destroy its uniqueness, because any explanation must be in terms of some general principle. That one substance can be changed into another is just such a principle. Having applied it to an instance of change that is by definition unique, one must then attempt to recover the lost uniqueness, which is done only by recourse to desperate measures, such as to say that the forms or accidents of the first substance remain, or that the change is total, not just in the sense that there is no remainder of the first substance, but in the sense that the matter of the first is changed into that of the second, and the same with the form. Theology, therefore, must not fall into the trap of attempting to explain the Eucharistic change. It must be left as ultimately a mystery. All that theology can hope to do is to throw some light on it by using the analogy of faith, and to show that it is not repugnant to reason, by providing for it a horizon of intelligibility.

However, within Aristotelianism, which, we repeat, provided the context of the debate, transubstantiation was the only way of protecting and stating the Eucharistic change and the consequent real presence as believed traditionally in the Church. We leave aside a purely "symbolic" presence as clearly at variance with this tradition. Companation and impanation, the serious alternatives to transubstantiation, were unacceptable, because they compromised the Eucharistic change in not allowing the ultimate reality of the consecrated bread and wine, which as ultimate must be one, to be the body and blood of Christ, or, as we would prefer to say, the sacrificed Christ. Hence the thrust of this critique is not simply to rule out transubstantiation, but while recognizing its service to the Church in the sixteenth century and therefore also to the Church of the present day, to show that its inadequacies for contemporary acceptance are too great to be borne. Thus we are moved to seek an alternative theology of the Eucharistic change in a new and more acceptable context of thought.

Such an alternative emerges, we suggest, from the theology of grace. It may be called a theology of sanctification. For this theology certain preliminary points have been made already in the critique of transubstantiation, but there are two further ones that we wish to present, and this we now proceed to do.

The first is that this theology will have to invoke the sacramental principle, viz., that what is represented under signs is rendered present and operative in reality. Applied to the Eucharist, this does not mean that the sacrificial death of Jesus is repeated historically; indeed this is ruled out both as fact and as possibility. The death of Jesus occurred only once historically, on Calvary; in the Eucharist it is re-presented in ritual, in which the words and actions of Jesus at the last supper are repeated. This act of ministry itself involves a certain presence of Christ, but over and above this, he is made present also in the bread and wine in his sacrificial death, in such a way that the participants, both by their assent and by their reception of Holy Communion, are joined to him in his act of self-offering to the Father, and so along with Christ are accepted by the Father. Just as the acceptance of Jesus by the Father on Calvary meant his being given again, as it were, for humans in the ministry of the Church, so the acceptance of the faithful in the Eucharist means that they leave the celebration charged with Christ's mission to the world. Note that what is primarily present in the Eucharist under the symbols is the sacrificial death of Jesus. Therefore the real presence means that Christ is present precisely in his sacrificial death for human beings. The real presence, then, is not an end in itself.

Obviously, whenever the Eucharist is celebrated it has its own historicity. When, therefore, we contrast the sacramental and the historical, we do not intend to deny to the sacramental its own historicity. We only want to deny that the sacramental repeats the historical precisely in the latter's historicity. With the term "sacramental" we affirm reality but deny historicity in this sense. The Eucharist, then, presents the death of Christ sacramentally, i.e., symbolically and really, but not historically.

The sacramental principle as operative in the Eucharist cannot be explained by philosophy, both because it is unique in itself, and because it goes beyond the experience on which philosophy, even metaphysics, is based. Metaphysics attains both humans in their spirituality and God, but cannot speak positively and directly about unique contingent interventions of God, among which the Eucharist is pre-eminent. The uniqueness of the mode of application of the sacramental principle to the Eucharist is appreciated when comparison is made with its application to baptism. There, too, a significant ritual involving a material reality (water) is performed, and also the spiritual event thus signified actually takes place; but in the Eucharist the sacramental event takes place not just in the believer, though that is where it takes place ultimately, but as means to that end it takes place first in the material realities of bread and wine, which are thereby elevated to a unique sacramental status. Here the sacrament consists not only in the ritual but also in the material realities used in the ritual.

Although what takes place in the Eucharist cannot be explained philosophically, it cannot, on the other hand, be dismissed as contrary to reason. While philosophy cannot explain the Eucharistic change, it can still be of assistance to Eucharistic theology. For example, it can influence discourse about it, in that it can uncover errors of logic, and also in that it can make important limiting statements about this-worldly reality, as, e.g., that bread and wine could not be changed into the sacrificed Christ in the historical sense, because only finite spirit, the spirit of a human person, is thus open to the infinite Spirit of God and therefore capable of this determination. The charge of philosophical impossibility can, however, be made against the theology of transubstantiation, because in seeing the four termini as this-worldly realities, it is forced into giving a philosophical explanation, which, as we saw, cannot stand up to criticism; but if the bread and wine can be said to retain their this-worldly reality in the Eucharist, and to be changed only in that they are identified really but not historically with a reality that transcends this world, then such an account of the Eucharist is immune from philosophical criticism.

A service philosophy can render Eucharistic theology is to provide a philosophical horizon against which the Eucharistic change can be grasped. In transcendental philosophy the authentic being of a thing is not so much what it is in and for itself as what it is for humans, in its meaning for them which is in part given and in part created by themselves. This distinction, between what is called the ontic and the ontological, will play an important part in our reflections about the Eucharist. In ancient times a horizon of intelligibility was provided by religious myths. Thus, for Jesus at the last supper the regulative myth was that of prophetic sign. When a prophet solemnly performed a symbolic ritual referring to a past or future event, he was believed actually to summon that event into present effectiveness. When the event lay in the past, the sign assumed the character of a memorial invested with this same effective power. It is important to realize that neither ancient mythology nor modern philosophy purported, or purports, to explain the Eucharistic change. Each merely provided, or provides, for it a horizon of intelligibility in a particular culture.

The second preliminary point, which goes back to the Eastern Fathers, is that a key to an understanding of the Eucharistic change is provided in the Incarnation, because there we have an instance, indeed the paradigm, of change from the sphere of the world to that of God. This view of the Incarnation is grasped in the light of two theological theses. The first is Rahner's thesis that the Incarnation is the unique and unsurpassable actualization by God of the potency of a human being for union with him;[4] the second is our own thesis that this union of Jesus with God was brought about by a unique and radical bestowal

---

4   Cf. Rahner, "On the Theology of the Incarnation," *Theological Investigations* 4, 105-20.

of the Holy Spirit, Spirit of Sonship, by the Father on the humanity of Jesus, in the one act creating it, sanctifying it and uniting it in person to the preexistent divine Son. From these the Incarnation can be seen as sanctification, indeed the paradigm of it, in that it is the most radical and complete possible instance of it.

This is shown in three steps. First, the Incarnation is the work of the Holy Spirit, the Sanctifier, whose task is to draw the creation into the life of God who alone is holy, to divinize the non-divine; second, properly speaking, only humans can be sanctified, since only they are matter with the openness to God necessary for the reception of the self-communication of God, and which traditionally is called spirit or soul; and finally, the sanctification of Jesus is the highest possible sanctification of a human being, since it alone terminates in unity of person with a divine person, viz., the Son.

To be grasped as a whole, the sanctification of Jesus must not be seen to stop short at the Incarnation, but must be appreciated to be brought to completion in his earthly life and his death. Another way of expressing this is to say that Jesus realized in his whole life the unique grace given him at his conception. The sanctification of Jesus through the course of his life was not simply the gift of God, but the mysterious conjunction and synergism of divine gift and human work which is the paradigm of every instance of the working of God's grace in humans. By his life-long obedience to the Father, which brought him to, and characterized, his death as the summation of his life, Jesus actualized the grace of the Incarnation, and thus sanctified himself (cf. Jn 17:19). There is no contradiction between the two statements: Jesus was sanctified by the Holy Spirit, and Jesus sanctified himself. Thus, the sanctification of Jesus is comprehended as begun with his conception and completed at his death. The theology of the death of Jesus as a sacrifice is included in the theology of sanctification, for both etymologically and theologically to sacrifice is "to do what is sacred,"[5] and when the sacrifice in question is the self-sacrifice of a human being, while it must be understood as the work of God accomplished through the Holy Spirit, it must also be understood as the self-dedication of the human to God, which to be authentic and total must be a devotion unto death.

To anticipate a likely objection, it should be said that the concept of sanctification should not be dismissed, because biblical and patristic,

---

5   Cf. L. Bouyer, *Rite and Man* (Notre Dame, Indiana, 1963) 79-80.

as even more irrelevant to modern thought than transubstantiation. In the first place the fact that it is biblical gives it a certain honor and distinction. It also expresses a profound truth that can be surrendered only with Christianity itself, for when all the reinterpreting has been done, we are left with the basic Christian concept of the human as finite transcendence grounded in, and ordered to, the infinite transcendence of God, and realized fully only in Christ. The realization of this transcendence towards God is the real content of the concept of sanctification. We have yet to explore the meaning of the sanctification of material objects, but we can already say that they are sanctified in that they are used by God as the necessary means (i.e., on the human side) by which God and humans in synergism realize this transcendence.

The sanctification of Jesus, paradigm of all sanctification, can be characterized as genuine change in that a reality belonging to the sphere of the world is caused to belong to the sphere of God. Two qualifications have to be made immediately. First, it is change *to* something new but not change *from* what it was originally. When something is changed from the sphere of the world to that of God it does not thereby cease to belong to the sphere of the world. Incompatibility could exist between the two spheres only if the transcendence of God were compromised or overlooked, or if a Manichaean view of the world were adopted. The transcendent God embraces all things as their creator, and when he intervenes graciously in the world, it can only be to draw it to a higher determination that leaves intact the perfections it already has. To use Aristotelian language to express an insight of transcendental theology, the sanctification of Jesus is not a change from one substance to another, but the determination of the potency of a substance in the highest possible way. That the humanity of Jesus did not cease to exist in the Incarnation was solemnly taught by the Council of Chalcedon. If his humanity had to cease to be what it was in order to be substantified by the divine Son, it would have been absorbed into the divinity, and there would have been only one nature, viz., the divine, in Jesus. This would be monophysitism, which was condemned by the Council. Secondly, the sanctification of Jesus does not imply an adoptionist Christology. It does not mean that Jesus existed first as a human person, and then, through the later action of the Holy Spirit, was made Son of God in humanity. There was no time of his human existence when Jesus was not Son of God.

These qualifications could create the impression that the sanctification of Jesus was no true change at all; but we must remember that his humanity could never of itself have attained the unity of person with the divine Son which it actually had, and therefore must have been changed by God. Secondly, and uniquely, it was a determination that terminated in another being, viz., the divine Son, even though the humanity did not cease to be what it had been all along. What would have been simply a human person, was, through sanctification, a divine person. This, above all, is why the sanctification of Jesus can be called a change. From this it is evident that the divine Sonship of Jesus is not something added extrinsically to his humanity, but is an intrinsic, though divine, determination of his humanity itself.[6] While it results in new and different being, it does not cancel out the original being. While from the standpoint of God it is the unsurpassable elevation of humanity, from the standpoint of the human it is the unsurpassable deepening of it, penetration to the depth and density of being consistent with incarnation.[7]

We have concentrated on the sanctification of Jesus because it is the paradigm of all sanctification. Ordinary people, too, are sanctified, with the Holy Spirit, who is sent by Christ and conforms them to him. With ordinary people, too, there is new being through sanctification, new height or depth (depending on one's standpoint), but not different being. They become a new creation in God, but still remain the simply human persons they always were. (We recall that it is this truth that Scholasticism strove to express when it characterized sanctifying grace as an accident and not a substance.) Even purely material objects when sanctified acquire new being, but for the moment we defer our consideration of precisely what this is. In all instances the continuing being in the sphere of the world is apprehended in the ordinary ways and is subject to worldly actions, such as eating and drinking. On the other hand, the new being, acquired in the sphere of God, is apprehended only by faith, through, of course, the sacramentality of the being in the

---

6   This statement should be interpreted in the light of what was said in chapters 5 and 7 about Christ's unique divine Sonship.

7   The statements of this paragraph need to be understood in the context of what was said in chapters 5 and 7 on Christ's unique created grace, the "substantial" grace of his humanity, bearing in mind the inseparability of created and uncreated grace, the latter, in this case being the gift of the divine Son himself to the sacred humanity.

world. In the case of humans (including Jesus) sanctification is an end in itself (or, ultimately, it is for the glory of God), and in all instances (i.e., Jesus, ordinary people and material objects) it constitutes the sanctified being as a sacrament placed in the world for the sanctification of human beings. The question as to precisely what the sanctified being is can be answered from the standpoint of either the sphere of the world or the sphere of God. If, however, one is pressed to give an ultimate answer to this question, one would have to opt for what the being is in the sphere of God, for being is determined in its relation to God, who is being, rather than in relation to the world, which only has being in dependence on him. However, to answer the question in this way is not to deny the continuing being that the being has in the world, for as we have said, there is no incompatibility between the two spheres. The sphere of God penetrates the sphere of the world. Thus sanctification both allows and requires the ultimate reality of a sanctified being to be one, and indeed what it is in the sphere of God. The supreme example of this is that without prejudice to the truth of less profound answers, the Christian must ultimately answer the question, "Who is Jesus of Nazareth?" by confessing, "He is the Son of God."

It remains to ask whether also the Eucharistic change can be characterized as sanctification. If an affirmative answer is indicated, we would then have at least the possibility of seeing that the bread and wine truly become the sacrificed Christ for the sanctification of humans without losing the reality they have in the world.

At the level of fact this question can be answered immediately. In recent times several theologians have collected testimonies of the Fathers, particularly Eastern Fathers, on the role of the Holy Spirit in the Eucharist.[8] Two clear affirmations emerge from these studies, first, that it is by the sanctifying power of the Holy Spirit that the bread and wine are changed into the body and blood of Christ, and secondly, that by the same sanctifying power the participants are gathered into

---

8   B. Brobinskoy, "Présence réelle et communion eucharistique", *Revue des sciences philosophiques et theologiques* 53 (1969) 402-20; J. Tillard, "L'Eucharistie et le Saint-Ésprit", *Nouvelle revue théologique* 90 (1968) 363-87; J. McKenna, "Eucharistic Epiclesis: Myopia or Microcosm?" *Theological Studies* 36 (1975) 265-84; E. Atchley, *On the Epiclesis of the Eucharistic Liturgy and in the Consecration of the Font* (London, 1935). An additional reference for this edition is N.S. Clark, "Spirit Christology in the Light of Eucharistic Theology" *The Heythrop Journal* 23 (1982) 270-84.

union with Christ in Holy Communion. In each instance the action of the Holy Spirit is an action of Christ which takes place in and through the Holy Spirit. On the basis of this statement of tradition we can confidently assert that the Eucharist is sanctification, sanctification by the Holy Spirit as sent by Christ, ultimately sanctification of those who participate in the Eucharist, and to this end sanctification of the bread and wine so that they are constituted the supreme sacrament of the sanctification of human beings, viz., Christ. All this is to be understood in the light of what we established in the previous chapter concerning the sending the Holy Spirit by Christ. It is seen to be sanctification from the consideration first, that it is done by the Holy Spirit, whose every action in the sphere of the world must be one of sanctification, secondly, that in the first instance it is an action of change which terminates in the sacrificed Christ, the very paradigm of sanctification, and thirdly, that ultimately it is the supreme sacramental action by which human beings are conformed to Christ, paradigm of sanctification.

The convictions of the East on this matter were given liturgical expression in the double epiclesis of the Eastern Eucharistic prayers. In the West, however, this important element of tradition was not so strongly preserved. If the Roman Canon, e.g., has an epiclesis at all, it is a very rudimentary one.[9] It was in order to incorporate more clearly this insight into the Western consciousness, for the consequent enrichment of Eucharistic faith, that the new Eucharistic prayers, composed as a result of the Second Vatican Council, were given explicit double epicleses.

The theologian will naturally want to look beyond tradition to the biblical witness that underlies it, and in this case such witness is provided in the statements of the New Testament that at the last supper Jesus pronounced blessings over the bread and wine and gave them interpretations relating to his sacrificial death. In the context of any Jewish meal the blessings over bread and wine are blessings of God, rather than of the bread and wine, but even so, those who eat and drink this bread and wine are believed thus to share in the blessings pronounced by the head of the family. In these blessings the presider communes with God, praising and thanking him. By eating and drinking the bread and wine those present are admitted to his communion with God and thus also share with each other in this communion.

9   Cf. J. Jungmann, *The Mass of the Roman Rite* 2 (New York, 1955) 233.

Here, then, the bread and wine are sanctified in the sense we have allowed to material objects. It was this religious ritual to which Jesus gave added significance when he said, "This is my body, this is my blood." The communion to which the twelve were admitted by eating and drinking *this* bread and wine was the consummation of Jesus' communion with God, because it comprised his self-offering to the Father in death and the Father's acceptance of this offering. Moreover, because of the redemptive and atoning quality of this death, which is indicated particularly by the word "blood", for them this admission to communion was reconciliation, overcoming the barriers erected by sin between themselves and God and thus also among themselves. Clearly, then, it was their sanctification. According to the Synoptic tradition, the last supper was a transformation of the paschal meal, and by his actions there Jesus had at the least invited identification of his approaching death with the sacrifice of the eschatological paschal lamb. Indeed, if this tradition is historically correct, it is more likely that he actually made the identification himself, in the meditation preceding the main part of the meal.[10] However, even if the presentation of the last supper as a paschal meal is a theological construction of the Synoptic tradition, based on the convenient proximity of Jesus' death to the celebration of the Passover, the statements made above about the bread and wine of the last supper remain valid. While, then, the action of Jesus was not a blessing of the bread and wine, it was clearly sanctification of them, for they were now given the most profound religious meaning and efficacy. We are here going beyond our earlier purely factual statement that the action of Jesus was sanctification of the bread and wine because it terminated in the sacrificed Christ, and are embarking on an explanation of how this sanctification was brought about. We shall not proceed with this point at this stage, being satisfied for the moment with having shown that our theology of the Eucharist as sanctification is rooted in the blessings and interpretations given by Jesus at the last supper.

The sanctification of humans that takes place in the reception of Holy Communion appears in the first instance to be a union of the communicants with the Holy Spirit; but the whole point of Holy Communion is that it is union with Christ. However, these two statements are not contradictory, but complementary. The Holy Spirit who comes to humans in Holy Communion comes as having definitively

---

10   Cf. Jeremias 218-20.

entered salvation history in being bestowed in all fullness as Spirit of Sonship on Jesus at his conception, thus establishing him as Son of God in humanity, and extended by him to us as the entelechy of Christ[11] in a sacramental action by which the Father draws us into his Sonship, thus uniting us to him. If this is true of every bestowal of grace, the distinctive feature of the Eucharist is that it alone contains and offers the whole saving mystery of Christ, Christ in his total availability, and this because, of all the means of grace, it alone signifies and presents Christ precisely in this fullness, i.e., in his self-offering to the Father in death and the Father's acceptance of this offering. Other means of grace, then, are all simply preparatory and derivative (paradoxically) in relation to the Eucharist. Any other kind of union with Christ in Holy Communion is unthinkable. The truth to be salvaged from those ultra-realistic statements of certain Fathers about the blood of Christ flowing in our veins or from the formula that in the Eucharist we eat the body of Christ and drink his blood is that they express the unbridgeable gap that exists between the Eucharist and all other means of grace. We have, in fact, arrived at a satisfactory way of interpreting this formula. Eating and drinking, as actions belonging to the sphere of the world, are centered upon the bread and wine, which continue to exist in this sphere after the Eucharistic sign has been constituted; but because in the sphere of God this bread and wine have been sanctified and changed into the sacrificed Christ, by this eating and drinking humans are sacramentally united with Christ in the way we have explained, i.e., they are united with Christ in his total givenness, therefore with Christ in the Spirit, whose activity is sanctification. The formula contains a kind of *communicatio idiomatum*, based on the unity of being (of which we shall say more later) of the bread and wine with the sacrificed Christ.[12]

---

11   See ch. 11.

12   The theology of the Eucharistic change presented here is the development of a widespread tendency that existed among the Eastern Fathers of the 5th c. J. Betz notes ("Eucharistie," HTG 1, 344-45) that the formulations attained at that time were unsatisfactory, because they contained a "Eucharistic dyophysitism" which was rightly rejected by the faithful and finally countered by the theology of John Damascene, in which the reality of the Eucharistic change came again to the fore. We would claim that the theology presented here brings the patristic movement noted by Betz to a conclusion in which the pitfall of dyophysitism is avoided. Likewise, points of similarity between this theology and that of Calvin, though real, are

Thus we are brought at last to the question, how are the bread and wine sanctified in the Eucharist so as to become the sacrificed Christ? The basic answer to this question, which will require elaboration, is that as inanimate objects they are sanctified through being made into a sacrament, indeed the supreme and unique sacrament, of the sanctification of humans. The bread and wine are sanctified through being incorporated into the total process of sanctification. This is done by investing them with deeper meaning, in the sphere of God, over and above that which they have, and retain, in the sphere of the world. However, this sanctification penetrates beyond the simple giving of new meaning and even of the new being it implies, and issues in actual *unity of being* of the bread and wine with the sacrificed Christ. Our reason for saying this is that this is how the words and actions of Jesus at the last supper must be understood in the light of the faith of the Church. The Eucharist would still have been the supreme sacrament of Christ if the sanctification of the bread and wine had stopped short at new meaning and its implied new being, as in the case of the water of baptism or icons, but the traditional understanding confesses the Eucharist as not only the supreme, but also the unique, sacrament of Christ. Like any other article of faith, the Eucharistic change remains constantly open to the process of reinterpretation, but this may not be done at the expense of the essence of the sacrament as grasped by the faith of the Church.

From the fact that it is precisely from investing them with new meaning that the Eucharistic bread and wine acquire new being an important corollary flows. Except for the case of purely private meaning, which does not apply here, meaning depends not only on the person who gives it but on the community that accepts it. It results from an understanding, almost a contract, in the community. For the twelve at the last supper, who formed the nucleus that was to be expanded later into the Church, the bread and wine would not have signified, and therefore would not have become, Jesus in his sacrificial death, had they not accepted this meaning from him in faith, however dimly they may have apprehended it at the time. Likewise in the Church the Eucharistic bread and wine signify and become the sacrificed Christ not because the minister acts from his personal faith but because he acts from the faith of the Church, in which he shares. If individual

---

superficial, since this theology penetrates to Eucharistic realism while his does not go beyond the realm of sign (cf. Betz 347).

Christians cease to believe, this does not affect the faith of the Church, which is indefectible, though for a person without faith there is no difference between the Eucharistic bread and wine and ordinary bread and wine, since their lack of faith incapacitates them from penetrating from the sphere of the world to that of God. The Eucharistic change and the consequent real presence, therefore, depend not simply on the exercise of God's power but also on the Church's faith, which, of course, is itself a result of God's gracious power. While the objectivity of the Eucharistic change and the real presence must always be upheld, this should not be at the expense of the dependence of the Eucharist on the faith of the Church. Since this point has been well made by others in other contexts, it will not require further treatment here.[13]

Let us now examine, briefly, the meaning of the Eucharistic bread and wine. Bread and wine signify at the first level human nourishment, and at the next level table fellowship, in the first instance between the individual guests and their host and thence among the guests themselves. In Jewish culture this fellowship is already something religious, and so in that setting the bread and wine are already sanctified, as is evident from the grace said before and after meals. In the context of a paschal meal they are further sanctified, through the interpretations given them by the head of the family in the course of the meditation. Whether the interpretation of the Eucharist in terms of the eschatological paschal lamb stems from Jesus himself or simply from the Synoptic tradition, when at the blessings of the last supper Jesus gave his own interpretations of the bread and wine, he deepened their meaning further still, so that now they signified himself sacrificed in death and therefore given totally for humans, to be appropriated by them communally by both their prayerful assent and their eating and drinking of the bread and wine. In each stage the new meaning, with its attendant being and efficacy, is by no means arbitrary, but is a further determination of meaning already possessed; but neither, on the other hand, is new meaning simply implicit in the old, for the new derives from the history of God's saving acts, which is contingent and free. Here we find a certain expression of the relation of nature and grace, new meaning being a determination of old without being either reduced to it or demanded by it.

---

13   Cf. E, Kilmartin, "Apostolic Office: Sacrament of Christ", *Theological Studies* 36 (1975) 243-64; McKenna, "Eucharistic Epiclesis: Myopia or Microcosm?"

It is clear that, except in the case of the Eucharist, the giving of new meaning, while it necessarily adduces new being,[14] does not result in unity of being between the sign and the reality signified. However, this limitation pertains to the nature of a sign. Something must now be said about the difference between a sign and a symbol. Given that in general a symbol stands closer to the reality signified than does a sign, for our present purposes we can define a symbol as a sign which has unity of being with the reality signified, and a simple sign as a sign in which this unity is lacking. Human beings do not have the power to bring about complete correspondence of being and meaning in the signs that they use, so that the distance that separates a sign from the reality signified can never be fully overcome. A symbol on the other hand, since it already possesses unity of being with the reality signified, communicates this reality in revealing its meaning. To this general statement two qualifications have to be made immediately. First, the meaning given to a sign is not necessarily arbitrary, but is often a determination of the meaning the sign already has. Secondly, the unity of being between a symbol and the reality signified can never be simple, but is dialectical, i.e., within the sameness of being there is an insuperable otherness.

Applying now our understanding of a symbol, we may say that in the sphere of the world a symbol is given only where there is already unity of matter and spirit, i.e., in a human being.[15] Only here is the depth of being, the spirit, symbolized in the other, the body, without prejudice to the profound unity of the being. If the sphere of God is allowed to penetrate the sphere of the world, the Incarnation then becomes the very paradigm of a symbol. The body of Jesus, joined in unity of being with the divine Son through his human spirit, is the symbol by which God is revealed and communicated to humans. When an ordinary person receives the Spirit in grace, their inner being is changed,

---

14 This can be illustrated by the well-known example of a wedding ring. The giving of meaning contained in the bestowal of the ring in the marriage ceremony adds new being to this ring for the bride and groom. It is no longer the same in being as similar rings awaiting buyers in the jeweler's window, much less is it the same as unfashioned gold from which such rings are made. We are saying that the new being of the Eucharist is much more than this kind of new being.

15 Cf. K. Rahner, "The Theology of the Symbol", *Theological Investigations* 4 (London, 1966) 221-52.

and their body becomes not a strict symbol, but a kind of symbol, of Christ and of God. (Here again we can see what Scholasticism was striving to express when it said that grace was an accident and not a substance.) Turning now to signs, we note that when purely material objects are invested with new meaning they become signs, but not symbols. To this the Eucharist is the sole exception, because in its case alone, by the power of God, the endowment of new meaning brings about complete correspondence of being and meaning. Because in the Eucharist there exists unity of being between the sign and the reality signified, the Eucharist is a symbol, even though this unity is not given at the start but is the end of a process. In this instance the process plunges to new, indeed unsurpassable, depth. While it includes all that belongs to signification, it is more than it and is unique, in that here alone signification becomes symbolization. Symbolization is arrived at over the road of signification. In none of the three instances given does the unity of the symbol and the reality signified abolish the dialectical otherness of the symbol. Specifically, in the Eucharist the symbolized reality, the sacrificed Christ, with whom the bread and wine are joined in unity of being, is revealed and communicated in the otherness of the symbol, the bread and wine.[16] From this reasoning alone we see that

---

16   At this point it will be apposite to quote from a book that appeared after the first edition of the present work, Louis-Marie Chauvet's *Symbol and Sacrament*, which was first published in French in 1987, "Because the mystery of the Eucharistic body of the Lord cannot be expressed on this terrain [viz., that of symbolism] unless it carries with it the symbolic richness of bread evoked all along the journey, it is clear that to express all its radicalness, not only can one no longer say but one must no longer say, 'This bread is no longer bread.' On the contrary, such a statement had to be made on the terrain of metaphysical substance since on this level it expressed the necessary implication of the *conversio totius substantiae* formulated dogmatically at the Council of Trent. On the altogether different terrain of symbolism and *due* to the fact that it is so different that the verb *'be' no longer has the same status it had at its origin* because the *Sein* is inseparable from the human *Da-Sein* and thus from language, from which it nevertheless remains distinct, to say that 'this bread is the body of Christ' requires that one emphasize all the more it is indeed still bread, but now *essential* bread, bread which is never so much bread as it is in this mystery." From Louis-Marie Chauvet, Symbol and Sacrament: A Sacramental Reinterpretation of Christian Existence, trans. Patrick Madigan and Madeleine Beaumont (Collegeville, Minn.: Liturgical Press, 1995) 400.

in the Eucharist the bread and wine must remain bread and wine in order truly to be the symbol of the ultimate reality of the Eucharist, the sacrificed Christ.

Linking now symbolization and sanctification in broad strokes, we may say that ultimately sanctification is the sanctification of humans, that human nature requires that this be done sacramentally, that in the Eucharist matter is elevated to the status of supreme sacrament, and hence in its own way sanctified, through the symbolization of God in it, and that this is done in a unique exercise of signification which perpetuates the paradigmatic symbolization of God that took place in the Incarnation and the death of Jesus. The sanctification of humans (including Jesus) can be called ontic sanctification, sanctification as it were from within, because it is a determination (by God) of their being-in-itself, through the communication of the Holy Spirit, but the sanctification of material objects is ontological sanctification, sanctification from without, since it is a determination of their being-for-humans, which is brought about by signification and, in the case of the Eucharist alone through the power of the Holy Spirit, by symbolization. The Eucharist, therefore, is the supreme and unique instance of ontological sanctification, and is not at all an instance of ontic sanctification (but is ordered to it). This is not to undermine in any way the reality of the Eucharistic change; rather it is to indicate how it can be conceived.

It is clear that ontic sanctification is the work of the Holy Spirit even though it normally requires the cooperation of humans; but that ontological sanctification is also the work of the Spirit is to some extent obscured by the nature of human intervention in this case, for it must be a human who invests objects with new meaning. However, in as much as these are used by God as sacraments for the sanctification of humans, the work of humans here must be seen not in isolation but as cooperation with God, therefore as synergism in which the action of the Holy Spirit anticipates and includes, without destroying, the action of humans. In the establishment of a sacrament, therefore, its meaning, precisely as meaning for humans, however exalted it may be by the use of analogy, must be the contribution of humans; the specifically divine contribution can only be grace. If these observations are correct of sacraments in which sanctification is brought about by signification, they are all the more so of the Eucharist, the unique sacrament in which signification becomes symbolization, for the paradigm of sanctification by symbolization, the Incarnation and the death of Jesus, is clearly the work of the Holy Spirit, and this without prejudice to the human work of Jesus. This enables us to see the Eucharist as a work of ministry, i.e., as a divine act mediated by humans for the sanctification of humans. At the last supper Jesus acted as the human who was unique bearer and sender of the Holy Spirit, and in celebration of the Eucharist in the Church the minister acts by virtue of the participation in Christ given him at ordination.

From the standpoint of the theology of sanctification we can now say something about the three traditionally recognized "bodies of Christ," the physical body, the Eucharistic body, and the mystical body which is the Church. The physical body was the supreme ontic symbol of God, in that by virtue of the Incarnation and the death of Jesus it was the ontic symbol of the divine Word, who is the revelation of the invisible and transcendent God. In order to be perpetuated for humans, the ontic symbolization of God in Christ was encapsulated in the ontological symbol of Christ that is the Eucharist. The Eucharist in turn calls into being the Eucharistic community, which is the Church, the community of humans who meet Christ, God and each other in this, the great sacrament. Because of their union through the Eucharist with the Holy Spirit, Spirit of Christ and of filiation, individual Christians become in their bodiliness a kind of ontic symbol of Christ and of God. This is true also of the Church as such, since in dependence on baptism and the Eucharist it possesses the Holy Spirit in its own way, which was expressed by St. Augustine in his statement that the Holy Spirit is the soul of the body of Christ which is the Church.[17] We cannot here go into the question of the relation of the individual Christian and the Church as symbols of Christ. We must be satisfied with observing that the Church is no more the symbol of the Holy Spirit than is Christ. In the Godhead only the divine Word can become symbol of God in the world, and the Holy Spirit, as Spirit of filiation, in each instance points away from himself to the Son. Symbolization of God is the first stage of sanctification, i.e., the constitution of a sacrament for the sanctification of humans, which reaches its completion when, responding to the offer of the sacrament, they have the Holy Spirit communicated to them by God. As paradigm of sanctification, Christ, together with the Eucharist, the individual Christian and the Church, each in its orientation to him and to each other, is actualized by the

____

17   *Sermo* 267 (PL 38, 1231).

Holy Spirit as symbolization of God, and is therefore directed beyond self as the sacrament of the sanctification of humans. To Jesus himself the Holy Spirit was communicated in an utterly radical, direct and non-sacramental way, and thus he was constituted the supreme sacrament for others, i.e., for the Church; and he achieves this effectiveness principally in the Eucharist.

The theology of the Eucharistic change presented here clearly owes something to the theology of transignification. While this represents an advance on transubstantiation, our avoidance of the term has been deliberate. First, the prefix "trans" links this theology too closely to transubstantiation, creating the impression that the bread and wine lose one signification in order to gain another. We hope to have shown that the bread and wine of the Eucharist lose nothing at all. The change that takes place in their signification is not a transition but a further determination and deepening of the meaning they already have. Secondly, the term "transignification" gives the impression that the new being of the bread and wine is fully explained by the giving of the new signification, just as transubstantiation claimed to do by the giving of new substance. We hope to have shown that this is not the case, and indeed that the uniqueness and ultimate inexplicability of the Eucharistic change lie in the fact that the Eucharist is the sole instance of symbolization (of God) in the realm of purely material reality. Whatever the disadvantages of the theology of sanctification, it does not labor under these particular drawbacks. Finally, the theology of sanctification is comprehensive, in that it does not stop short at what happens to the bread and wine, but more importantly, indicates also what happens to those who participate in the Eucharistic celebration.

The theology of the Eucharist as sanctification was not simply plucked out of the air: it was suggested in the first instance by the liturgy, specifically by the new Eucharistic prayers composed after the Second Vatican Council. These led back to the Fathers, where a rich and promising theology of the Eucharist and the Holy Spirit was found, a theology that harmonized with the theology of grace we have drawn from the same sources. Behind them stands the figure of St. Paul telling us that Christ is our sanctification (1 Cor 1:30) and that we are saved through sanctification by the Spirit (2 Thess 2:13). Developing this theology, we arrived at the concept of the Eucharist as ontological symbol of Christ and hence of God, i.e., a sign that is one in being with the reality signified, and so reveals and communicates it. This needs to be understood in terms of the broader concept of sanctification. The bread and wine become the ontological symbol of Christ through sanctification by the Holy Spirit, and Christ is conveyed to the communicants by the communication of his Spirit to them by the Father. This symbol is as much a process as a being, a process engaging God and humans, in which they commune with each other in Christ the mediator. As performed by God it is his sacramental self-communication to humans; as performed by humans it is their sacramental entering upon an intimate relationship with God and fellow-humans. The sanctification conveyed in the Eucharist is Christ, the same total sanctification that first placed him in the world as sacrament of salvation for humans. The difference is that the ontic sanctification of the historical Jesus is preserved for the time of the Church by being made ontological, i.e., attainable through signs. While the Eucharist remains a mystery elusive to understanding, theology has its part to play, for the mystery is to some degree elucidated by use of the analogy faith provides in the Incarnation as sanctification, and further, a horizon of intelligibility is given in that humans constantly invest the signs that surround them in the world with new meaning and being. The Eucharist stands out from this horizon in that in it alone, by the sanctifying power of the Holy Spirit, being is made to correspond completely to endowed meaning, so that it is more than a sign of Christ, it is the symbol of Christ. Finally, the theology of sanctification allows us to see the Eucharistic change in its proper perspective, not as a wonder existing for itself, but as a moment of the total process of the sanctification of humans, i.e., the sanctification of the Church, a process whose sacramental form is indicated by the nature of humans themselves.

With the theology of the Eucharist as principal sacrament of grace we conclude this part of our book. It remains, in the next, and last, part, to integrate into our synthesis the questions that have preoccupied Western thought on the theology of grace. These have to do mainly with the part played by humans in the encounter of God with them in grace.

PART V

FURTHER QUESTIONS IN
THE THEOLOGY OF GRACE

13 DIVINE SOVEREIGNTY AND HUMAN FREEDOM

The first of the remaining questions to which we must give specific attention is that of divine sovereignty and human freedom. The word "sovereignty" is chosen deliberately as our keyword, because it is less open to objection than "predestination" or other similar biblical words, with which, however, it shares the disadvantage of being somewhat anthropomorphic. The main problem about "predestination," which occurs in verbal form with the meaning "fore-ordain" in Acts 4:28, Rom 8:29-30, 1 Cor 2:7 and Eph 1: 5,11, is that by force of the word itself the notion is conveyed of a decision on the part of God that is anterior to all action on the part of humans and determinative of such action. It is much stronger in meaning, therefore, than "foreknowledge," another biblical word sometimes used in conjunction with it. Thus, while we know that in fact human freedom is preserved under divine predestination, it is extremely difficult to retain the idea of freedom in the face of the vividness and unqualified simplicity of the concept of predestination. Another difficulty (not unconnected with this) is that despite its biblical origin the term "predestination" has had a most unfortunate record in the history of heresy. Although there is an important Catholic doctrine of predestination, viz., that God wills all people to be saved and predestines some to glory (to which we shall return soon), the doctrine that is more usually conjured up by the word is that God predestines some (and only a few at that) to glory and the rest to damnation. However, this latter version is more accurately labeled "double predestination," an expression whose meaning should be clear even from the brief account given above.

The concept of sovereignty, on the other hand, contains nothing explicit about unfreedom on the part of subjects, though it is true that in the ancient world sovereignty had slavery as its normal correlative. The word "sovereign" (*despotēs*) is used in the New Testament of God (Lk 2:29; Acts 4:24; Rev 6:10), of Christ (2 Pet 2:1; Jude 4) and of earthly slave-owners (1 Tim 6:1, 2; Tit 2:9; 1 Pet 2:18). A major theme of the New Testament is that in Christ God has set us free, i.e., free from slavery, specifically slavery to sin (Jn 8:34), passions and pleasures (Tit 3:3), corruption (2 Pet 2:19), the Mosaic Law (Gal 5:1) and the elemental spirits (Gal 4:3, 9). This means that on the basis of faith we are no longer slaves but sons and daughters, i.e., of God (Gal 4:7, Rom 8:15) and brothers and sisters in the Lord (Philem 16). Because, however, of the lack of complete precision in the concept of sovereignty, as spoken of above, it was also possible in this predominantly Pauline theology to say that believers are slaves of God (Rom 6:22; Eph 6:9), of righteousness (Rom 6:18), of Christ (1Cor 7:22) and of all people (Mk 10:44; 1 Cor 9:19). This, however, is not true slavery. It is only said to be slavery in order to make the point, in the most forcible possible way, of the totality of the dedication of faith. As free self-dedication, it is in fact the opposite of slavery, which is enforced subjection (cf. 2 Pet 2:19). Faith makes us children of God, and children are free (Mat 17:26). Thus the New Testament itself presents us with the teaching that God is sovereign but that those who submit to his sovereignty are free, both because they do this freely, and, more fundamentally, because God's sovereign action creates their freedom. The sovereignty of God, therefore, is different from that of earthly rulers who vaunt their authority over those forced to be their subjects (Lk 22:25), thereby degrading them. While God's sovereignty is incomparably greater than theirs, it founds and continually enhances the freedom of those who accept it in faith, and so, as it appears in Christ, i.e., as his divine authority, is revealed as humble service (Mk 10:45; Jn 13:14). Hence, while presenting the sovereignty of God as absolute, Scripture at the same time presents freedom as a great gift of God to humans, and indeed as a gift that flows from God's sovereign action toward them.

While we rightly speak of divine sovereignty and human freedom as pertaining to the being of God and humans respectively, we should not lose sight of the fact that in each the attribute in question is not static but dynamic, and so is revealed in its operation. Thus the sovereignty of God (the Father) is manifest in his choice of humans, which, as we see from the introduction to the Letter to the Ephesians (1:3-14), as well as from the other texts cited above, is directed in the first place to Christ, and only thence to others, and then precisely in their unity with him through freely rendered faith. Thus, despite its limitations, we find ourselves having recourse once more to the idea of predestination, because it does at least designate the action of God as the sovereign choice of humans in Christ, shorn now of all implication that the choice is made atomistically and arbitrarily. This basic theme we have expounded already under another rubric, viz., anointing. Further, the human freedom of Jesus, far from being destroyed by his unique grace, is seen to be founded and brought to completion by it in the faith and obedience that characterized his life; and likewise the freedom of ordinary people is elicited in their lives by the grace that is extended, even anonymously, from him to them. When predestination is placed in the correct, i.e., Christological, perspective, it loses the horrendous character that otherwise attaches to it, and it begins to take on, as it should, overtones of the love and providence of God.

It is clear from what has been said that it is precisely God the Father who makes the choice of humans for salvation. In addition to the texts already cited the following also bear this out: Lk 18:7, Rom 8:33, Col 3:12; 1 Thess 1:4; Tit 1:1; Jas 2:5; 1 Pet 1:2; 2:9-10. An apparent exception is Mk 13:27 (and parallel), where the chosen are said to be the elect of the Son of Man, but it is clear from v. 20 that they are such because chosen by God. The basis of this choice is not the works of humans but the sovereign freedom of God. The chosen, therefore, may truly be said to be "chosen by grace" (cf. Rom 11:5- 6). The making of the choice is thus removed entirely from the sphere of the world, so that in Eph 1:4 it can be said to have been made "before the foundation of the world." However, the fact that it is made in Christ means that it is realized in the world, and indeed through the sacramental bestowal of the Holy Spirit (1 Thess 1.4; 1 Pet 1:2). The purpose of the choice is variously stated to be: that people might be saved through sanctification by the Spirit and belief in the truth (2 Thess 2:13); that they might be rich in faith and heirs of the Kingdom (Jas 2:5); for sanctification by the Spirit, obedience to Jesus and sprinkling with his blood (I Pet 1:2), i.e., for covenant relationship with God (cf. Ex 24:8) in the Spirit through the mediatorship of Christ; and that they might be God's people and receive mercy (1 Pet 2:9-10), i.e., again, for covenant with God. Underlying these statements is a ground bass: God's choice is the initiatory action of the eschatological covenant in which his Spirit is poured out on humans through Christ in the prevailing covenant attitude of *hesed*, i.e., merciful love on the part of God and faith on the part of humans. This Spirit, we are told in Rom 8:14, 15 and Gal 4:6, is the Spirit of filiation, who makes us adopted children of God the Father (Rom 8:23; Gal 4:5). As we have seen, our faith, as response to the Father in his Spirit, both brings about this filiation (cf. Gal 3:26) and flows from it. Bearing in mind that it was the bestowal of this Spirit in all fullness on Jesus that made him the unique Son of God, and the statement of Ephesians that God, the Father of Our Lord Jesus Christ (1:3), destined us in love to be his children through Jesus Christ (1:5), we find the most comprehensive statement of the purpose of God's choice to be: that we might be his children in the Son through the bestowal of his Spirit of filiation. This filiation we possess now in that we already have the first fruits of the eschatological Spirit, but at the consummation of the eschaton we shall possess him more fully still, and therefore only then will our filiation be fully established and revealed (cf. Rom 8:19, 23). Within the eschaton a tension exists between the present moment and the consummation, with our filiation related to both.

In Rom 8:29 the divine foreknowledge and predestination are ordered to our divine filiation in Christ. In the next verse the stages in the realization of this predestination are given as calling, justification and glorification. Omitted here is sanctification, which belongs immediately after justification (cf. Rom 6:19, 22, 1Cor 1:30, 6:11). Whereas election and predestination belong simply to the sphere of God, calling takes place in the sphere of the world, through the preaching of the gospel (Rom 9:24; 1Cor 7:20-24; 2 Thess 2:14; 1Tim 6:12). Here it is the Father who calls, but clearly this can happen only in the calling by Christ, since it is he with whom humans are confronted in preaching. In this connection the saying, "Many are called but few are chosen" (Mt 22:14), is of interest. Here "many" is a semitism for "all." There is no limitation on the number to whom the Gospel is preached; but those who respond in faith, thereby revealing themselves to belong to the chosen, are relatively few.

If the question of the reconciliation of the divine sovereignty and human freedom is to be discussed rewardingly, the starting-point should be the history of the doctrine of grace, viz., what this history has to say about predestination and the universal salvific will (cf. 1 Tim 2:4) on the part of God, and the distinction, dating from the sixteenth century, of efficacious and sufficient grace, which normally are understood as categories of created actual grace.

A certain doctrine of predestination is supposed in the gospels, and begins to emerge explicitly in the thought of St. Paul in Rom 8:28-30 and 9:6-29. This is determined further still by St. Augustine, who exchanges Paul's collective perspective for an individual one and realizes that the nature of God requires predestination to be absolute.[1] Although the Church affirms the universal salvific will more strongly than Augustine did, its doctrine of predestination is basically taken from him (cf. DS373, 397, 623-33, 641, 974, 1177, 1522-23, 1540, 1556, 1565, 1567, 2005, 2432). It can be summarized as follows:

1. God wills that all people be saved, and so extends to all the offer of salvation.

2. In order to be saved, people must cooperate with God by freely accepting his offer of salvation.

3. If a person is lost, their loss is not because of any failure on God's part, but because of failure on that person's part, in freely refusing cooperation. In this case, therefore, the blame rests on that person alone.

4. If a person is saved, their salvation is entirely the work of God, so that their free cooperation is included in the gift of salvation. In this case, therefore, praise is due to God alone, who has predestined this person to salvation.

This doctrine presents daunting problems in the order of understanding, and the only light that we can shed on it is to show, as we soon shall, that reflection on the nature of both God and the human person leads to the conclusion that the solution for which theologians have so long striven not only has eluded them in fact but is in principle impossible. The various heresies that have appeared on this matter in the course of the history of dogma are such precisely because they attempt to offer solutions for an insoluble problem. To discuss them we must first say a word about the distinction of efficacious and sufficient grace. These categories apply both to individual acts that advance a person toward salvation and hence by definition require grace (technically called salutary acts), and to salvation as a whole. Efficacious grace, as the name indicates, is grace that works, i.e., grace that actually brings about the work desired by God. Sufficient grace, as the name also indicates, is grace genuinely proportionate to the desired work but in fact does not succeed. However, its assured sufficiency guarantees that its failure is due not to any lack on God's part, but simply to a free human refusal to cooperate with it. It is correct, therefore, to link efficacious grace with predestination and sufficient grace with the universal salvific will, provided this is not taken to mean that efficacious grace (for individual acts) is given only to the predestined or that

---

1   Cf. Ch. Baumgartner, *La Grâce du Christ* (Tournai, 1963) 69.

the predestined are given only efficacious grace (i.e., that those who are saved never sin). It is important that sufficient grace be grasped under its positive aspect, viz., its sufficiency, and not under its negative aspect, i.e., its failure. Only thus is the universal salvific will preserved as a genuine positive element of the doctrine, and a heretical version, viz., double predestination, avoided.

It will also be helpful to make some brief comments on certain questions which always arise in a discussion of predestination. Despite the many attempts to do so, we are not entitled to make any statement as to the number of either the predestined or the damned. The text of Mt 22:14, "Many are called, but few are chosen," has often been invoked as an assertion that the number of the damned far outweighs that of the predestined, but in fact the text has nothing to do with predestination, being concerned, as we have seen, with the relatively small number of those who respond to the word of preaching. It is therefore useless to speculate on this matter; nor can one know with absolute certitude (that of faith) whether oneself is predestined, though there are signs, the same as for knowing whether one has fellowship with Christ in this life, that give rise to a justified relative or moral certitude (cf.1 Jn 4:7-21). Neither are we entitled to make the judgment that any particular person is damned, or to hold that there definitely are some damned. On the other hand, the condemnation of apocatastasis (restoration, i.e., universal salvation consequent on an eventual bringing of hell to an end) at the sixth century Synod of Constantinople (DS 411) forbids us to say that all people are guaranteed salvation and that therefore no one can be ultimately damned. While we do know that many are saved (cf. Rev 7:9), salvation and loss are best grasped as existential possibilities presenting themselves to every person as the only ultimate alternatives, and calling for a decision of repentance and faith (cf. Deut 30:19).

The various attempts to solve the problem of the divine sovereignty and human freedom have all foundered on the effort to integrate these elements within a single theological system, for the relationship of God and the human, which is what is in question here, is essentially mysterious and ultimately impervious to systematization. Thus, these attempts will finish up by stressing one of the elements to the detriment, even the loss, of the other.

One type of solution takes its inspiration from St. Augustine, who himself so stressed predestination that he compromised the universal salvific will. This type will be developed further in the same direction, presenting an exaggerated or anachronistic Augustinianism called "predestinarianism." Jansenism, in holding that for fallen humanity the only true grace is efficacious grace, denied sufficient grace and the universal salvific will. This is only one step from the extreme position of Calvin, who held double predestination. In these views the sovereignty and freedom of election of God are exalted, but the freedom of humans and hence their cooperation in their salvation is denied. This means that the true nature of the human being as spirit is not recognized.

The alternative type of solution is that of St. Augustine's adversaries, the Pelagians and, more importantly, the Semi-Pelagians, on whom we shall center our attention here. With them it was the universal salvific will that was stressed. A human being is saved when they consent to the grace of salvation offered them by God. It is the consent of humans, therefore, added to the grace, that makes the latter efficacious. There is no efficacious grace given simply as such. Hence, there is no predestination. In this system, which merits the label "spiritual democracy," human freedom is exalted, but the sovereignty of God and his freedom of election are compromised. Even if it is recognized that God plays an essential part, human beings save themselves in this system, for it is their consent which gives the last determination to the grace of God. The fundamental error of this system is that it destroys the true nature of God, for in placing humans in their freedom outside God's sovereignty it reduces God to a demiurge. This is done as soon as human consent is said to add something to the grace of God which the latter does not possess of itself.

Where one alters human nature, as in Jansenism, one inevitably alters the nature of God also; and likewise to alter the nature of God, as in Semi-Pelagianism, is to alter also human nature. This is because in both systems God and humans are simply grouped together, whereas in reality they are separated by a chasm which is bridged only by the totally gratuitous grace of God, and this despite humans' natural community with God which is expressed in Scripture by the word "spirit," in Aquinas by the statement that humans have a natural desire of the beatific vision, and in Rahnerian theology by its assertion of the "supernatural existential." In the end, therefore, despite their vastly diverging moral implications, Jansenism and Semi-Pelagianism are not so very different from each other. In Jansenism it is in the sphere of

God that God and humans are grouped together, for grace is held to be due to human nature; in Semi-Pelagianism they are grouped together in the sphere of the world, for God is reduced to the level of a power operating within worldly categories. Whether it is in the sphere of God or the sphere of the world that they are put together is of small account, for the end result is the same: the nature of each is destroyed. It has been well said of Baius, predecessor of Jansen, that he was "the Pelagius of Paradise."[2] It is only when the true natures of both God and humans are respected that progress is made at all possible; but ironically it is precisely then, that the only progress that emerges is the realization that reconciliation of the divine sovereignty and human freedom is impossible in principle.

In addition to these solutions, which have been rejected by the Church as heretical, we must consider briefly Banezianism and Molinism, the two classical "Catholic" solutions from the late sixteenth century. These are called Catholic in the sense that they at least tried to take all the essential elements of the problem into account though in fact neither succeeded in doing so; and hence they ultimately reduce to forms of Predestinarianism and Semi-Pelagianism respectively, though neither of them has in fact ever been condemned. Thus, the Dominican Thomist Báñez held that predestination is antecedent to God's knowledge of human merits, and that efficacious grace differs intrinsically from sufficient grace because the former confers the salutary act itself while the latter does not. Efficacious grace is a "physical premotion" (*praemotio physica*), i.e., a created grace which infallibly moves a person to perform a salutary act, but moves them precisely in their freedom. The immediate objection one might make to this is that here human freedom remains only an assertion, without its due place in the system. Whatever its intentions, Banezianism, then approximates to the later Jansenism. The Jesuit Molina, on the other hand, held that God by use of his "middle knowledge" (*scientia media*), i.e., his knowledge of "futurables" (i.e., those things or states that would come to pass if certain conditions were fulfilled), a class of beings standing midway between possible and simply future beings, selects for creation only that order in which he sees that his will is actually carried out, i.e., when those whom he wills to consent to the grace of salvation are foreseen actually to do so. This system divided into two, viz., simple Molinism, in which predestination takes place

2   Cf. N. Abercrombie, *The Origins of Jansenism* (Oxford, 1936), 90.

on the basis of a person's foreseen merits, and Suarezian congruism, in which predestination is antecedent to these merits. Despite the ingenuity of Molinism, it is undeniable that in its various forms grace is rendered efficacious by human consent, and so it reduces to a form of Semi-Pelagianism. Applying here what we said above of the radical similarity of Jansenism and Semi-Pelagianism, in both Banezianism and Molinism the real transcendence of God over humans is compromised. This constitutes the ultimate reason for the abandonment of both systems in modern times. Theologians now seek, if not a solution, at least an insight precisely on the basis of the transcendence of God.

In both these systems the grace in question is created grace, and in Banezianism the distinction of efficacious and sufficient grace is qualitative. Even today there are theologians holding no brief for Banezianism who say the same thing, on the grounds that the only alternative is Semi-Pelagianism.[3] Thus, they say, efficacious grace must include the salutary act itself and therefore the free human consent, while sufficient grace will include neither; otherwise it is human consent which makes grace efficacious and and so becomes the determining factor in salvation, which is Semi-Pelagianism. In Molinism, on the other hand, there is no qualitative difference, the grace of God being determined from sufficiency to efficacy by human consent; but an attempt, albeit unsuccessful, is made to rebut the charge of Semi-Pelagianism by saying that the sovereignty of God is preserved in the provision that he sovereignly creates the order in which he foresees this to happen.

Granted that there is a grace which is efficacious and also a grace which is sufficient but not efficacious, we cannot avoid the question as to the nature of the distinction between them. To say that there is no qualitative distinction is apparently to adopt a Semi-Pelagian position; but to say that there is, is to opt for Jansenism, for a system in which the human person always cooperates with the grace which includes their consent and never with the grace which does not, unquestionably compromises human freedom. Here, therefore, we are on the horns of a dilemma. The only way out is to broaden the context in which the question is put. Theologians agree that hitherto the debate has taken place in the context of created grace, which in any case is clear enough from the fact that the question of distinction is asked at

---

3   E.g. Baumgartner 307.

all. The fact that in this context the two answers which emerge as the only alternatives are equally unacceptable shows that the question is actually unanswerable in the given context, that the context itself is deficient, and that a new context must be sought. But, granted that efficacious and sufficient grace must belong to the same order, i.e., both are created grace or both uncreated grace, and given the simplicity of God, where real distinction is impossible, the question assumes a new aspect when put in the context of uncreated grace, which is identical with God himself. Then efficacious and sufficient grace become terms to describe the different possible outcomes of the mysterious interaction of the transcendence of God (shorn now of all anthropomorphism) and human freedom. Where the outcome is a salutary act, the grace must be said to be efficacious, and to include free consent in the sense that divine being in its transcendence must embrace all human being, so that the ultimate praise goes to God alone; but where the outcome is refusal and sin, the grace must be said to have been truly sufficient, so that it is seen that the human and not God is to blame for its failure. In fact, however, each grace is identical with God himself in his self-communication to humans, which requires for its realization free human cooperation.

Rahner among others has shown that the problem of divine sovereignty and human freedom is insoluble in principle because the transcendence of God requires that finite being have an existence which at the same time is dependent on him, i.e., finite being is a participation in infinite being (otherwise we have atheism), and independent of him, i.e., finite being is itself and not God (otherwise we have pantheism).[4] This may be seen from a consideration of the following statement: the fullness of being is God plus finite being. If finite being is here thought to add something to God, it is thereby exempted from his sovereignty and he is reduced to a demiurge, since his existence precisely as God, i.e., as fullness of being, is denied. This is atheism. But if to avoid this conclusion finite being is equated with nothingness, i.e., mere appearance lacking substance, all being is thereby recognized as infinite, i.e., as God. This is pantheism. Finite being, we must therefore conclude, while being truly itself, adds nothing to God and falls completely under his sovereignty. The intellectual difficulty stems from the fact that at the heart of finite being is mystery: the dialectic of dependence on, and independence of, God in regard to being. Because there is nothing

---

4   K. Rahner, "Grace and Freedom," SM 2, 426b.

in finite being more fundamental than this dialectic, there exists no principle that encompasses both elements, and so the possibility of an explanation is ruled out completely.

What has just been said about the being of finite being will necessarily embrace also its operation. The operation of finite being is therefore to be attributed to finite being as truly its own, but at the same time is subjected to the sovereignty of God, so that ultimately it must be attributed to him as his operation. When we come to speak specifically of a human being in their characteristic operation, viz., freedom, the same considerations apply. The free operation of a human being, therefore, is most truly their own but at the same time must be attributed to God as included under *his* free operation (viz., creation). Further, what applies at the level of "nature" will also apply at the level of the "supernatural," so that whatever is achieved in relation to a person's salvation is truly their work but at the same time completely the work of God in grace. The human person "realizes" the grace of God, i.e., they appropriate it and translate it into genuine human reality, which, however, never stands as a rival to God but is a deeper participation in God's being than would be possible for subhuman (i.e., non-spiritual) being or for a human without grace, because it is a participation in this being in the precise manner in which, properly speaking, it is possessed by God alone, viz., as triune. The all-important difference is that the human participates in this being, whereas God possesses it in all fullness. The more humans submit themselves to the sovereignty of God the more they establish their proper nature as human beings, viz., spirit, or capacity for God. There is a direct, not an inverse, proportion between their affirmation of dependence on God, i.e., subjection to him, and their affirmation of independence of him, i.e., the achievement of their proper nature as human. The unsurpassable instance of this is Jesus himself, whose unique unity of being with God is explained by the fact that he realized his unique grace (viz., that of the Incarnation) through seeking not his own will but that of the Father (cf. Mk 14:36) and treading the path of obedience through life to death on the cross (cf. Phil 2:8). This stands in remarkable contrast to Nietzschean man, who asserts independence in the face of God but who thereby becomes a monster. Sin, the way in which a human asserts their independence of God through rejecting their dependence on him, is merely self-destruction. This provides the key to the solution of the problem of the necessity of attributing a person's sins, as human acts, to God. While such acts must be attributed to God materially and in terms of their positive content, they cannot be so attributed in their formal character of sin, where they are non-being, negation, a falling-away from being.

It remains to show how these reflections fit into the synthesis of the theology of grace offered in this book. Despite the wide acceptance of the contrary view, it is clear that there can be no qualitative distinction between efficacious and sufficient grace, since they are not distinctions within created actual grace but rather ways of characterizing the self-communication of God to humans in uncreated grace in its success and its failure respectively. While we will return to this theme later, our reflections so far have sufficed to justify already the conclusion that there is no such thing as actual grace at all, in the sense of a created passing grace distinct from created sanctifying grace. What scholasticism has identified as created actual grace in the two subcategories of efficacious and sufficient grace we can dispense with altogether and replace with the self-communication of God to humans in uncreated grace in its dynamic aspect of seeking to evoke a response from them. Scholasticism was, of course, aware that within its scheme sanctifying grace alone was not enough to account for all the works of grace, e.g. the repentance of a sinner, an act for which grace was necessary but sanctifying grace was by definition absent. Within this context the existence of actual grace has been defined against Pelagianism and Semi-Pelagianism, and such definitions are appealed to by theologians of the Scholastic tradition precisely to protect positions such as that exemplified above. This concern is safeguarded in our system by the declaration that the self-communication of God comes to humans first as an offer calling for and enabling a response, an offer which presupposes in them nothing of stable being in the sphere of God (as we call it), or sanctifying grace (as Scholasticism called it), or divine filiation (as the New Testament calls it). It is this self-communication of God which, as we have shown already, as bestowal brings about in humans for the first time the new being spoken of above, and this through the medium (or sacrament) of the offer precisely in its acceptance by humans. Efficacious and sufficient grace, therefore, remain for us the ways of characterizing the success and the failure respectively of the self-communication of God at the critical point of meeting humans in their freedom. If it is successful, we must acknowledge that its success is due entirely to God, without prejudice to the fact that on another plane it must be said to be entirely due to the human person; and if it fails, its failure is due entirely to that person and not at all to God, for from God's standpoint it lacked nothing required for its success.

A further observation in regard to efficacious and sufficient grace may be made from the starting-point of our statement that the offer of grace by Christ is the sacrament of its bestowal by the Father. When grace is merely sufficient there takes place only the offer of grace. Its refusal by the human being precludes the bestowal by the Father. When grace is efficacious the bestowal actually takes place. To the refused offer of grace, then, is linked sufficient grace, and to the bestowal of grace is linked efficacious grace.

The one grace to which we have returned is the self-communication of God, or, more precisely, the communication by the Father of the Holy Spirit in the sacrament of Christ. In our system we have safeguarded in our own way the concerns of Scripture, which are expressed in such anthropomorphic terms as foreknowledge, election, predestination and universal salvific will, and also the concerns of theology, which have been expressed in such terms as sanctifying and actual grace, and efficacious and sufficient grace. Our synthesis allows only one real distinction within grace, a distinction which must always be upheld, because it corresponds to the insuperable distinction of God and the human, which remains such even in the Incarnation. This is the distinction of the self-communication of God on the one hand and the self-transcendence of the human on the other, the latter, of course, always understood as response to, and appropriation of, the former, and embracing both the new being of the human whether in becoming (formation) or constitution, and their action, their movement toward God.

14 GRACE AND HUMAN STRIVING

Under this heading there are four matters requiring treatment, and so we now proceed to present them, in logical sequence. These are: concupiscence and integrity (on which, in relation to Jesus, something has already been said in Part Two), perseverance, actual grace, and fundamental and final option. We begin with concupiscence and integrity.

As human beings find themselves in the world prior to their acceptance of grace, they see their life characterized by factors which at a deeper level can be grasped as aspects of a single reality. These are division within self, in which idealism is countered by selfish desire (particularly when it comes to action), and death, as it exerts its influence over life, particularly in the form of dread. In Scripture the first of these counter-forces is called "concupiscence," in the sense of "sinful desire." Concupiscence and death are connected in that inner division issues finally in the radical dissolution of the person which death has every appearance of being. That St. Paul saw the connection between them is evident from his statement in Rom 8:6 that "to set the mind on the flesh is death." Consequences of sin, they are overcome by the supernatural gift of grace, in as much as it includes, as subsumed, lower gifts proportioned to this task and called "preternatural" because unattainable by human nature and gratuitous, yet pertaining to the perfection of nature rather than to the self-communication of God. It is best to see them as dynamisms of grace. Their bestowal in this life is only partial, their fullness being reserved for the eschaton. They are identified as freedom from concupiscence, and immortality. Clearly, the death which is the outcome of concupiscence is not just death in its physical constitution, which is unavoidable, but the death of the sinner, which is the total loss of the person, of which concupiscence as inner division is the beginning. It is the death of eternal perdition. Therefore, the immortality meant here is not immunity from dying; nor is it the natural immortality of the soul. It is a reality generally grasped as the reunification of body and soul which is believed to take place at the general resurrection.

Like their opposites, freedom from concupiscence and immortality are aspects of a single reality, viz., the unification and perfection of the person as such, with immortality understood as the eschatological aspect of freedom from concupiscence. For this reality there exists a traditional positive name, viz., "integrity." Immortality is suitably explained as the unification and perfection of the just person within self given completion and permanence in death, which, though it appears to be a shattering blow from without, is here transformed to become the all-inclusive act of self-surrender to God in faith (and love) on the part of that person and their completion through grace on the part of God. This unification will establish the person in the fullness of their being, which will include perfection in their social as well as individual character. The social aspect, guaranteed by the doctrine of the communion of saints, needs to be preserved if we are to have an authentic contemporary hermeneusis of the idea of the general resurrection. Integrity as we would understand it, while embracing the eschatological dimension, relates primarily to human life in the world (which also, of course, has a social aspect), and refers to the healing, the integration, the making-whole, the unification and perfection of the person in their natural endowment, and not, therefore, precisely in their communion with God. It will come to expression in their highest activity, viz., love of God above all things, which will include, of course, love of neighbor. This activity, it should be realized, is empowered directly by grace elevating nature; but in so far as it presupposes the healing of nature it depends on the gift of integrity.

The concept of the perfection of the person simply in their nature, meaningful enough for Scholasticism with its closed concept of human nature, is more difficult to sustain in transcendental theology, where this nature is understood precisely in terms of its orientation to God. Even here, however, there is need for distinction between what is simply achieved by and in human beings, as, e.g., knowledge of the world; what is achieved by and in humans and is at the same time (though with a priority of order) the self-communication of God, viz., grace; and what is achieved by and in humans and is given with and through this self-communication but is not identical with it, viz., integrity. For want of suitable alternatives the words "natural," "supernatural" and "preternatural" must continue to apply respectively to these realities, even though the terms are now seen to be rather inadequate in themselves. To present the same situation in other terminology, we might point, respectively, to that (in humans) which is achieved simply in the sphere of the world; to that which is achieved in both the sphere of the world and the sphere of God (in that the latter penetrates the former); and to that which is achieved in the sphere of the world *because* of its penetration by the sphere of God. For the sake of clarity it should be added that it is not strictly logical to oppose integrity to concupiscence as usage prompts us to do. The precise opposite of integrity is the disorder in human being, while the precise opposite of concupiscence is love, though, as we have pointed out, this love requires the person to be elevated by grace as well as healed by integrity. Grace (as possessed by humans and subsuming integrity) and love on the one hand, and disorder and concupiscence on the other, are related as being and operation. We will now look briefly at the contrast of love and concupiscence as the alternative motives of action.

Whilst never losing sight of the importance of particular acts or of the motives for which they are done, Scripture attaches the greatest significance to the over-all stance that a human adopts toward God. This matter is found in Scripture as the doctrine of the "heart" of the human person. The heart is the spiritual center, hidden from the sight of others, hidden even from oneself (1 Cor 4:3-5), but patent to the eyes of God. Above all, it is as God sees the heart that he will judge a person (Deut 8:2; 10:16-17; 1 Kings 8:39; 1 Chron 28:9; 2 Chron 6:30; Ps 17:3; 44:21; 139:23; Prov 21:2; 24:12; Jer 17:10; 20:12; Lk 16:15; Acts 1:24; Rom 8:27; Rev 2:23), but unfortunately this heart is corrupted by sin (Jer 17:9). In the teaching of Jesus (Mt 15:18-20) the wrongful actions by which a person is defiled are seen as proceeding precisely from the heart.

According to Deuteronomy (6:4-5), the principal business of a person's life is to love God, and indeed with their whole heart. This deep love, which finds expression in the observance of the commandments, is response to the prior love of God, in which he chooses Israel for covenant (4:32-40; 7:6-8, etc.). Jesus unites the great commandment of Deuteronomy with that of Lev 19:18, which enjoins love of neighbor, to form the great single commandment that he gives to his followers (Mk 12:28-31 and parallels). Here we have the basic and all-comprehending moral teaching of Christianity. St. Paul goes on to say that whatever a person does should be done out of love (1Cor 16:14). In Gal 5 his well-known contrast of the flesh and the Spirit furnishes the contrast of concupiscence and love: concupiscence as "concupiscence of the flesh" (v. 16), and love as heading the list of "the fruit of the Spirit" (v. 22) (see also 1 Thess 4:3-12, especially vv. 5 and 9 for the contrast of concupiscence and love in Paul).

In the writings of St. Augustine concupiscence and love appear as motives of action, and indeed as the only alternatives.[1] He believed that goodness of motive was what distinguished a good act from a sin. For him anyone who did not explicitly believe in Christ was an unbeliever, and therefore was incapable of the faith, and hence of the love, that was required by Scripture for an act to be acceptable to God and to escape being a sin. All the acts of unbelievers, therefore, were sins. The sinning believer also lacks the love to perform truly good acts, but they retain the faith that allows them to have at least imperfect love, and this enables them to avoid further sin in their apparently good acts. Augustine could see no medium between love and concupiscence, between a salutary act and a sin. This was because the distinction of the natural and the supernatural was not available to him. This distinction was the achievement of the Scholastics, and it allowed a mid-position, viz., a naturally good act, performed from a motive of natural love, which, though less than the supernatural love of God above all things, was enough to save an act from being a sin. Significantly, however, the Scholastics did not posit a natural virtue of love of God above all things corresponding to the supernatural one. This was because such a love, possible for a person with the gift of integrity (which was not given in the concrete without grace), was not possible for them in their fallen state. The love of God above all things is the love for God in which even one's love of self is referred to God. The reign of concupiscence in the fallen human being makes this love impossible unless they are healed by God. This God has done through the gift of grace. As Aquinas points out, however, the love that flows from grace differs from the hypothetical love that would flow from integrity (without grace). The latter would attain God only as "the principle of natural

---

1   Cf. *Epistola* 217: 4, 12 (PL 33, 983); *Enarratio in psalmum* 118: 22, 7 (PL 37, 1565-66); *Sermo* 159: 3, 3 (PL 38, 869); *De diversis quaestionibus ad Simplicianum* 1, 3 (PL 40, 113); *Enchiridion ad Laurentium* 30 (PL 40, 246-47); ibid. 121, 32 (PL 40, 288-89); *De natura et gratia* 70, 84 (PL 44, 290); *De perfectione iustitiae hominis* 6, 15 (PL 44, 298); *Contra duas epistolas Pelagianorum* 1, 2, 5 (PL 44, 552); ibid. 11, 9, 21 (PL 44, 586); *Contra Julianum Pelagianum* 4, 3, 21 (PL 44, 749); ibid. 4, 3, 33 (PL 44, 755); *De gratia et libero arbitrio* 17, 13 (PL 44, 901).

good," while the former attains him as "the object of blessedness," with whom "a person has a certain spiritual fellowship."[2] In other words, the love flowing from grace is truly personal, uniting the person to God precisely as he is in himself, and it can only be response to his love.

It is true, therefore, to say that love triumphs over concupiscence, provided that this love is recognized as a free human act as well as the gift of God. It was this requirement that Baius and later the Jansenists did not fulfill in their (erroneous) interpretation of the theology of Augustine. For them love and concupiscence were irresistible forces determining the human will from within. They considered that freedom under grace was sufficiently guaranteed if the person were not moved by external force. In their view, a person was free provided they willed a thing self, even if the willing were brought about by necessitation. To take an example from modern life, they would have said that a drug addict is free: no one forces them to take drugs; they take them because they want to.

The Catholic response to this rejects the notion of freedom just outlined and declares that human freedom under grace is a freedom from necessitation as well as from coaction (DS 1939, 2003). Grace is not necessary for a good act, i.e., for an act contributing to the fulfillment of human nature (cf. DS 1934, 1936, 1937), and though grace is necessary for a salutary act it is not precisely the grace of justification that is required (cf. DS 1525, 1526). Hence the supernatural virtue of love is not necessary for either a good or a salutary act, though it is necessary, as we will see later, for a meritorious act, i.e., for an act by which a person grows in their friendship with God. Hence an act does not need to be motivated by love in order to escape being a sin. Theologians have long discussed the question as to the kind of intention of love that is necessary to render a good work of a just person meritorious. The most widely accepted opinion (and also the most common-sense one) is that no special intention is necessary, and that it suffices that the work be done from habitual charity, i.e., simply by a person in "the state of grace." It is argued by some that the authentic Thomistic position on this is that in these circumstances love will always exercise an actual, even if implicit, influence on the act. However, it is also true that the more a Christian's acts proceed from the explicit motive of love of God (and neighbor), the more meritorious they will be. This is because love provides the highest, and therefore the

---

2   *Summa theologiae* I-II, 109, 3 ad 1.

most personal, of all possible motives for action. Even an "anonymous" Christian is capable of acting from this motive, i.e., from a love that in fact is directed to God and neighbor and inspired by grace though present to consciousness in other terms.

It is love of God above all things that integrates the other virtues, the possession and practice of which constitute the realization of the human. Persons, then, are unified, made integral and whole, when they thus love God. The presence of this ability to love, therefore, means that basic integrity has been established. However, neither the presence nor the absence of this ability can be conclusively demonstrated in particular instances; rather, we must be satisfied, as in the case of knowledge of justification, with signs that give rise to no more than moral certainty. The basic integrity of which we speak is not complete in this life. It is always under threat; it can be lost, and when it is, it needs to be regained. On the other hand, it can be increased; and while the increase must be attributed to the action of grace, it must also be attributed to our own efforts in response to, indeed enabled by, grace. Hence it is by loving that integrity is increased. A person grows in self-possession through loving. And their self-possession reaches its completion in the act of dying, so that it is there that at last a person is able to express self fully in a single act, which is an act of love. The Christian doctrine of grace therefore has this to say to the secular person about the human wholeness they so earnestly desire: it is achieved only asymptotically throughout life; while it is a human achievement, it is in the first instance the gift of God; and it is brought about not through self-seeking but through loving.

In itself the word "concupiscence" denotes spontaneous inclination, prior to reflection, toward either good or evil, though in normal usage it is restricted to the inclination to evil. In Scripture it is the inclination to sin, even the power of sin working in humans (Gen 3:7,10 [cf. 2:25]; 8:21; Jer 17:9; Sir 15:14; Rom, 1:24; 6-8 [cf. 5:12]; Gal 5:16; Eph 2:3; Col 3:5; 1 Thess 4:5; 1 Tim 6:9; 2 Tim 2:22; Tit 2:12; 3:3). It is unlikely that Paul identifies concupiscence completely with sin, though he does link them closely. Rahner sees the tendency to identify the two in Paul as arising from the practice, initiated by St. Augustine, of applying the classical passage, Rom 7:14-25, to the justified person, in which case the sin there spoken of can only be concupiscence.[3]

---

3   Cf. Rahner, "The Theological Concept of Concupiscence," *Theological Investigations* 1, 347, note 2.

Luther understood Paul in this way, and thus concluded that a person remains in reality a sinner after justification. It is better to see Paul as speaking here in the name of the unregenerate or of Adam considered not as a particular person but as the spokesperson of humankind. For Paul sin is not so much a state as a power, and so will include concupiscence; but in Rom 7:8 he distinguishes them, and he recognizes concupiscence as remaining in the justified even though for him, as we will see, justification means the destruction of sin (Rom 13:14; Gal 5:16; Eph 4:22). The Council of Trent declared (DS 1515) that when Paul calls concupiscence sin, as he does, e.g., in Rom 6 and 7, the Church understands this in the sense that concupiscence derives from sin (i.e., from original sin) and leads to sin (i.e., to personal sin). The fact that Paul sees concupiscence as a power working in people against their real interests reflects perhaps the rabbinic tendency to mythologize concupiscence.[4] This tendency has been pursued into modern times, but with harmful results for evangelization, standing as it does in opposition to the scientific world-view and offering a way out of accepting personal responsibility for sin. Our task, then, will be to interpret Scripture's mythological statements about concupiscence in an anthropological way.

Rahner treats concupiscence anthropologically when he speaks of it as "man's spontaneous desire, in so far as it precedes his free decision *and resists it.*"[5] Desire precedes decision in that spontaneous apprehension of the object by the subject's appetitive power is the presupposition of the intellectual act; and desire resists decision in that the exercise of freedom by which a person attempts to dispose of self as a whole through placing self before God and making an existential decision about him is not entirely successful. The basic reason for this partial failure is the finiteness of the human being, which implies in them a real distinction of essence and existence, with essence achieved only asymptotically in the concreteness of existence. Rahner expresses the same idea with the aid of the terminology of "nature" and "person:" a person experiences great difficulty in adequately expressing their person, i.e., that which they desire to become, in their nature, i.e., that with which they are endowed. Concretely for a human being, their finiteness is given in the exhaustive binding of their spirit as form to the matter of their body. Here form finds itself resisted and

---

4   Cf. W. Davies, *Paul and Rabbinic Judaism* (London, 1965) 21.

5   Rahner 360.

only partially successful in bringing itself to actualization in the "other" of matter. The sharpest, but by no means the only, expression of this dualism in the human is the resistance they encounter in self of the sensitive to the spiritual. It is wrong to conceive the sensitive and the spiritual in humans as fundamentally opposed: in fact they are fundamentally ordered to each other in that every human act involves both. The disorder, therefore, exists at a less profound level. When Paul opposes flesh and spirit, these are for him religious, not anthropological, concepts. The flesh is the whole person in contrast to spirit, which is God. Hence the flesh, which includes the person's spirit, is the human being in their apartness from God, i.e., in their sinfullness. Certainly Paul sees the rebellion of the lower human appetites as an expression of sin, but it is only one of several expressions, and it is an expression precisely of sin, i.e., of something which ought not exist.

It is important to note that the reality which we call concupiscence is experienced as a force countering evil as well as good inclinations. Humans find it difficult not only to be as good but also to be as evil as they might wish. (This will be applied when we come to speak of the theological distinction of sins.) While integrity is the perfection of nature by which obstacles to freedom for self-orientation for good are overcome, there exists also a kind of perverted integrity by which the human inclination to wholeness is gradually replaced by a spiritual death-wish which facilitates self-disposition for evil.

The fact that concupiscence derives from their finiteness shows that it is a natural condition of human beings. From this we see that the healing of concupiscence will be preternatural and hence gratuitous. It may be asked whether integrity is not owing to humans because of the fact that every nature will have the right to its own integrity. Is it not against the wisdom of God to create a nature that without his further help must remain forever divided against itself? It is a false approach to attempt to answer this question in terms of the abstract principle which it contains; rather, it should be answered in terms of God's concrete plan of creation, salvation and fulfillment. As a sinner, a human being has no claim on the healing and saving grace of God, which in this setting (comprehended by the Pauline usage *charis*) remains absolutely gratuitous. From the point of view of concrete human nature, however, humans would indeed have been frustrated had God not come to their aid with the preternatural gifts, for this frustration is inseparable from the nature of finite spirit, which, however, is such not fortuitously but precisely for the vocation of union with the infinite spirit of God. The purpose of the entire intervention of God in the sphere of the non-divine is that the self-communication which takes place in God and is identical with him might be participated in by non-divine being, so that God might be all in all (cf. 1 Cor 15:28). This involves and explains the creation of the world and of humanity its supreme representative, which as spirit in the world is alone capable of this participation. The giving of the preternatural and the supernatural gifts, therefore, must be seen as moments of this plan. Its gratuitousness, which must always be upheld in this setting also, here resides precisely in the sovereign freedom of God in adopting and embarking on the plan, a freedom which does not apply to the self-communication within the Godhead itself. Integrity is given only *ad integritatem naturae*, for the perfection of nature, and therefore its loss does not mean, as Luther, Baius and the Jansenists believed, that human nature is thereby intrinsically corrupted, though it is "wounded." The naturalness of concupiscence raises again the question of its relation to sin. This relationship arises from the actual supernatural vocation of humans, without which there could be no question of sin. Because humans experience concupiscence as an impediment to the realization of this vocation, it is for them a negative existential, just as grace is their supernatural existential. A contemporary hermeneusis of the doctrine of original sin does not favor a state of original justice from which humanity, in the person of Adam, fell. If this doctrine is now to be understood somehow in terms of the need of all people for the salvation of Christ, the experience of concupiscence is to be seen as the manifestation of this need. It is not, of course, an unambiguous manifestation, for concupiscence continues to exist even in those who have been justified. The gifts of grace and integrity do not simply remove concupiscence: they only mitigate it; but the stronger presence of concupiscence in humans without grace, though not demonstrable empirically, allows us to retain a sense in which concupiscence can still be said to flow from original sin as well as to lead to personal sin. It is in this sense that we accept the statement of Scheffczyk, that the naturalness of concupiscence is only its formal and structural component, while its material reality comes from the tendencies released by sin. We endorse also his further observation that the continuance of concupiscence in the justified enables them to be conformed to the sufferings of Christ and thus to share in the redemption.[6]

Thus we conclude our observations on the subject of concupiscence. Since concupiscence constitutes the main obstacle to humans' perserverance in good, it is appropriate that we pass on now to our second point, the question of perseverance.

So far when discussing the necessity of grace for good, salutary or meritorious activity, we have considered this necessity only in relation to discrete actions. Clearly, however, this does not fully meet the requirements of real situations in life. We must now, therefore, take up the question of the necessity of grace for living in obedience to God for the whole of life, or at least for a lengthy part of it. This has indeed been a traditional question for theology, put precisely in the form of a question about perseverance "for a long time" (latin: *diu*). Connected but not identical with it is the question about perseverance at the moment of death, called "final perseverance." As a matter of terminology we will be satisfied with speaking simply of "perseverance" (whether life-long or not) and "final perseverance." What the question will entail for us is the demand for a theology of fundamental and final option as alone doing justice to the nature of the human as spirit in the world. We will not go into the question of the nature of the good on which this perseverance is centered, beyond saying that it is the moral law as taught by the Church, which derives ultimately from the moral teaching of Christ, and which, absolutely speaking, is discoverable by reason. And we will regard perseverance as continuing despite light infringements; that is to say, it is destroyed only by a serious infringement (a theme to which we will return soon).

Against the Pelagians and the Semi-Palagians the ancient Church taught the necessity of grace for salvation (DS 225- 27, 241, 380). Since humans are not saved unless they cooperate with grace, the necessity of grace here is precisely for the salutary observance of the law, i.e., for its observance in a way conducive to salvation. This raises the question: given that grace is necessary for the precisely salutary observance of the law, is it necessary also for its observance simply in itself? This question can only be put when the distinction of the natural and the supernatural is appreciated, which was not the case at the time of the Pelagian and Semi-Pelagian controversies. However, when the Council of Trent came to restate the Church's position on

---

6   Cf. "Concupiscence," SM 1, 404a, b, 405a.

this matter at the close of the Middle Ages (by which time the distinction had become common property), it was content simply to resume the doctrine of the ancient councils (DS 1541, 1572). It is therefore not immediately clear whether the Church's teaching on the necessity of grace for the observance of the law applies to the substance of the law or only to the manner of its observance. However, an examination of the early documents referred to above reveals that grace is there declared necessary not only for the gaining of eternal life but for the overcoming of concupiscence. And concupiscence militates against the observance even of the substance of the law (cf. the classical text, Rom 7:14-25, where, as we have said, the "I" is best understood as referring to the unregenerate human being, whose problem is not the manner of observance but the observance itself). Hence we are justified in concluding that the necessity of grace refers not only to the manner of observance but to the substance of the law. Since concupiscence remains after justification, even the justified need grace in order to persevere; and if *they* need it, the unregenerate need it all the more.

Within Scholasticism the nature of this grace was a matter of dispute. In this context the view of Aquinas, that it is habitual rather than actual grace, is to be preferred, both because the grace must be commensurate to a state, and because habitual or sanctifying grace includes love of God above all things, which is required to counter the concupiscence that poses the threat to perseverance in the first place.[7] This means that the ability to persevere is given with the grace of justification. Certainly, the Church taught, against the Protestants and the Jansenists, that the justified have the capacity to avoid sin (DS 1536, 1568, 2001). It is not at all difficult to incorporate this position into our theological synthesis: the Gift of the Holy Spirit, love of the Father, changes the very being of humans as they respond, making them children of God and evoking from them the love of sons and daughters, which empowers them to overcome all obstacles to their relationship with God and to remain in the observance of the law. Conversely, the person who does not possess this divine filiation is not capable of the stable love of God that is proof against temptation. From this it follows that there is no such thing as a purely secular holiness. If a person in fact lives in obedience to the moral law this is because they are given the grace to do so. As we have seen, the possession

---

7 *Summa Theologiae* I-II, 109, 3.

of this grace is not restricted to identifiable Christians but is extended also to "anonymous" Christians.

The sin that a person is able to avoid through this grace is serious sin, not light or venial sin. Trent taught that for the justified to abstain from all light sin would require a special privilege, such as was granted to Mary (DS 1573). The reason given for this by Aquinas is the inability of the justified to overcome the disordered movements of sensuality in their totality even though they do have the power to win through in each individual case.[8] This is an aposteriori statement, i.e., flowing from Christian experience, rather than an apriori one. Even in those who appear fully committed to Christ the power of concupiscence is of such strength that they are unable to avoid all light sins.

The teaching of the Council of Trent continues with the assertion that even the justified cannot persevere in good unless they receive a "special help from God" (DS 1572). Nothing, however, is said about the nature of this help. The need for it arises from the continuance of concupiscence in the justified, to which witness is borne both by experience and by the statements of Scripture, which urge Christians (whom we must presume to be justified) to avoid sin and pray for perseverance (Gal 5:16-25; Eph 6:10ff; 1 Cor 10:13). This immediately raises the question, if a special help over and above sanctifying grace is needed by the justified for perseverance, what becomes of the position just reached, that the power to persevere is bestowed by sanctifying grace? Scholasticism after Trent answered this question by distinguishing between the radical and the complete power of perseverance, and saying that the former is bestowed by sanctifying grace, the latter by the special help. The foundation for this assertion is the fact that the grace of justification heals concupiscence only partially, so that the special help is needed for the cure to be complete, i.e., in the sense that the justified can be successful in carrying out their resolve to avoid sin (they cannot, of course, hope to avoid temptation). The special help, moreover, belongs to the category of actual grace, for it is invoked not continuously but only at certain times, when needed. This is because concupiscence, which it counters, asserts itself in a critical way only from time to time. The power of perseverance, therefore, quite fittingly includes both an habitual and an actual element.

Underlying these statements we discern not apriori principle but a reflection of actual Christian experience. Our relationship with God is

---

8   Ibid. I-II, 109, 8, and 74, 3 ad 2.

personal. In this relationship we are both free and at the same time impeded by concupiscence. From our side alone, therefore, the relationship will not be fixed, but will wax and wane and at times be placed in jeopardy. Even on God's side the relationship will vary, not through any imperfection in God, but rather because of his sovereign freedom, which allows him to take unpredictable initiatives. From both sides, therefore, the relationship will be variable, and from our side it will be exposed to threat. That sanctifying grace is declared to bestow the basic power of perseverance is recognition of the fact that between the just and God there exists a basically stable bond and relationship; that the special help is also declared to be necessary is recognition of the flux that exists in this as in all personal relationships (as opposed to the fixed steadiness of impersonal relations) and the danger to which it is exposed from the human side. The doctrine of the special help, therefore, is recognition of the precisely personal nature of the relationship between the just person and God. An analogy may be taken from a marriage in which one partner is stronger than the other: between them there exists a bond, which is, however, sometimes under threat because of the character of the weaker partner; at these times the stronger partner must act with particular tact and love in order to help the other rise to a love by which the crisis will be overcome and the bond preserved. Since the fidelity of the stronger partner is assured, the continuance of the bond will depend on maintaining the character (and consequently the commitment) of the weaker partner at or above a certain critical level. In this analogy (which is an apt one because it closely parallels the covenant relationship of grace) the character of the weaker partner (upheld by the love of the other) stands for sanctifying grace (the habitual element), and the efforts of the stronger partner at times of stress stand for the special help (the variable element). The reality surpasses the analogy in that God is the founder of whatever good there is in a human being. His merciful love is the explanation of the new being of the human person, of their commitment to him in faith, hope and love, of the bond that exists between them, and of the special efforts by which they are rescued at times of crisis.

Once we see the personal reality that is expressed by the doctrine of the special help it is not difficult to incorporate it into our synthesis. Scholasticism found it necessary to distinguish between sanctifying grace and the special help as habitual and actual grace respectively because this was the only way in which it could attempt to do justice to the situation within its chosen context of created grace (granted that the special help is recognized as an internal help and not just as a providential disposition of external factors). Once we broaden the context, a different answer becomes possible without prejudice to the doctrine. By his merciful love for humans, which is the Gift of the Holy Spirit, the Father so transforms them that they become his children, and the relationship of loving filiation is set up between them and God. This relationship, however, is placed in jeopardy because of their frailty (concupiscence). When this threat becomes acute, God sustains the relationship by loving them all the stronger (with all that this entails by way of providential action) and thus enabling them to rise to a love that conquers difficulties. Here it will be seen that the periodic nature of the special help is maintained without any need to distinguish between an habitual and an actual gift within the category of created grace. The power to persevere is established with the change of the person into a child of God through the reception of the Holy Spirit, love of the Father, and Spirit of filiation; it is completed by the intensification of this love at the times when this is required. There is, admittedly, a distinction here, but it is the one we have upheld throughout the presentation of this theology, viz., the love of God, identical with the Holy Spirit (corresponding to uncreated grace in Scholasticism) on the one hand, and the change in the being of the person consequent upon receiving that love (corresponding to created [habitual] grace in Scholasticism) on the other; but we do not invoke a distinction of actual and habitual grace within the context of created grace as Scholasticism did.

Scholasticism taught that the grace of justification bestows the right to claim the special help when needed. This statement, which to Protestants smacks of legalism and Semi-Pelagianism, nevertheless contains a truth that must be preserved. We would prefer to express it thus: the gift of filiation denotes for the adopted child a community of life with the Father which allows them to call on the Father with filial confidence, as no outsider (someone who is not a son or daughter) could do. This position is unexceptionable, for the confidence of the child is based on what they have received and appropriated, certainly, but only as the grace of God—it is not based on anything that they have of self.

We now consider briefly a gift referred to in passing by Trent as "the great gift of perseverance" (*magnum perseverantiae donum*) (DS 1566).

By this is meant actual perseverance, which includes perseverance at the moment of death, or final perseverance. Neo-Scholasticism, basing itself on the teaching of the Council, related sanctifying grace and the special help on the one hand and the great gift on the other in the following way: the former pair between them constitute only the *power* of perseverance, while the latter constitutes *actual* perseverance. A person may be *able* to persevere without *actually* persevering. The great gift is precisely the actualization of the power of perseverance. Of the three, then, only the great gift can be said to be efficacious grace. Final perseverance must be considered as a distinct element because it involves eschatological salvation. Thus the moment of death is recognized as qualitatively different from the moments that conclude any other long spans in a person's life. As the theory of final option asserts, at death a just person will normally gather up and reaffirm the whole direction in which their life has been moving, viz., toward God. Because final perseverance has this meaning, it may be said to be given only to the predestined and hence not to be an object of merit. The teaching and the theology of the great gift fit readily into our synthesis when account is taken of the positions already reached on the divine sovereignty and human freedom, on God's election of humans in Christ, and the theory of final option. The great gift is nothing other than the Gift of the Holy Spirit, love of the Father for humans, by which a person is helped through life and especially at their last moment to rise to a love of God that makes of their life a journey toward God and of its end a definitive reaffirmation of that chosen orientation.

Although final perseverance cannot be merited, Catholic spirituality encourages us to pray for it constantly as "the grace of a happy death." The Christian commitment of our lives should give rise to the consoling hope that God who began the good work in us will bring it to completion (cf. Phil 1:6). The doctrine of the special help also should have a bearing on our spiritual life, since it directs us again to those parts of Scripture and the liturgy where we are exhorted to pray frequently, even daily, for the gift of perseverance, and never, in Semi-Pelagian fashion, to take our relationship with God lightly or for granted. Christians should pray continually for perseverance, as perseverance in faith, hope and love, perseverance in their life's vocation, and perseverance at the moment of death.

As we have had occasion to mention actual grace several times already in relation to the question of the necessity of grace for perseverance, it will be appropriate now to give some attention to our third point, the question of actual grace itself. In Scholasticism the term "actual" in this context is meant to distinguish this grace from "habitual" grace, habit and act being contrasting and complementary concepts. Moreover, within the concept of the supernatural habit itself a distinction is made between the entitative habit, viz., sanctifying grace, and the operative habits, viz., the infused virtues. Hence actual grace, as the grace required for salutary acts, is opposed not only to sanctifying grace, but, more directly, to the infused virtues from which these acts flow. Against Pelagianism and Semi-Pelagianism the necessity of grace for every single salutary act has been defined (cf. DS 225ff., 373ff., 1551ff.), and in this sense the existence of actual grace must be said to be of faith. However, it must be borne in mind that as a real distinction the distinction of habitual and actual grace must, and in fact does, belong to the usual Scholastic context of created grace. If a new context is chosen, viz., that of the self-communication of God, the question of the distinction of actual and habitual grace may, and indeed must, be put anew, without prejudice to the doctrine that grace is needed for every salutary act.

The Scholastic theologians were divided on the question as to precisely what must be included under the concept of actual grace. Some held that for every single salutary act a distinct actual grace was necessary. Just as the divine concourse was required in each instance for a finite being to pass from potency to act, so a supernatural divine concourse was required for the performance of every salutary act, and with this concourse actual grace was identified. Others took the view, called Thomistic because Aquinas did not recognize an act as salutary unless it flowed from a constituted habit,[9] that the infused habits, entitative and operative, provide sufficient explanation for the vast majority of salutary acts, since these habits are not static but dynamic in character. This view did not deny the necessity of the concourse, but refused to recognize precisely it as the grace in question. On this

---

9   While Aquinas recognizes that for the disposition of the soul for a habit (in this case sanctifying grace) it cannot be required that some other habit be already present (*Summa Theologiae* I, 109, 6), he several times enunciates the principle that habit, along with faculty, is the principle of the act (Ibid. I, 83, 2; I, 87, 2; I, 93, 7; I-II, 49, introduction).

view, which is to be preferred both because it does greater justice to the supernatural habits and because it better fulfills the requirement that "beings are not to be multiplied without necessity," there are only three graces that would have to be admitted as purely actual, in the sense that they are not adequately explained by supernatural habits. These are the special help and final perseverance, of which we have spoken already, and lastly what is called "prevenient" grace. The latter is usually understood as the grace which by definition precedes and anticipates (*praevenire*) all action of the will in regard to God, e.g., the grace that wakens a person spiritually for the first time (cf. DS 1525). H. Bettenson has pointed out that in the writings of St. Augustine, from whom this doctrine stems, the passive voice of *praevenire*, *viz.*, *praeveniri*, as used in this connection has the meaning "to be started," "to be set going," so that prevenient grace not only anticipates but actually starts the will of the person on their movement toward God.[10] From these remarks it is clear that prevenient grace will precede the existence of any supernatural habits in a human person, and therefore could be understood by Scholasticism only as a strictly actual grace. As we have already fitted the special help and final perseverance into our synthesis, it remains now only to do the same in regard to prevenient grace.

From the side of God prevenient grace may be identified without further ado as the Gift of the Holy Spirit offered to humans in the sacramentality of Christ. By definition the only basis in a human being for the acceptance of this grace is their spirit as capacity for God ("as he is in himself," as Rahner maintained in his theology of the "supernatural existential").[11] As they cooperate with the grace of God offered to them and accepted by them, it is possible (even likely) that there will be a delay in time before justification takes place, i.e., before they are able to rise to the love of God which both flows from and brings about justification. During this time, however, we should see the supernatural habits as beginning to be formed within them. We have expressed this concept elsewhere in this book as the divine filiation of the human person, in formation as distinct from constitution. However, these

---

10   H. Bettenson, *Documents of the Christian Church* (London, 1963) 55, note 1.

11   For an explanation of the qualification added here see my later article, David Coffey, "The Whole Rahner on the Supernatural Existential," in *Theological Studies* 65 (2004) 95-118.

habits in formation only partly explain the continuance of a human's response as it approaches nearer and nearer to love of God above all things. At the same time these acts, as increasing response to the proffered love of God, transcend the habits in formation and draw them in their train so that the habits approximate more and more to sanctifying grace and the infused virtues, or as we would prefer to say, to divine filiation and the faith and love of sons and daughters.

In this way not only do we incorporate prevenient grace and the subsequent "co-operating" grace into our system, but we arrive at a position where we are able to say something about actual grace in general. To situate our observations within the Scholastic framework for a moment, we espouse, as a number of neo-Scholastic theologians have done by means of the concept of *habitus in fieri* (habits in becoming or formation), a compromise between the position of Aquinas, for whom every salutary act had to flow from a corresponding habit, and those theologians who required no habits at all and were satisfied with understanding actual grace simply as *"esse fluens"* (flowing or passing being, which appears to be a contradiction in terms.) More importantly, if we wish to retain the category "actual grace" for the purpose of designating those instances of grace where a salutary act cannot be explained fully or even at all in terms of supernatural habits, we must realize that it does not denote a passing grace distinct from habitual grace in the context of created grace. Only two graces remain in our synthesis, and they are closely related, the second the result of the first: the Father's Gift of the Holy Spirit, Spirit of filiation, and the new being of divine filiation brought about in humans by the reception of this Spirit. Actual grace reduces simply to the former in the case of prevenient grace, and to a combination and interaction of both in the case of subsequent grace.

We pass on now to our fourth, and last, point, the theology of fundamental and final option. The anthropological considerations involved in the treatment of this question will serve to unify our remarks on the three previous points.[12]

---

12 Because my thinking on it has developed over the years, the presentation of this point undergoes here a substantial revision of what I wrote in the first edition. See my article, David Coffey, "Rahner's Theology of Fundamental Option," *Philosophy & Theology* 10/1 (1997) 255-84, and my book *The Sacrament of Reconciliation* (Collegeville, Minn.: Liturgical Press, 2001) 18-27.

In presenting now a theology of fundamental and final option it will not be necessary to start from the very beginning, since the essential work has already been done by others,[13] and since even in this book the themes on which such a theology draws have already been presented, so that it now remains only to gather them together and orientate them to this new end. In the following reflections, therefore, use will be made of positions attained on such matters as the universality of the call to salvation, anonymous Christians, the biblical doctrine of the human heart and the theology of concupiscence. Closely connected with our theme is the question of the theological distinction of sins, which we will therefore consider at the same time. While there exists wide agreement as to the general contours of option theology, there is still room for difference of opinion on significant matters of detail.

Psychologists have long been unhappy at the naivety of the view that the meaning and value of a person's life are determined simply by the objective nature and the deliberateness of their discrete actions. A human being possesses a center, an ego, which is formed over a long period through the interaction of highly complex forces. Attitudes and actions must always be seen in relation to this center: they both flow from it and contribute to its formation and consolidation. The core of the human person, then, is both revealed and shaped through their activity, which lies toward the periphery of their being. One therefore rightly expects consistency rather than anarchy in a person's actions. However, we must beware of any tendency toward a mechanical application of principles to the conduct of a person. No one can really predict how a human being will act in a given situation or pass judgment on their action. All we have here is an explanation that lends reason and coherence to human actions, shows how they can be truly personal, and redeems them from arbitrariness. It is also possible, of course, that the patterns of action, the attitudes and even the basic orientation of a person may be weakened and even reversed.

This view is endorsed by transcendental philosophy, which understands human persons in terms of their transcendental orientation to Being. They actualize themselves in terms of this orientation by acting within the categories imposed by their historical existence. Transcendental theology takes up this view, identifying as God the

---

13 E.g., on fundamental option: Fransen, Glaser, von Hildebrand, Rahner and Reiners; on final option: Boros, Glorieux, Rahner, Schmaus, Schoonenberg.

goal of the person's orientation and asserting that the actualization takes place in their personal history of salvation through the action of grace and their cooperation with it. Thus, while the individual actions of a person, even those directed to God, are confined within categories, their being remains transcendentally referred to God. It is precisely this insight that we preserve when we assert the sacramentality of grace: while the offer of grace is made necessarily in a sacrament belonging to the world, for example (and supremely) the humanity of Christ, the bestowal of this grace is done transcendentally (but still in the sacrament) by the Father, which is clear from the fact that thus the Father makes of the person precisely a son or a daughter. The major architects of Western Christian thought, Augustine and Aquinas, have recognized, each in his own way, the basic orientation of the human person to God, and hence taught that on every person lies the necessity of making a profound choice of God (which they could only see as a particular and directly intended act) and that people who fail to make this choice thereby expose themselves to eternal loss.[14] Since this applies to every person, its application outside Christianity calls for a theology like Rahner's theology of the anonymous Christian. We know that God wills the salvation of all (see 1 Tim 2:4), and so gives all the opportunity for this. Here we have the beginnings of fundamental option theology.

From Scripture we recall the doctrine of the heart of the person, outlined earlier in this work, in which the person is asserted to possess a spiritual center, which is open to the eyes of God alone, and from which their actions radiate. From Scripture also, with the aid of modern theology, we have presented a theology of concupiscence, in which the resistance encountered by the human spirit in realizing itself in the "other" of matter comes to the fore and presents a reason for the impossibility for a person to dispose of self entirely before God in a single act. Scripture also characterizes certain sins as unforgivable, thus consigning them to a much more serious category than, e.g., those other grave sins listed in the Pauline literature as excluding from the Kingdom of God (1 Cor 6:9-10; Gal 5:19-21; Eph 5:3-5). These are blasphemy against the Holy Spirit (Mk 3:28-29 and parallels),

---

14 For Augustine see E. Portalie, *A Guide to the Thought of St. Augustine* (Chicago, 1960) 271-73; for Aquinas, D. Coffey, "The Salvation of the Unbeliever in St. Thomas Aquinas and Jacques Maritain," *The Australasian Catholic Record* 41 (1964) 193-98.

apostasy (Heb 6:4-6), and "mortal" sin (1 Jn 5:16-17). It is generally agreed that the unforgivableness of these sins stems neither from the sins themselves nor from any refusal of forgiveness on God's part, but from the fact that those who commit them have effectively blocked themselves off from the grace of God.

We are thus entitled to claim Scriptural basis for the assertion that even in what Catholic teaching has called "mortal" sin there is scope for differentiation of levels of alienation from God, measured not so much by individual acts as by the stance over against God which these both reflect and bring about. With this observation we introduce the theme known as the theological distinction of sins. In light of what we now know, it might be desirable to restrict the term "mortal sin" to the three "unforgivable" sins of Scripture and refer to those others by which charity is lost as "grave sins." The remainder, "venial" sins, are more fittingly called "light" or "non-grave." Those in which the matter is grave but the sin is not (because of diminishment of responsibility), could be called "mitigated" should it seem too dismissive to refer to them simply as "light."

A difficulty raised by this is that, as grave sin is by definition definitive, it is not possible to have degrees of alienation from God: one is either alienated or not.[15] We take it that by definitiveness here is denoted the irreversibility and completeness consequent on a total total rejection of God. In order to reply we must adopt a more nuanced approach than is evident in the objection. An act is definitive, though only in a relative sense, if it engages a person's core freedom (as it is aptly called). In the realm of sin, and according to the traditional view, this was done if the three requisites of grave matter and full knowledge and consent were verified. Such an act was judged definitive in the sense that the person had destroyed in self the divine life previously enjoyed through grace. This is all that the traditional view had in mind; in fact it was the only kind of definitiveness that it knew. But from psychology we now know that this may not be enough to engage core freedom, for what Rahner calls an "imposed necessity " (not so much at the level of the act as at the level of the person) which would lessen or remove personal guilt, might have come into play. Examples

---

15   In this section we take into account the objections raised by R. McCormick, "Notes on Moral Theology: January-June, 1968," *Theological Studies* 29 (1968) 680-81, from B. Schüler, "Todsünde - Sünde zum Tod?," *Theologie und Philosophie* 42 (1967) 321-40.

of what is meant here are provided in the *Catechism of the Catholic Church* when it lists "affective immaturity, force of acquired habit, conditions of anxiety or other psychological or social facts that lessen or even extenuate moral culpability."[16] Evil acts affected by any of these factors do not engage core freedom, and so cannot be considered to be mortal sins or to be definitive in any sense at all.

According to Aquinas, as we have seen, charity, as both virtue and act, is the love of God "above all things." It is by charity, "faith working through love" (Gal 5:6), therefore, and only by it, that God can be embraced as the ultimate end of human life, for the ultimacy in question here consists precisely in the reference of all things, including ourselves, to the supreme good that only he can be. The fundamental option, therefore, must consist in the virtue and act of charity, and it is changed by grave sin—any grave sin—because it is by this alone that charity is expelled from the human heart. But grave sin, as Aquinas taught, is not easily committed. As he wrote,

> Though grace is lost by a single act of mortal sin, grace is not lost easily. For it is not easy for a person possessing grace to perform such an act, the reason being their inclination to the contrary. As Aristotle said in 5 *Ethics* (ch. 6), it is difficult for a good person to do things that are not good.[17]

(Note that Aquinas here speaks at the level of the person rather than of the act alone.) Charity, therefore, to which the human person is inclined by virtue of the supernatural existential, is of its nature stable, and its opposite, grave sin, can only be definitive in the sense that the sinner is utterly incapable of regaining charity by their own unaided power. The grace of God, however, is always offering; and the basis on which it is received is the faith and hope, albeit uninformed, that remain after sin (see the Council of Trent, DS 1544, 1577, 1578) and both permit and encourage repentance.

Because this faith and hope provide a link, however tenuous, with God, the fundamental option for God, while lost, cannot in this situation be said to be totally eradicated. For that to be done, sins against hope and faith would have to be committed. Only in that case can

---

16   *Catechism of the Catholic Church* 2352. The Catechism is here only speaking about one specific grave sin, but there is no reason against applying its statement more generally.

17   *De veritate*, q. 27, a. 1 ad 9.

the sinner be said to have disposed of self entirely in rebellion against God. And this self-disposition occurs only at the end of a process, not in an isolated act. Even then, the possibility of repentance and conversion cannot be ruled out, however unlikely it might seem. Such is the power of grace. An absolutely definitive option against God can only be achieved (if that is the right word), if the complete destruction of a fundamental option for God is ratified by dying the death of a sinner, in other words, by a final option against God, for only at this moment, Rahner writes, "man is freed from his attachment to all that is individual"[18] and thus enabled and obliged to make a final choice for or against God. Whether the latter option ever occurs is known only to God.

It may be further objected that the view of the human person presented here is too Platonic, i.e., that the human spirit is envisaged as the prisoner of the body, released in death. In fact, however, the anthropology implicit in our position is closer to that of Aristotle, in which the soul is the form of the body. However, it differs from the latter in that the spirit is regarded not just as informing, i.e., as the source of power, but as itself increasing and gathering in being through its dependence on matter and in response to the grace of God offered continuously in the sacraments that comprise our world. This is the anthropology of Rahner and Teilhard. In it death comes as the completion of the actualization of the spirit and hence of the person. True, death results from forces that are natural and sub-personal, e.g., old age, disease, or accident, but these merely provide the occasion for precipitating that act which cannot avoid being the affirmation of self as built up in one's personal history, and which, if it is also an affirmation of God, cannot fail to involve grace. From this it will be clear that we cannot accept the view of nature and grace that sees the person as left mostly to self, with grace offered only on occasions. While we must defend nature against Luther and all who regard it as destroyed by original sin, we must remember that in fact it never exists by itself. Humans and their world are stamped by the two realities of grace and sin; and every person lives in this milieu, bathed as it were in the grace of God. At times its claim on them will be urged dramatically, but far more often its voice will be subtle, discerned in the ordinary events and encounters that make up daily life.

---

18   K. Rahner, "Death," SM 2, 61b.

Besides according well with the sources, the theology presented above fits readily into our synthesis. The fundamental option of a person, attained (normally) over a period coinciding with the development of adult moral responsibility at whatever age this occur (perhaps the late teens or the early to mid twenties in our culture), and identical with "faith working through love," is the transcendental result of their continuing categorial response to the offer of grace, the Gift of the Holy Spirit, in the sacraments of grace that constitute their world. This option is a possibility for every person whether they be engaged by Christianity or not. Apart from the setbacks caused by sin (which can nevertheless be overcome), their life can be a growing affirmation of God in faith, which results in a deepening sanctification brought about by the Father through his bestowal of the Holy Spirit. This affirmation reaches its absolutely definitive form in the act of the death of a just person, in which their personhood, both in its natural dimension and particularly in its divine filiation, is brought to completion, so that the person thus gains a definitive position and effectiveness in the communion of saints, a position which is recognized by the Church in its practice of the canonization of saints, the most favored and outstanding of the children of God.

15 JUSTIFICATION, SANCTIFICATION AND GLORIFICATION

These themes are linked by St. Paul (Rom 6:19, 22; 1 Cor 1:30; 6:11), and also belong together logically. They occupy the last place in our presentation not because they are unimportant but because this is their appropriate position in the exposition of the theology of grace in the perspective which we have adopted. In fact they are very important. No theology of grace could claim to cover the essential ground unless it gave them due attention. We therefore consider them now, in the order given above.

The importance of the theme of justification in the theology of grace lies in the fact that it has to do with being made acceptable to God through the forgiveness of one's sins. It comes to us in the New Testament as part of the polemical thought of St. Paul against Pharisees and Judaizers, particularly in his letters to the Romans and the Galatians. It is the application of an image, viz., that of a court in which the accused, who stands for the unregenerate person, awaits their verdict from the judge, who stands for God. Amazingly, the judge declares the accused acquitted although in fact they are guilty. The action of the judge, who is "just" or "righteous" (Rom 3:26; 2 Thess 1:5; 2 Tim 4:8), is "justification" (Rom 4:25; 5:18), by which the judge "justifies" the accused (Rom 3:30; 4:5, etc), thus making them "just" (Rom 1:17), in possession of "justice" or "righteousness" (Rom 4:3-6) like the judge himself (Rom. 3:5, 25). For the sake of clarity we draw attention particularly to the distinction here of justification, the action of God, and justice, the attribute of God and of the justified person.

Actually, Paul has borrowed this image from his adversaries, who have used it for their own presentation of what happens in justification. The fact is that it is better suited to their account than to his. The situation can be likened to a duel, where the opponent has the choice of weapons. We need to remember this, for it means that Paul is using an image which is in fact imperfect for the conveying of his teaching. The Pharisaical version presents justification as based on a person's works, and Paul shows his understanding of this doctrine in Rom 2:13-16. The idea is that the one who observes the Law in all fullness is the true just person, and their justice will be acknowledged and declared by God in the eschatological judgment. This justification is forensic only, i.e., it is simply a declaration of existing justice, and it is eschatological, i.e., it happens at the end on the basis of the life that has preceded it.

Paul wishes to present a radically different concept of justification. For him no one can be just on the basis of works; rather, all people are sinners and stand in need of the redemption that comes from Christ (cf. Rom 1:18-3:24). Justification, then, comes not through works but from the mercy of God on the condition of faith, a faith which is an admission of powerlessness to win justice by oneself (Rom 3:28; 4:1-8; 9:30-32; 10:3; Gal 2:16). Justification, then, is an effective action of God, the actual forgiveness of sins, not the declaration of an existing justice. Paul makes the image refer to the present life, not to a future vindication (Rom 5:9); and to the sinner, not to the just person (Rom 4:5). Justice follows justification; it does not precede it. For Paul justice too is different from what it is in the Pharisaical theology: it is grace, a gift from God, not something which people can have of themselves.

To convey his ideas Paul must break through the limitations which the image imposes on him. The main one is that justification will continue to appear to be merely forensic. In order to overcome this he uses particularly vivid language when speaking of justification. Thus, e.g., in Rom 5:19 (see the whole passage vv. 12-21) he asserts the reality of one's justification in contrast with the reality of one's sinfulness. What emerges from this is a strong impression of the gratuitous and paradoxical character of justification: it comes as a gift, and as the opposite of what one would expect. Further, the nature of faith is not fully expressed in the image. We know from elsewhere that faith is the total response of a person to the grace of God, but in the image it appears only on the basis of the contrast with works. The result, inevitably, is a one-sided presentation.

It is to other images used by Paul that we must turn if we are to gain a completely unambiguous statement of the reality of the destruction of sin and of the renewal which take place with the bestowal of grace by God. Thus in Rom 8:1-2 he speaks of being "in" Christ Jesus, of having "life in Christ Jesus," and thus being freed, by the law of the Spirit, from the law (the Mosaic Law) which brings sin and death, so that there remains no condemnation for this person. Other writings of the Pauline corpus support this statement. Thus Eph 4:22-24 speaks of "putting off" the old corrupt nature, of being "renewed" in the spirit, and of "putting on" the new nature "created" after the likeness of God in true justice and holiness. And Tit 3:5 speaks of God as saving us not because of deeds done by us in justice but through his own mercy, by the washing of "regeneration and renewal in the Holy Spirit," which he poured out on us richly through Christ so that we might be "justified by his grace." It is highly significant that in two of the three texts quoted here the forgiveness and renewal are attributed to the reception of the Holy Spirit. It is beyond doubt, then, that these are intended as actual realities and not as merely forensic entities.

Paul links the justification image with Christ, who is never far from his mind. In Christ the justice of God is revealed (Rom 3:25; 2 Cor 5:21), and God has constituted him our justice (1 Cor 1:30). For our sake he took our sins upon himself, so that when we are justified our justice comes about through our association with him (2 Cor 5:21) through faith. Our justice is not our own but his (Rom 8:1, 3-5; 2 Cor 5:19-21). Here our image breaks down, as it labors under the double limitation of having only forensic concepts at its disposal, and of being referred primarily to one who was sinless, and to whom, therefore, the idea of justification simply does not apply. At this point it is better to put the image aside and look at the reality to which it points, viz., the fact that a person is justified through their solidarity with Christ. To be "in Christ" conveys for Paul something real as well as mystical. It means that the Spirit who is totally his is given, through him, also to us, but that whereas in his case the Spirit's work was simply that of sanctification (and indeed in the most radical possible way), in our case it includes justification as a prior moment (not in time but in order) (1 Cor 1:30). At this point we must resume the, theology of divine filiation, for the Spirit's work of sanctification is that of creating divine filiation, fully and uniquely in the case of Christ, and by participation in the case of others. By now we have moved far from the justification image. In the mind of Paul the difference between the two is not that only the justification image starts with humans as alienated from God, for the filiation image begins at the same point, i.e., with humans (but not Christ) presented as slaves (of sin) (Rom 6:17,20; Gal 4:3, 9; 5:1; Tit 3:3), the contrast of slave and son being an obvious one in the households of Paul's communities (Rom 8:15; Gal 4:2). Despite the fact that use of the slave-son image here is not fully logical (the master, sin, being different from the father, God, in the application), this image adds the dimensions of liberation and adoption to that of forgiveness contributed by the justification image. Admittedly, with talk of adoption we are again in the realm of forensic language, but this drawback is overcome by the consideration that the adoption in question is brought about not through a legal decree but through a real bestowal of the Spirit of filiation. (It remains, however, an adoption, for it supervenes only after an initial period of alienation from God.)

At the Reformation the Protestants exploited the basic inadequacy of the justification image in Paul, and presented it as positively teaching a merely forensic justification. This was not because they shared the ideas of the Pharisees and Judaizers against whom Paul was writing. Indeed the Christian equivalents of these latter would be the Pelagians, who stood at the opposite pole to the Protestants. The idea of forensic justification suited the Protestants because it allowed justice not to be real at all. (In the Pharisaical concept it was real but purely human). This was important for them because of their belief that human nature had been totally corrupted by original sin. Since humans must remain always sinners, God could not really justify, i.e., change, them, but he could declare them just and impute to them the merits of Christ. Then they would be simultaneously a just person and a sinner (*simul justus et peccator*). The Council of Trent rejected this doctrine (DS, 1515, 1561, 1580).

At this point we do well to resume the theology of Aquinas. The will of humans and the will of God, he says, differ in that whereas the former is attracted by an existing good, the latter simply creates the good that is loved.[1] (Aquinas recognizes that the will of humans also is creative of good, but insists that it cannot fully create the good that it loves. This recognition is important, for it is an acknowledgement of the creative power of human love.) From this it can be seen that a purely forensic justification by God is impossible. God cannot love humans without that love being creative and effective. He cannot forgive them, in an act of merciful love, without their being truly forgiven and really different in their being as a result.

The doctrine of justification fits readily into our synthesis. Its concern is to emphasize that the grace of God finds the human person a sinner, whose sin is overcome in their being assimilated to Christ, in whom the justice of God himself is made present. This victory over

---

1   *Summa Theolgiae* I-II, 110, 1.

sin, so the doctrine continues, is an act of God, not of humans; but humans plays their part, by cooperating with God by repentance and faith. The grace of justification is identical with that of divine filiation, bestowed by the Father in the Holy Spirit, Spirit of filiation, who confers this grace as liberation from the slavery of sin and as adoption as a child of God, a share in the Sonship of Christ, not just in name but in very truth.

The justification theme began with an image, which had to be interpreted and applied, but with the next theme, sanctification, we are dealing with an idea that applies directly. The vocabulary used by Scripture in relation to this theme involves words for the state (holiness), the adjective (holy), the verb (to sanctify) and the action (sanctification). In the Old Testament "holy" meant basically "other" or "apart" and was applied primarily to God, precisely in his distinction from humans and their world. The modern equivalent of the holiness of God, therefore, would be his transcendence. The term, then, denoted his very essence, his divinity. In this connection we note that the term "Holy Spirit" indicated simply the divine Spirit, or the Spirit of God.

As applied to creatures "holiness" indicated their assimilation to the sphere of God, and "sanctification" the action of God by which this is done. Any person or thing set aside for divine worship or service thus became holy. In all likelihood the idea of holiness as a freely rendered spiritual dedication of oneself to God derived from this, for it was fitting that a person who had been given over to God should endorse their consecration with a life of freely given service, an idea which lies at the heart of the liturgy and theology of infant baptism today. It is important to note that this ontological holiness, as we may call it, preceded moral holiness and provided its basis. Pelagianism is thus excluded at the outset from the idea of genuine human holiness. It is recognized to be a gift, a grace, flowing from the divine election, and human contribution to it can be seen only as cooperation. At this point we resume the theology of sanctification presented earlier in this book, when we discussed the Eucharist. According to this, for persons sanctification means the determination of their being in the sphere of God, their acquisition of being as supernatural fulfillment of nature, with the latter understood as openness to, or capacity for, God; and for objects sanctification is also an acquisition of being, viz., their constitution as the sacraments through which God does this.

Israel was holy, because it belonged to God by election and covenant (Ex 19:6), and as its successor the Church is holy (1 Pet 2:9), as are its individual members, who are called "saints" because chosen by God and dwelt in by his Spirit (1 Cor 3:16-17). Above all, Jesus is called the Holy One (Rev 3:7), because of his oneness with God. He is also called the Holy One of God (Jn 6:69) and the holy servant (Acts 4:27,30), expressions of his unique origin and relation to the Father. In Lk 1:35 he is called holy because made so by the Holy Spirit. We saw in our theology of the sanctification of Jesus that he is the holy one par excellence, because the bestowal of the Holy Spirit, Spirit of Sonship, on him by the Father was radical and total, with the result that he was made unique Son of God.

As we have seen, one's first contact with God is with the Holy Spirit, who as Spirit of filiation makes them a child of God united to the unique Son (one Spirit in Christ and in Christians) and thus brings them into community of life with the Father. From this we readily see that as the one who assimilates humans to the sphere of God it is precisely the Spirit who is the Sanctifier (Rom 15:16; 2 Thess 2:13; 1 Pet 1:2). At the same time we must bear in mind that the Father sanctifies, in the sense that it is he who acts through the Spirit (1 Thess 5:23), and that also Christ sanctifies, in that it is he who offers the Spirit in grace. Humans are sanctified only if they accept this offer and cooperate with grace. Hence it is not in any way Pelagian to say that there is also a sense in which humans may be said to sanctify themselves. This they do by their free response of faith and the good works that it implies (Rom 6:19, 22-23; 1 Cor 6:10-11; 1 Pet 1:14-16) as well as by the avoidance of sin (1 Thess 4:3; 1 Cor 6:18-19).

The principal matters pertaining to sanctification have been covered already earlier in this work, but there remain two topics which require some attention. The first of these is the question of the gifts of the Holy Spirit, i.e., the spiritual gifts given by the Holy Spirit. These fall into two categories, the first of which has to do with gifts given principally to the individual person rather than to the community. We express the matter thus in order to avoid giving the impression that there is any such thing as a purely personal spiritual gift. No Christian is isolated from the community of the Church, and whatever gifts he or she has relate in some way to the community. These are normally called the seven gifts of the Holy Spirit, and scriptural basis for them is given in Is 11:2, in which the Hebrew text lists six gifts of the Spirit to be borne by the future Messiah and borne in the past by his renowned ancestors: the wisdom and understanding of Solomon, the counsel and might of David, and the knowledge and fear of God of Moses, Jacob and Abraham. To these the Septuagint adds piety, a reduplication of the fear of God, thus bringing the number up to seven. The Council of Trent taught that they belong to the interior renewal of justification (DS 1528; cf. 178).

The number and nature of the gifts have been matters of dispute, but the theology of Aquinas on this has received general acceptance.[2] According to him, they are seven in number, they are created gifts, and their function is to heighten the sensitivity of a person to the inspirations of the Spirit, thus facilitating acts of virtue. While they are present in all the just, they come more into play in the higher reaches of the spiritual life, by giving an increased openness to God and holding concupiscence in check. They enable persons to discern with more certitude the will of God for themselves in the puzzling situations in which they so often finds themselves in life. We look to Jesus in the Gospel to see the principal example of this. His unerring instinct to discern, and his courage to carry out, the course of action indicated by the Kingdom is yet another sign that he was indeed the Christ, prime bearer of the messianic gifts of the Spirit.

In assimilating the teaching and theology of the gifts into our synthesis, we are satisfied with observing that since grace is the love of God for us (the Holy Spirit), a love which evokes from us an answering love, anyone who possesses this grace will be disposed to seek the detailed will of God in the subtle ways known to love. The more intensely one loves God, the more sensitive one will be to his inspirations, discerning his will with clarity where a less graced person will do so in obscurity and difficulty. Such a person will make a ready response to the promptings of the Spirit. There is a sense, therefore, in which we would want to endorse the teaching of Aquinas that the gifts are created. While they are best understood in terms of a loving relationship between God and the human person in the bond of the Spirit, they are located at the human end of the bond, in spiritual sensitivity. There is no need to limit their number, artificially, to seven.

1 Cor 12 is devoted to the other kind of gifts of the Holy Spirit, the "charisms," given to individuals primarily for the building up of the community, the Church, e.g., the gifts of apostleship, prophecy,

---

2   Cf. ibid. I-II, 68; II-II, questions 8, 9, 19, 45, 52, 121, 139.

teaching, etc. (cf. vv. 27- 31). Here too a balance must be struck between the public and the private character of the gifts. While these ones exist for the sake of the Church, the fact that they are possessed by individuals shows that God wills that individuals be sanctified personally by accepting their particular responsibility for the community.

The Councils of Florence and Trent taught that certain of the sacraments, viz., baptism, confirmation and order, imprint on the soul a "character," i.e., an indelible spiritual sign, which constitutes the explanation of their unrepeatability (DS 1313, 1609). Comparable with these is the "bond" of marriage, by which the unity and indissolubility of Christian marriage are expressed. The tendency to understand these realities in terms of elaborate metaphysical categories is not only baffling to anyone holding a modern anthropology, but also quite unnecessary. As P. Fransen has pointed out, the teaching of Trent on this matter is by no means to be regarded as a canonization of Scholastic speculation. It is better to regard the unrepeatability of these sacraments as based on the divine fidelity, and to accept their visible rites as those by which persons are "characterized," i.e., publicly entrusted with positions entailing particular responsibilities and rights in the community of grace.[3]

We come now to the second, and final, topic referred to above as remaining to be treated in relation to sanctification, viz., the value of human cooperation with grace. In the first place this resumes the idea, mentioned above, of self-sanctification, understood in an orthodox way free of Pelagianism, and also points to the intrinsic character of the reward of good actions as cooperation with grace, i.e., they result in an increase or growth, from within, of the person's being in the sphere of God. Secondly, it raises the question of merit, which at first sight appears to introduce an extrinsic element, as though a person's reward could adequately be compared to wages paid for work done. This is unfortunate, for all extrinsicism must be eliminated from the consideration of our relationship with God, since human nature must be understood as capacity for God. Merit, however, does introduce the element of justice (in the sense not of righteousness but of fidelity in giving another what is their due). A person's reward is based on the justice of God. The person is free, and never more so than when they become a child of God, so that their actions performed under this grace actually require that God recognize their value with him.

3   Cf. "Orders and Ordination," SM 4, 342a, b, 325a.

Both ideas, cooperation and merit, were repugnant to the Reformers, the first because of their belief that human nature was corrupted by original sin, and the second because it appeared to destroy the gratuitousness of grace in making it a matter of justice. Since we are striking the latter objection now for the first time, we shall have to give it our attention. In what follows we shall be at pains to reconcile the claim of the righteous person on the justice of God and the gratuitousness of their reward.

The Old Testament taught the justice of God, who rewards the good and punishes the wicked. It was only gradually, with the Book of Ezekiel, that the concept of individual, as distinct from group, responsibility, was attained; and the problem posed by the fact that the good appeared to suffer and the wicked to prosper was solved only by the emergence, in the Books of Daniel and Wisdom, of the doctrine of the immortality of the soul, which made it possible to see God's justice as taking effect in the next life. In the New Testament the Kingdom is presented as the reward of virtue (Mt 5:1-10; 7:21), and the King (the Son of Man) is depicted as a just judge (Mt 25:31-46). St. Paul is important in this connection, for elsewhere he appears as the champion of the gratuitousness of grace and of the sovereignty of God. In Gal 6:7-9 he sketches a teaching of responsibility and retribution. He speaks of the reward of the just person under various images: the court of justice (Rom 14:10; 2 Cor 5:10); the claim of the son as an heir (Rom 8:17); the athletic prize (1 Cor 9:24-25; 2 Tm 4:6-8); and weightlifting (as training for bearing the weight of glory in the life to come) (2 Cor 4:17). The term "merit" is not biblical, originating with Tertullian, who, it is thought, may have been a lawyer; but as we have just shown, the reality for which it stands is biblically based. For the same reasons as in the case of Paul, it is interesting to note that St. Augustine also had a doctrine of merit.[4] The Scholastics, principally Aquinas,[5] discussed the question of merit in the light of the distinction of condign and congruous merit (*meritum condigni* and *meritum congrui*), the former based on justice and the latter on liberality. The justice involved in condign merit is either that of equality, i.e., between the work and the reward, or of proportion, where there exists a proportion but not equality between the two. The first is verified only in

---

4   Cf. J. Rivière, "Mérite," DTC 10/1, 643-51.

5   Cf. *De veritate* 27. 1, 2, 3; *Summa theologiae* I-II, 114, 6; III, 19, 4, and 48, 1.

the case of Christ, who by virtue of the Incarnation placed a work that strictly earned his exaltation to the right hand of God. The Incarnation also had the effect of making Christ the head of the Church, thus conferring on him the capacity to act as the representative of other people before God. Precisely as representative, then, he was able to merit condignly not only for himself but for others. (An example that illustrates this would be that an ordinary member of a group of workers has no right in justice to claim the wages of the group on their behalf, but their constituted representative does have this right.) Condign merit of proportion is verified in the case of ordinary Christians on the basis of their divine filiation. The fact that they are sons and daughters does not give them the representative character of Christ, the unique Son, but it does at least create a proportion between themselves and God which bestows a new dignity on them and on their good actions. As explained above, they can merit condignly only for themselves, not for others. Whatever merit they earn for others, then, is congruous not condign. In Scripture God has bound himself, in justice therefore, to reward their good deeds, but his action goes beyond the mere making and honoring of a decree; in making people his children (through faith, hope, love and sanctifying grace), he sets up in reality the basis of the justice by which he is bound. Further, while a person who has sinned seriously is capable of performing under grace salutary acts of penance by which their lost filiation is eventually regained, precisely meritorious acts require that this filiation be already constituted. Hence a person in the state of sin cannot perform a meritorious act.

Luther was being consistent when he denied the possibility of merit. If human nature was corrupted by original sin, and if justification was only forensic, there was no possibility of setting up a proportion between human beings and God, and hence no basis for a doctrine of merit. In condemning his doctrine and presenting its own, the Council of Trent spoke only of condign merit. It taught (DS 1582) that the just person merits for self an increase in sanctifying grace, eternal life, even the "gaining" of eternal life (if they have died in grace), and an increase in glory. Evident here (and also in DS 1535, 1545-1550 and 1574) is the Council's concern to maintain both the intrinsic character of merit and the continuity between grace and glory, and at the same time to avoid giving the impression that final perseverance itself can be merited, since the latter belongs, as we have seen, to the predestined alone. Whatever the criticisms one might want to level at the apparent legalism and extrinsicism of the Scholastic theology of merit, one should recognize that it does bring out the representative character of Christ, and also the fact that justice must be acknowledged as an element of the situation where the grace of God really changes a person. The quarrel with Protestantism on this score should be fought not on this but on the previous ground of the ontological character of justification. If the latter is real, then God in his justice is bound to recognize it to be so. At the same time Scholasticism was able to show that the claim in justice does not eliminate or diminish the gratuitousness of grace, for the bestowal of divine filiation, which provides the basis for this claim, is itself grace. As Augustine put it, "When God crowns our merits he crowns nothing other than his gifts."[6]

So far as our synthesis is concerned, the value of a person's cooperation with grace should be seen to flow from the reality of the divine filiation which their response to grace brings about and thenceforward constantly deepens. And since under grace a person makes of self in this life what they will be in the next, their relationship to God in heaven will depend on the depth of divine filiation attained in their life and their act of dying.

On the question of the revival of merit after penance for sin, the alternative opinions are those of Suarez and Aquinas.[7] The former held that merit lost through sin is restored in the same degree as was present before the sin, and indeed is increased through the sacrament of penance. Obviously this opinion is based on a legalistic and extrinsicist concept of merit. Aquinas on the other hand held that the restoration of merit depends on the degree of commitment and love with which the sinner turns again to God. Since it sees merit and sanctification as personal realities, this opinion is to be preferred.

We turn now to the third theme, glorification, which is a modification of the concept of glory. In Scripture "glory" is "the divine mode of being."[8] Unlike holiness, which characterized God in his separation from the world, glory connotes, as pertaining to his essence, his living and saving relationship to humanity, and so is often presented as entailing visibility, in the form of brilliant light. Paradoxically, however, this serves to emphasize further the transcendence of God over

---

6   *Epistola* 194, 5, 19 (PL 33,880).

7   Cf. M. Schmaus, *Katholische Dogmatik* 4/1, 595.

8   G. Kittel, *Theological Dictionary of the New Testament* 2 (Grand Rapids, 1966) 247.

humans. As the powerful presence of God awaited the eschaton for its full revelation and operation, glory was an eschatological concept. On that day we would "see" God and "give glory" to him, i.e., acknowledge his majesty with fitting humility and honor. Because of the unity of Jesus with God, he shared the divine glory. For the fourth evangelist, with his realized eschatology, this was situated already in the earthly life, where, however, it was beheld only with the eyes of faith (Jn 1:14; 2:11; 11:4; 12:23-24). Otherwise, the glory of Jesus was connected with his resurrection (Rom 6:4; 1 Pet 1:21) or parousia (Mk 8:38; 10:37; 13:26 and parallels). Not only will we *see* the glory of God, but through our solidarity with Christ in the Spirit, which we possess now, we will, and to some extent already do, *participate* in it (2 Cor 3:7-18, Eph 3:16-17; 1 Pet 4:14). Our "glorification" will be brought to completion in our own resurrection, to take place at the parousia (Rom 8:17; Phil 3:21; Col 3:4). The concept of glory as shared in by humans, then, has to do with the whole process of their divinization, their participation in God. To some degree we have covered this already, in our treatment of sanctification. It remains, however, to consider the eschatological completion of the process, signified particularly in the resurrection of the body. And it remains also to consider the participation of the infra-personal world in this process.

It is not possible in a work of the present scope to do more than make a cursory statement on the question of the bodily and general resurrection. It must suffice to say that this image entered the Jewish religion in the second century before Christ probably from Persian sources and under the inner impulse of the necessity of finding a way to vindicate those who had not merely died but had done so in bearing witness to the covenant, viz., the martyrs under Antiochus Epiphanes.[9] The image served to express, far better than its alternative, the immortality of the soul, could have done, the political and religious hopes of the Jewish people for eschatological restoration and salvation. In the New Testament, in conjunction with the complementary ideas of the ascension and the sending of the Spirit at Pentecost, it served first of all as the vehicle of expression of what would otherwise have been inexpressible, viz., the transformation of Jesus in his death, i.e., his completion by the Father, in person and grace as Son of God

---

9   Cf. X. Léon-Dufour, *Resurrection and the Message of Easter* (London, 1974) 19; W. Marxsen, *The Resurrection of Jesus of Nazareth* (London, 1970) 134.

in humanity, and the revelation and making present and effective of himself to his community in this Sonship through the power of the Spirit as Spirit of Christ, experienced as the outpouring of grace, the call to personal faith and the impetus to missionary activity. The result was that thenceforward this community was to hold itself to be the community of salvation, with the Savior present in power in its midst through the Spirit. Secondly, the image served to focus the community's attention on a future fulfillment over and above that which comes with individual death. While divine filiation and community in the Spirit are begun in this life, their completion as the work of the Spirit in fully identifying the community with the unique Son belongs to the eschaton (Rom 8:11, 17, 13, 29).

Once we have appreciated the mythological character of many of the thought forms of the New Testament, studied their origins and understood something of what they strove to express, it is no longer possible for us to accept a purely literal understanding of such things as a triumphant return of Christ to earth, a general physical resurrection, and judgment by Christ. This makes it all the more imperative to discover what is meant by these images. For a long time the answer to this question was obscured by a highly individualistic and atomistic understanding of what happens to the just person after death. It was believed, and officially taught by Pope Benedict XII, that either immediately or upon purification they were admitted to the beatific vision of God, which they enjoyed thenceforward for all eternity without the mediatorship of any creature (DS 1000- 1002). This teaching must be understood within the limits of the Scholasticism of its day, presenting the beatific vision as being, like grace, a work of God in his unity, common to the three divine persons. As it stands, it is incapable of assimilating the glorification themes listed above. It was only with a piece of work by Alfaro (which we have referred to earlier[10]) that a satisfactory solution has become possible. Alfaro's study led him to the conclusion that without prejudice to the official teaching, the beatific vision is mediated to the just in heaven by the incarnate Son who even there is the only one who knows the Father (cf. Mt 11:27; Jn 1:18). This means that the work of the Holy Spirit and of Christ, far from being discontinued in heaven, reach their completion there. A moment's reflection is enough to show that the reduction of Christ in heaven simply to our companion fails to do justice to the "one mediator

---

10   Cf. notes 14 and 15, Chapter 5.

between God and humans" (1 Tim 2:5). We recall also that the Holy Spirit is called by Paul "earnest" or "first fruits" (Rom 8:23; 2 Cor 1:22; 5:5; Eph 1:14), the implication being that in heaven we receive him in fullness; and that when Scripture speaks of heaven as the vision of God it is precisely the Father who is meant (Mt 18:10; 1 Jn 3:2). In this view God is everlastingly Trinitarian, not just in himself but in his dealings with humans. In more recent times Church teaching has more than once stressed the inner consistency between grace and glory, the only element acknowledged to be different being the difference in the condition of the human person.[11] In offical teaching this difference is expressed by means of the "light of glory" (lumen gloriae) (DS 895), which is an "ontological specification of the mind"[12] making it possible for humans to see God directly. If grace, then, is truly Trinitarian, as we hope to have shown in this work, glory too must be the same. Finally, the philosophical objections to distinct roles of the three divine persons in grace and glory, based on the conception of God's action as efficient causality, have, as we have seen, been superseded through the introduction of the concept of divine formal causality.

These reflections place us in a position to say that we reduce the eschaton when we depict it as succeeding the present age historically. Of course, it has been realized from the time of the Fourth Gospel that the eschaton penetrates the present age. Many, however, taking literally the apocalyptic descriptions of the synoptic Gospels (cf. Mk 13 and parallels), have thought that in addition to this there is to be in the future a cataclysmic divine intervention, involving a general resurrection, the parousia and judgment, which will place an end to human history. These elements of the eschaton as presented in the Gospels are conveniently grouped under the single idea of general resurrection, to which the resurrection of Christ is related as inauguration to consummation.[13] We would like to suggest that when the eschaton is presented in Scripture in this way it is best interpreted as God himself, in his holiness, his otherness from the world, his transcendence, heaven. This is where Christ now belongs, in that his human life is over and he has passed to the Father. Those who lived and died in Christ are there too, i.e., with him and in him through the Spirit (cf.

---

11   Cf. notes 12 and 13, Chapter 5.

12   K. Rahner, "Beatific Vision," SM 1, 153a.

13   Cf. Pannenberg, 66-68.

Eph 2:6, where the present is understood in the light of the future). They have entered upon the definitive stage, where the parousia has been taking place from the moment of Christ's death. They constitute with him the definitively eschatological community, which, however, is constantly being augmented through the deaths of individual just persons. It is precisely this community which constitutes the consummation spoken of above. We on earth are justified, sanctified, glorified even (Rom 8:30), on the basis of our faith and divine filiation. We belong to the eschatological community, and the eschaton really touches us already. We do not, however, belong yet to its definitive stage, which we shall do only through our death. It is not, therefore, an historical aeon which separates the present from the eschaton, but the personal time of one's own life. This suggested solution puts aside such questions as whether the human race will come to an historical end, as not answered by the revelation (though in principle it is answerable by science). This means that the question as to whether the augmentation of the definitive community will ever come to an end must also remain unanswered by theology. Such a question, however, appears insignificant alongside the assertion that this community is constituted substantially by the death of Christ, when he joins the just who have died before him, saved by his grace. Further, this solution does not abolish the intention of the teaching of the particular and general judgments. The former has to do with the value of the individual person's life, the latter with their aggregation to the definitive eschatological community. Thus is acknowledged, in spiritual as in all other matters, both the individual and the social character of the human person.

It remains now only to add a word about the participation of the infra-personal world in the process of glorification.[14] Speaking first of glorification as a present reality, we point to the visible aspect of grace, present at its strongest in the Eucharist. This granted, we must admit that grace will be visible also in lowlier manifestations, in keeping with other (non-Christian) religious systems and even with anonymous Christianity, without going so far as to claim that the presence of grace can ever be thereby demonstrated incontrovertibly. This whole position is based on the conviction that the world is the extension of the human body, and that through their body, therefore, the human person is related spiritually to the world as a whole. When in response to grace they truly love God they will also love self, the neighbor and the

14   Cf. J.B. Metz, *Theology of the World* (New York, 1969).

world, for these loves are inseparably united. And these latter loves will be manifest in the world, for they will result in work and in unselfish cooperation with the neighbor in accepting responsibility for perfecting the world ("art" in Aristotle's sense), repairing, tending, planning, developing and directing it. The grace of humans, then, will be manifest in the order and progress of the world. The present glorification of the human person in grace will redound upon the world. On the other hand the selfishness and sin of humans will also be manifest in the world, in the harm done to it ("violence" in Aristotle's sense), e.g., the pollution of the environment and the ultimate folly of war, where humans fall to destroying each other, the hard-won fruits of work and even the world itself. Gen 3, concerning Adam in the garden, and Gen 8-9, concerning Noah, both suggest that there is a definite connection between the spiritual conditon of humans and the state of the world.

As to the participation of the world in the eschatological glorification of humans, Paul in the classical text, Rom 8:18-23, presents the world as, far from being destroyed, sharing in its own way in the definitive redemption. Aquinas has reaffirmed this position in his commentary on the text in the final chapter of the *Summa contra Gentiles*. Since, however, we are unable to accept as literally true the mythological account of the occurrence of the eschaton as anticipated by Paul and endorsed by Aquinas, we must ask what we are to make of the assertion of the participation of the world in the eschatological glorification. Lyonnet, commenting on the same text, says that the world is to be redeemed as a consequence of the redemption of humans, and particularly of their bodies, i.e., that which they have from and of the world, and that thus the world will be transformed, not annihilated, though in its own way, of which we are told nothing.[15] The only illumination we can add to this is taken from Rahner's theology of death.[16] He holds that as the human person is related through their body to the whole world, and as the particular relationship to the body is ended with death, the spirit of a person just dead, instead of becoming a-cosmic, enters into a relationship of openness to the world as a whole. While Rahner is unable to be specific as to what this entails, what he says is undoubtedly correct, unless one is prepared to accept the alternative view of the soul, viz., the Platonic, in which the soul is

---

15   Cf. S. Lyonnet, "The Redemption of the Universe," *The Church: Readings in Theology* (New York, 1963) 136-56.

16   Rahner, *On The Theology of Death* 27-34; "Death," SM 2, 58b - 62a.

seen as essentially alien to the world. He goes on to say that the spirit of a person who has died becomes "a codetermining factor of the universe precisely in the latter's character as the ground of the personal life of other incarnate spiritual beings."[17] Thus the transformation of the world is its building-up, through the aggregation of humans to the definitive eschatological community, precisely as "world," i.e., the Germanic *wer-ald*, or "age of man," i.e., the arena where authentically human life is led at every level, including (and particularly) the highest, viz., that of love of God and neighbor. (Hence the concept of "world" is to be contrasted with the purely geographical concept "earth.") It is necessary, however, to remove from this conception all suggestion of a Marxist earthly paradise. The ultimate end of humanity is to sit with the Father in the heavenly places in Christ Jesus, to whom each person is united, with their fellows, in one Spirit (cf. Eph 2:6, 18).

---

17   Rahner, "Death" 60a.

CONCLUSION

By way of conclusion we now draw together and restate in briefest and simplest form the principal themes of the theology of grace that have emerged in the course of our study. In the Godhead the Holy Spirit proceeds as the mutual love of the Father and the Son. When God directs his love beyond himself, he does this so that created being, through human being its highest representative, may share in its own way in the inner life of the Godhead. He wills the non-divine only to divinize it, in the human. His love, therefore, will first call into being whatever is to belong to the sphere of the non-divine; then it will call humans alone into the inner sanctum where God has his being. Humans will experience this love as grace, for not only can they lay no claim to it, but they are found by it averted from God. Drawn through their response of faith into the Godhead, they encounter this love as it there primordially exists, i.e., as the Holy Spirit, love of the Father for the Son. Humans are therefore drawn into union with the rightful object of this love, the Son. For them the Holy Spirit is Spirit of filiation.

The Father makes this offer of love to humans in a range of sacraments, of which the highest is Christ, principally, in the time of the Church, in the Eucharist. His plan is that in a single instance, that of Jesus, his bestowal of love be so radical as to be non-sacramental; in the one act it calls Jesus into being as a human, sanctifies him, and unites him in very person to the divine Son. Jesus is Son of God in humanity. In the course of his life, a life of obedience to the will of the Father, he realizes this unique grace, so that in his death the divine Sonship is fully realized in him. He is then, as human, as fully at one with the Son in the Trinity as it is possible for a human to be, and he returns the Father's love for him, the Holy Spirit, as his own love for the Father. Yet, as a human loving the Father, he in that same act loves his fellow humans, and so becomes the sacramental source of the Holy Spirit, now Spirit of Christ, for them.

Christ, therefore, offers to other humans the Holy Spirit as his own. If they respond in faith, the offer becomes for them the sacrament of the Father's bestowal of the same Spirit on them as Spirit of filiation, making them sons and daughters of the Father, in the unique Son.

The reality we call grace, which we might otherwise conceive simply as the merciful favor of God, is revealed, therefore, to be a divine person, the Holy Spirit, the love of the Father and the Son in the Trinity, and to be grace for humans because he is for him the Spirit of filiation, raising them to union with the incarnate Son. The only other reality to which we give the name of grace is the transformation of the human being self, the created reality identical with their divine filiation, the result of the bestowal of the Spirit on them. We thus arrive at a comprehensive and quite simple conclusion, which hopefully would satisfy even so severe a critic as Barth: the grace of God is the Gift of the Holy Spirit.

BIBLIOGRAPHY

Except for those works marked with an asterisk, the following are modern works to which I have referred in the text and notes of this book. Those marked with an asterisk, though not referred to in the text or notes, I have considered specially deserving of mention.

Abercrombie, Nigel. *The Origins of Jansenism.* Oxford: Clarendon Press, 1936.

Alfaro, Juan. "Christo Glorioso, Revelador del Padre." *Gregorianum* 39 (1958): 222-70.

Atchley, E. G. Cuthbert. F. *On the Epiclesis of the Eucharistic Liturgy and in the Consecration of the Font.* London: Oxford University Press, H. Milford, 1935.

Balthasar, Hans Urs von. *Love Alone: The Way of Revelation.* Edited by Alexander Dru. London: Burns & Oates, 1968.

———. *Elucidations.* Translated by John Riches. London: S.P.C.K., 1975.

———. *Engagement with God.* Translated by John Halliburton. London: S.P.C.K., 1975.

Barth, Karl. *Church Dogmatics,* Vol. 4, Part 1, The Doctrine of Reconciliation. Translated by Geoffrey W. Bromiley. Edinburgh: T & T Clark, 1956.

Baumgartner, Charles. *La Grâce du Christ.* Tournai: Desclée, 1963.

Bender, Wolfgang. *Die Lehre Über den Heiligen Geist bei Tertullian.* Munich: Max Hueber Verlag, 1961.

Bettenson, Henry. *Documents of the Christian Church,* 2nd ed. Oxford: Oxford University Press, 1963.

Betz, Johannes. "Eucharistie." In HTG 1:336-55. Edited by Heinrich Fries. Munich: Kösel Verlag, 1962.

Boros, Ladislaus. *The Moment of Truth: Mysterium Mortis.* London: Burns & Oates, 1965.

Bouyer, Louis. *Rite and Man: Natural Sacredness and Christian Liturgy.* Notre Dame, Ind.: University of Notre Dame Press, 1963.

Bobrinskoy, Boris. "Présence réelle et communion eucharistique." *Revue des sciences philosophiques et théologiques* 53 (1969): 402-20.

Brown, Raymond E. *The Gospel According to John, XIII-XXI.* The Anchor Bible. Garden City, N.Y.: Doubleday, 1970.

———. *The Birth of the Messiah.* Garden City: N.Y.: Doubleday, 1977.

Chauvet, Louis-Marie. *Symbol and Sacrament: A Sacramental Reinterpretation of Christian Experience*. Translated by Patrick Madigan and Madeleine Beaumont. A Pueblo Book. Collegeville, Minn.: The Liturgical Press, 1995.

Clarke, Thomas E. "Some Aspects of Current Christology." In *The Encounter with God: Aspects of Modern Theology*, edited by Joseph E. O'Neill, 33-58. New York: Macmillan, 1962.

Coffey, David M. "The Salvation of the Unbeliever in St. Thomas Aquinas and Jacques Maritain." *The Australasian Catholic Record* 41 (1964): 179-98, 265-82.

———. "The Gift of the Holy Spirit." *Irish Theological Quarterly* 38 (1971): 202-23.

———. "The 'Incarnation' of the Holy Spirit in Christ." *Theological Studies* 45 (1984): 466-80.

———. "The Theandric Nature of Christ." *Theological Studies* 60 (1999): 405-31.

———. "The Spirit of Christ as Entelechy." *Philosophy & Theology* 13 (2001): 363-98.

———. "The Whole Rahner on the Supernatural Existential." *Theological Studies* 65 (2004): 95-118.

———. *"Did You Receive the Holy Spirit When You Believed?": Some Basic Questions for Pneumatology*. The Père Marquette Lecture in Theology, 2005. Milwaukee, Wisc.: Marquette University Press, 2005.

———. "A Trinitarian Response to Issues Raised by Peter Phan." Theological Studies 69 (2008): 852-74.

Cullmann, Oscar. *The Christology of the New Testament*. New Testament Library. Translated by Shirley C. Guthrie and Charles A. M. Hall. London: SCM, 1963.

Davies, William D. *Paul and Rabbinic Judaism: Some Rabbinic Elements in Pauline Theology*. London: S.P.C.K., 1965.

Dondaine, Hyacinthe F. *La Trinité (Saint Thomas D'Aquin, Somme Théologique)*, Vol. 2. Paris: Desclée, 1946.

Dunn, James D. G. *Jesus and the Spirit*. London: SCM, 1975.*

Ernst, Cornelius.   *The Theology of Grace*. Cork: Mercier, 1974.*

Fenton, John C. *The Gospel of St. Matthew*. Harmondsworth: Penguin, 1963.

Flick, Maurizio, and Alszeghy, Zoltan. *Il Vangelo della Grazia: Un Trattato Dogmatico*. Florence: Libreria Editrice Fiorentina, 1964.*

Fransen, Peter. *The New Life of Grace*. Translated by George Dupont. London: Geoffrey Chapman, 1969.*

———. "Orders and Ordination." In SM 4:305a-327a.

Grillmeier, Aloys. "Dogmatic Constitution on the Church, Chapter II." In

Commentary on the Documents of Vatican II, Vol.1. Edited by Herbert Vorgrimler, 153-85. Translated by Adolphus Lalit, Kevin Smyth and Richard Strachan. London: Burns & Oates, 1967.

Gutwenger, Engelbert. *Bewusstsein und Wissen Christi: eine dogmatische Studie.* Innsbruck: Rauch, 1960.

Hahn, Ferdinand. *The Titles of Jesus in Christology.* Translated by Harold Knight and George Ogg. London: Lutterworth, 1969.

Haspecker, Josef. "Bund." In HTG 1:197-204. Edited by Heinrich Fries. Munich: Kösel Verlag, 1962.

Jeremias, Joachim. *The Eucharistic Words of Jesus.* Translated by Norman Perrin. London: SCM, 1966.

Jungmann, Joseph A. *The Mass of the Roman Rite: Its Origins and Development*, Vol. 2. Translated by Francis A. Brunner. New York: Benziger, 1955.

Kasper, Walter. *Jesus the Christ.* Translated by V. Green. London: Burns & Oates, 1976.

Kelly, John N. D. *Early Christian Doctrines*, 5th ed. London: Adam & Charles Black, 1977.

Kenny, John P. *The Supernatural.* New York: Alba, 1972.*

Kilmartin, Edward J. "Apostolic Office: Sacrament of Christ." *Theologcal Studies* 36 (1975): 243-64.

Kittel, Gerhard. *Theological Dictionary of the New Testament*, Vol. 2. Translated and edited by Geoffrey W. Bromiley. Grand Rapids, Mich.: Eerdmans, 1964.

Koch, Robert. "Spirit." In *Encyclopedia of Biblical Theology* 3:869b-889b. Edited by Johannes B. Bauer. London: Sheed and Ward, 1970.

Latourelle, René. *Theology of Revelation: Including a Commentary on the Constitution "Dei Verbum" of Vatican II.* New York: Alba House, 1966.

Lentzen-Deis, Fritzleo. *Die Taufe Jesu nach den Synoptikern: Literarkritische und gattungsgeschichtliche Untersuchungen.* Frankfurt am Main: Josef Knecht, 1970.

Léon-Dufour, Xavier. *Resurrection and the Message of Easter.* Translated by R.N. Wilson. London: Geoffrey Chapman, 1974.

Lonergan, Bernard, J.F. *Insight: A Study of Human Understanding.* San Francisco: Harper & Row, 1958.

―――. *Method in Theology.* London: Darton, Longman & Todd, 1971.

Lubac, Henri de. *The Mystery of the Supernatural.* Translated by Rosemary Sheed. New York: Herder and Herder, 1967.

Lyonnet, Stansislas. "Péché. IV. Dans le Nouveau Testament." *Supplément au Dictionnaire de la Bible* 1, Fascicle 38: 486-567. Paris: Libraire Letouzey & Ané, 1963.

————. "The Redemption of the Universe." In *The Church:Readings in Theology*: 136-56. New York: P.J. Kennedy, 1963.

Malmberg, Felix. *Über den Gottmenschen* (Quaestiones Disputatae 9). Basel: Herder, 1960.

Margerie, Bertrand de. "La doctrine de saint Augustin sur l'Ésprit-Saint comme communion et source de communion." *Augustinianum* 12 (1972): 107-19.

McCormick, Richard A. "Notes on Moral theology: January-June, 1968," *Theological Studies* 29 (1968): 679-741.

McDonagh, Enda. *Gift and Call: Towards a Christian Theology of Morality*. Dublin: Gill and Macmillan, 1975.

McIntryre, John. *The Shape of Christology*. London:SCM, 1966.

McKenna, John H. "Eucharistic Epiclesis: Myopia or Microcosm?" *Theological Studies* 36 (1975): 265-84.

McKenzie, John L. "Covenant." *Dictionary of the Bible*: 153-57. London: Chapman, 1965.

Marxsen, Willi. *The Resurrection of Jesus of Nazareth*. Translated by Margaret Kohl. London: SCM, 1970.

Metz, Johannes B. *Theology of the World*. New York: Herder and Herder, 1969.

————. "Konkupiszenz." In HTG 1: 843-51. Edited by Heinrich Fries. Munich: Kösel Verlag, 1962.

Muck, Otto. *The Transcendental Method*. Translated by William D. Seidensticker. New York: Herder and Herder, 1968.

Mühlen, Heribert. *Der Heilige Geist als Person*. Münster: Verlag Aschendorff, 1963.

————. *Una Mystica Persona*. München: Verlag Ferdinand Schöningh, 1968.

————. "Person und Appropriation. Zum Verständnis des Axioms: In Deo omnia sunt unum, ubi non obviat relationis oppositio." *Münchener Theologische Zeitschrift* 16 (1965): 37-57.

Muldoon, Thomas. *De Gratia Christi*. Theologiae Dogmaticae Praelectiones, Vol. 5. Rome: Officium Libri Catholici, 1965.*

Müller, Max, and Halder, Aloys. "Person. 1. Concept." In SM 4: 404a-409b.

North, Robert. "Soul-Body Unity and God-Man Unity." *Theological Studies* 30 (1969): 27-60.

O'Collins, Gerald. *Foundations of Theology*. Chicago: Loyola University Press, 1971.

————. *The Easter Jesus*. London: Darton, Longman & Todd, 1973.

Orsy, Ladislas M. "Common Sense about Sin." *The Tablet*, 9 February, 1974: 125-128.

O'Shea, Kevin, F. "The Reality of Sin: A Theological and Pastoral Critique." *Theological Studies* 29 (1968): 241-59.

Pannenberg, Wolflhart. *Jesus - God and Man*. London: SCM, 1968.

———. "Person." RGG 5 (3rd ed.): 230-35.

Parente, Petrus. *De Deo Uno et Trino*. Turin: Marietti, 1956.

Penido, Maurillo T. L. "Gloses sur la Procession d'Amour dans la Trinité," *Ephemerides Theologicae Lovanienses* 14 (1937): 33-68.

Portalie, Eugène. *A Guide to the Thought of Saint Augustine*. Translated by Ralph J. Bastian. Chicago: H. Regnery, 1960.

———. "L'onction du chrétien par la foi." *Biblica* 40 (1959): 12-69.

Powers, Joseph M. *Eucharistic Theology*. New York: Herder and Herder, 1967.

Prestige, George L. *God in Patristic Thought*. London: S.P.C.K., 1936.

Rahner, Karl. *On the Theology of Death* (Quaestiones Disputatae 2). Translated by Charles H. Henkey. Edinburgh: Nelson, 1961.

———. *The Trinity*. Translated by Joseph Donceel. London: Burns & Oates, 1970.

———. "Theos in the New Testament." In *Theological Investigations*, Vol. 1. Translated by Cornelius Ernst. London: Darton, Longman & Todd, 1961: 79-148.

———. "Some Implications of the Scholastic Concept of Uncreated Grace." In ibid.: 319-46.

———. "The Theological Concept of Concupiscence." In ibid.: 347-82.

———. "The Eternal Significance of the Humanity of Jesus for our Relationship with God." In *Theological Investigations*, Vol. 3. Translated by Karl H. and Boniface Kruger. London: Darton, Longman & Todd, 1967: 35-46.

———. "On The Theology of the Incarnation." In *Theological Investigations*, Vol. 4. Translated by Kevin Smyth. London: Darton, Longman & Todd, 1966: 105-20.

———. "The Theology of the Symbol." In ibid.: 221-52.

———. "Dogmatic Reflections on the Knowledge and Self-Consciousness of Christ." In *Theological Investigations*, Vol. 5. Translated by Karl H. Kruger. London: Darton, Longman & Todd, 1966: 193-215.

———. "Reflection on the Unity of the Love of Neighbor and the Love of God." In *Theological Investgations*, Vol.6. Translated by Karl H. and Boniface Kruger. London: Darton, Longman & Todd, 1969: 231-49.

———. "Anonymous Christians." In ibid.: 390-98.

———. "Atheism and Implicit Christianity." In *Theological Investigations*, Vol. 9. Translated by Graham Harrison. London: Darton, Longman & Todd, 1972: 145-64.

————. "On the Theology of Ecumenical Discussion." In *Theological Investigations*, Vol. 11. Translated by David Bourke. London: Darton, Longman & Todd, 1974: 24-67.

————. "Anonymous Christianity and the Missionary Task of the Church." In *Theological Investigations*, Vol. 12. Translated by David Bourke. London: Darton, Longman & Todd, 1974: 161-78.

————. "Observations on the Problem of the 'Anonymous Christian.'" In *Theological Investigations* , Vol. 14. Translated by David Bourke. London: Darton, Longman & Todd, 1976: 280-94.

————. "Jesus Christ in the Non-Christian Religions." In *Theological Investigations*, Vol. 17. Translated by Margaret Kohl. London: Darton, Longman & Todd, 1981: 39-50.

————. "Beatific Vision." In SM 1: 15lb-153b.

————. "Death." In SM2: 58b-62a.

————. "Faith. 1. Way to Faith." In ibid.: 310a-313b.

————. "Grace and Freedom." In ibid.: 424a-427b.

————. "Missions. II. Salvation of the Non-Evangelized." In SM 4: 79b-81a.

————. "Revelation. II. God's Self-Communication." In SM 5: 353b-355b.

————. "Transcendental Theology." SM 6: 287a-289b.

————. "Selbstmitteilung Gottes." In LTK 9: 627.

Rivière, Jean. "Mérite." DTC 10/1: 574-785.

Rondet, Henri. *The Grace of Christ*. Translated by Tad W. Guzie. Westminster, Md.: Newman Press, 1967.

Scheeben, Matthias J. *Handbuch der Katholischen Dogmatik*. Gesammelte Schriften, Vol. 6, Part 1. Freiburg im Br.: Herder, 1954.

————. *Die Mysterien des Christentums*. Gesammelte Schriften, Vol. 2. Freiburg im Br.: Herder, 1958. (*The Mysteries of Christianity*. Translated by Chril Vollert. St. Louis: Herder, 1954.)

Scheffczyk, Leo.   "Concupiscence." SM 1: 403b-405a.

Schillebeeckx, Edward. *Christ the Sacrament of Encounter with God*. Translated by Paul Barrett. English text revised by Mark Schoof and Laurence Bright. London: Sheed and Ward, 1977.

————. *The Eucharist*. Translated by N.D. Smith. London: Sheed and Ward, 1968.

Schmaus, Michael. *Katholische Dogmatik,* Vol. 1, Part 1, 4th ed., Gott der Dreieinige. Munich: Max Hueber Verlag, 1948.

Schoonenberg, Piet. *The Christ*. Translated by Della Couling. London: Sheed and Ward, 1972.

Schüller, Bruno. "Todsünde—Sünde zum Tod?", *Theologie und Philosophie* 42 (1967): 321-40.

Simons, Eberhard. "Personalism." In SM 4: 419b-423b.

Stévaux, A. "La doctrine de la charité dans les Commentaires des Sentences de Saint Albert, de Saint Bonaventure et de Saint Thomas." *Ephemerides Theologicae Lovanienses* 24 (1948): 59-97.

Taille, Maurice de la. "Actuation créée par Acte incréé." *Recherches de science religieuse* 18 (1928): 253-68.

(English: "Created Actuation by Uncreated Act." In *The Hypostatic Union and Created Actuation by Uncreated Act*. Translated by Cyril Vollert. West Baden Springs, Ind.: West Baden College, 1952.)

———. *Theological and Pastoral Orientations on the Catholic Chrismatic Renewal (Malines)*. Notre Dame, Ind.: University of Notre Dame Press, 1974.

Tillard, Jean M.R. "L'Eucharistie et le Saint-Ésprit", *Nouvelle revue théologique* 90 (1968): 363-87.

Verhees, Johannes J. "Heiliger Geist und Inkarnation in der Theologie des Augustinus von Hippo. Unlöslicher Zusammenhang zwischen Theologie und Ökonomie." *Revue des Études Augustiniennes* 22 (1976): 234-53.

Westermann, Claus. *Isaiah 40-66*. Translated by David M. Stalker. London: SCM, 1969.

Yarnold, Edward. *The Second Gift: A Study of Grace*. Slough, St. Paul Publications, 1974.*

GENERAL INDEX

A

Abercrombie, N. 262
accident 71
Alfaro, J. 83, 305
Antiochus Epiphanes 304
apocatastasis 260
appropriation 26
Aquinas, St. Thomas 52, 73, 80, 99,
    107, 272, 279, 280, 284, 286, 288,
    290, 296, 299, 303
ascension of Jesus 189
Atchley, E. 241
Augustine, St. 22, 34, 39, 42, 50,
    211, 212, 229, 250, 258, 260, 272,
    274, 288, 301, 303

B

Baius, M. 262, 273
Báñez, D. 262
Banezianism 263
Bardenhewer, O. 163, 164, 170, 173
Barth, K. 17
Basil, St. 81
Baumgartner, C. 79, 259, 263
beatific vision 81
Bender, W. 212
Benedict XII, Pope 305
Bettenson, H. 285
Betz, J. 244
Boethius 72
Bonaventure, St. 51
Boros, L. 102, 287
Bouyer, L. 238
Brobinskoy, B. 241
Brown, R. 160, 190

C

Calvin, J. 261
Cappadocian Fathers 21
causality
    efficient 69
    formal 70
    personal 69
character, sacramental 300
Clarke, T. 89
Clement of Alexandria, St. 207
Coffey, D. 61, 79, 285, 286, 288
concupiscence 103, 278
covenant 75
Cullmann, O. 152
Cyril of Alexandria, St. 79, 95, 125,
    176, 211

D

Davies, W. 275
death 185
de la Potterie, I. 126, 128, 129, 130,
    136, 137, 146, 152, 153, 161, 201,
    203
de la Taille, M. 81, 84, 139
De Margerie, B. 23
Dibelius, M. 161
distinction of sins, theological 289
divine acts
    constitutive and concomitant 36
    essential 35
    notional 35
Dondaine, H.-F. 33, 40

E

entelechy 221

Mühlen, H. 26, 38, 55, 70, 92, 93,
 124, 155, 165, 166, 167, 201, 203
Müller, M. 73
Mystici Corporis 147

O

O'Collins, G. 157, 187
option
 option final 291
 option fundamental 291
Origen 95, 209

P

Pannenberg, W. 73, 74, 94, 152, 156,
 157, 158, 159, 187, 306
Parente, P. 41
Pelagians 261ff.
Pelster, F. 89
Penido, M.T.-L. 42, 51
Pentecost 188
per filium 21
perseverance 283
Person 72
Peter Chrysologus, St. 123, 134
Peter Lombard 80
Pius XII, Pope 83, 147
Portalie, E. 288
predestinarianism 261
Prestige, G.L. 20
processio operati 30
processio operationis 31
psychological analogy 38

R

Rahner, K. 18, 27, 60, 70, 81, 82,
 84, 85, 96, 99, 102, 103, 111, 184,
 196, 222, 224, 237, 247, 265, 274,
 276, 287, 291, 306, 309
Reiners, H. 287
resurrection of Jesus 187
Richard of St. Victor 42

Rivière, J. 301
Rondet, H. 79

S

sacrifice for sins 189
Scheeben, M. 121, 129, 156, 165,
 168
Scheffczyk, L. 103, 277
Schillebeeckx, E. 232
Schmaus, M. 26, 287, 303
Schoonenberg, P. 18, 99, 225, 287
Schüler, B. 289
Semi-Pelagianism 261
Semi-Pelagians 261
Simons, E. 74
sinlessness of Jesus 102
special help 282
Spirit Christology 135
Stévaux, A. 48
Suarez, F. 303

T

Teilhard de Chardin, P. 291
Tertullian 211
theandric operation 194
Tillard, J. 241
transcendental theology 70, 74, 77
transignification 251
Trent, Council of 302

V

Verhees, J. 163
von Balthasar, Hans Urs 181

W

Westermann, C. 153
W. Marxsen, W. 304